Holocaust
Voices

Holocaust Voices

An Attitudinal Survey of Survivors

Alexander J. Groth

Professor Emeritus,
University of California, Davis

with the assistance of John R. Owens
and Marilyn A. Groth

Humanity Books

an imprint of Prometheus Books
59 John Glenn Drive, Amherst, New York 14228-2197

Published 2003 by Humanity Books, an imprint of Prometheus Books

Holocaust Voices: An Attitudinal Survey of Survivors. Copyright © 2003 by Alexander J. Groth. All rights reserved. No part of this publication may be reproduced, stored in a retrieval system, or transmitted in any form or by any means, digital, electronic, mechanical, photocopying, recording, or otherwise, or conveyed via the Internet or a Web site without prior written permission of the publisher, except in the case of brief quotations embodied in critical articles and reviews.

Inquiries should be addressed to
Humanity Books
59 John Glenn Drive
Amherst, New York 14228–2197
VOICE: 716–691–0133, ext. 207
FAX: 716–564–2711

07 06 05 04 03   5 4 3 2 1

Library of Congress Cataloging-in-Publication Data

Groth, Alexander J., 1932–
    Holocaust voices : an attitudinal survey of survivors / Alexander J. Groth
        p. cm.
    Includes bibliographical references and index.
    ISBN 1–59102–155–3 (hardcover : alk. paper)
    1. Holocaust, Jewish (1939–1945)—Personal narratives. 2. Holocaust survivors.
I. Title.

D804.3.G77 2003
940.53'18—dc22

                                                                                    2003016787

Printed in the United States of America on acid-free paper

This work is dedicated to the memory of

Szmuel Zygielbojm

CONTENTS

PREFACE

The original idea for this project—an uninhibited overview of the Holocaust by a large number of its surviving victims—goes back nearly thirty years. For many reasons, all connected to the author's personal and professional circumstances, this design could not be realized in those earlier years. It awaited retirement from my teaching position at the University of California, Davis, in the 1990s.

In the eventual completion of this project I am indebted to many persons. But, before gratefully acknowledging my obligation to them, I must mention first the names of those family members whose memory in the years of the Holocaust inspired and sustained my efforts. Above all, my thoughts turn to the figure of my mother, Maria Hazenfus-Gross, whose heroism and singular enterprise saved my life on many occasions during those murderous times. They also turn to the memory of my father, Jacob Goldwasser, martyred by the Nazis in the Krakow ghetto, and to the memory of his two brothers, Marian and Adam Goldwasser, both of whom died, unmarried and childless, at the hands of Nazi executioners; both had made heroic attempts—all that human love could possibly inspire—to save me, their only nephew, from the predators of the Final Solution.

My thoughts turn also to the memory of my grandparents, Isaac and Adela Hazenfus; they ran a grocery store, *Wenecja* ("Venice") in the heart of Warsaw before the war. I could never forget the twinkle of my grandfather's marvelous smile, his great sense of humor, all his good-natured practical jokes and funny remarks, even in times so desperate that they virtually defy description; or the kindly seriousness of my grandmother and the anguished figure of their son, my uncle Henryk Hazenfus, a scholar and marvelous young linguist conversant in many languages. I go back to the summer of 1942 in the Warsaw ghetto, when my grandfather refused to abandon my then-blind grandmother and joined with her, heroically, before a Nazi firing squad.

I also recall the figure of another martyr, Dr. Maksymilian Zirler, physician, a man of great learning and wisdom, and my stepfather and role model during those times. Nor could I forget those who had given me so much when they had so little themselves in the immediate postwar years: my aunt, Gienia Goldwasser, in Israel, and my great-uncle, Abe Buterweiser, and his wife, Sarah, in the United States.

I owe a great debt of gratitude to my colleague, Professor John R. Owens, who recorded and coded all the observations in this study, helped me develop the several scales in it, carried out many of the calculations reported here, and also did almost all the tabular presentations. I am also greatly indebted to my beloved wife, Marilyn A. Groth. She contributed much to the substance and form of our questionnaire and helped with a variety of tasks connected with this project—beyond, of course, her critically important moral support.

I am very grateful to my longtime colleague in the Department of Agricultural Economics at UC Davis, Professor Richard Green, who ably assisted in matters relevant to the statistical aspects of this study. Profuse thanks are likewise due to the former chair of the political science department at UC Davis, Professor Larry Berman, for his generous assistance and unflagging encouragement. I also greatly appreciate the assistance of our current political science chair, Walt Stone, and my colleague of many years here, Ed Costantini.

Special thanks go to several other very helpful persons: cousins Max Erlichman, Wolf Erlichman, and Anne Sone, as well as Pnina Zilberman, Director of the Toronto Holocaust Educational and Memorial Centre, for their critical assistance with the survey of Canadian survivors; President Jack Mandel and Frances Mandel, as well as Secretary-Treasurer Joe Nussbaum and Anne Nussbaum, for equivalent help with the American Congress of Jewish Survivors of Los Angeles; Tova Weiss, Coordinator of Holocaust Programming at the Jewish Federation of Scranton, Pennsylvania; Lisa J. Culhane, Assistant Director of the Anti-Defamation League of Denver, Colorado; and Dr. Lawrence Weinbaum of the World Jewish Congress, who generously assisted me with the interviews of several survivors residing in Israel. I am indebted to Dr. Michael Winter of the UC Davis Shields Library for his bibliographic assistance and for his insightful advice. Michael Koch was most helpful in analyzing some of the data. The assistance of John E. Daniels is likewise gratefully acknowledged, as is that of Zoe Clemons and of Dr. Sylvia Hacker. My colleague, Professor Larry L. Wade, as he has done on so many past occasions, read the whole manuscript and made many very valuable and creative suggestions.

I am indebted to Dr. Ann O'Hear at Humanity Books for insightful comments and suggestions, and I very much appreciate the sympathetic interest of its president, Dr. Paul Kurtz. Special thanks go to Benjamin Keller for his great help with the manuscript.

Above all, of course, I wish to express profound appreciation to our survivor respondents—anonymously to all those who did not wish to be identified by name as well as to those who agreed to have their identities disclosed. To relive the experience and to reflect, once again, upon the meaning of the Holocaust was clearly very painful for people so personally wounded by the Final Solution. Still, their contribution to the reckoning of history is priceless. I am honored, beyond all words, by the effort, the trust, and the faith that the survivors gave me in the preparation of this study. All acknowledgments notwithstanding, any mistakes and shortcomings in this study are the sole responsibility of its author.

The list of names that follows here includes only those persons who returned their questionnaires and who gave permission for their names to be listed. To them, and to those who preferred to remain anonymous, I am most grateful. In a few cases, questionnaires were sent by persons who did *not* live in Nazi-occupied areas at any time during the Holocaust but who felt a sense of affinity with the survivors by virtue of their own origins or family ties. These replies were not included in our study because the purpose here was to discover the reactions of those who had had at least some direct and personal experience of Nazi treatment of European Jewry and in countries in which the Final Solution took place.

Bernard Abend
Jack P. Ashley
Claire Baum
Helena Baumwirt-Shapiro
Cesia Beckerman
Esther Bem
Barbara Berliner
Louis Berliner
Marcel Biener
Eugelina Billauer
Richard Billauer
Felix Brand
Irene Butter
Felicia Carmelly
H. Chandler
Bela Cislowski
Judy Cohen
George Corey
Irene Csillag
Elisabeth F. de Jong
Samuel Z. Doro
Kurt S. Drechsler
Serena Drechsler
Josef Drobiarz
Leo Egan
Maynard Eisinger
Michael Englishman
Mary Enzsol
Jane Erbs
Sidney Erbs
Morris Fasen
Helene Feilenbaum
Aron Fellenbaum
David Feuerlicht
Fay Feuerlicht
Arthur File
Bella File
George Fine
Shary Fine

Ralph Fischer
Rosette Fischer
Frances Flumenbaum
Samuel Flumenbaum
Anna Fox
Dora Franen
Samuel Franen
David Frankel
Helen Frankel
Miriam Frankel
Arnold Friedman
Renée Ganz
Aron Gepner
Harry Glaser
W. E. Glied
Joseph Goldfarb
Paula Goldstein
Regina Goldstein
Henry Goldwyn
Lillian Goldwyn
Stanley Goodrich
Elly Gotz
Bernice Greenbaum
Roman Greenbaum
Felix Greenspan
Ben Grohman
Ibolya Grossman
Morris Gruda
Mary Gruen
Sigi Hart
Rose Heiferling
Henry Helfing
Fanny Hellman
Louis Hersh
Mina Hersh
Sara Hertzberg
Magda Hilf
Phillip Hirsch
Regina Hirsch

Ervin Hoenig
Herbert Hofman
M. Ickowicz
Wolf Ickowicz
Rodak Helen Izso
Jutta Jason
Eugene Jason Jaszcovits
Edith Jelinowicz
George Judkiewicz
Bella Kalka
Paul Kalka
Moishe Kantorowicz
Jerry Kapelus
Harry Keil
Cesia Kingston
Max Kingston
Motek Kleiman
Arnold J. Klein
Mary Klein
Morris Klein
Julian Kleinberger
Al Kleiner
Arthur Kleinhandler
Mary Kleinhandler
Nechemia Knobel
Sol Koral
Rachelle Kujawski
Wolf Kujawski
Harry Langsam
Paul Laufer
Barbara Lee
Bernard Lee
Sam Liberman
Charles Ligeti
George Lubow
Judy Lysy
Bernard Marco
Sally Marco
Helen W. Margines

Daniel Markowicz
Helen Markowicz
Martin Maxwell
Leo Mittler
Edith Mora
Peter Mora
Helen Moss
Sol Moss
David Moszkowicz
Sam Nortman
Joseph A. Nussbaum
Henri Opas
Lola Orzech
Stanley Orzech
Leopold Page
Gina Parker
Philip Polus
Ben Popowski
Naftali Rathaus
Sol Rattner
Tova Rattner
Maria Rebhun
David Rendel
Molly Rendel
Pola Ritter
Coenraad Rood
Olga Rosen
Sam Rosen
Bronia Rosenblum
Dorothy Rottman
Judith Rubinstein
George Salamon
Moritz Salz
Leslie Samuel
Irving Schaffer
Vera Schiff
Joe Schifman
Ryva Schifman
Magda Schuller

H. Schusheim-Beigel
Helen Schwartz
Josef Schwartz
Sara Schwartz
Daniel Schweitzer
George L. Scott
Bernard S. Secinowicz
Karl Shanofsky
Alex Shelunchik
Adele Silber
Isaac Silber
Edith Silver
Henry Silver
Nusia Silver
Sol Silver
Peter Silverman
Sid Spektor
Irwin Spielman
Manny Steinberg
Israel Stuhl
A. Szedlecki
Harold Tabak
George M. Tamari
Ilse M. Thompson
Joseph A. Tochterman
Joseph Tomashov
Leslie Trattner
Magda Trattner

Mike Traurig
Martin Twersky
Vini Ungar
Leonard Vis
Frieda Wald
Jack Wald
George Waldbaum
Lili Weinberg
Gerta Weintraub
M. Weintraub
Ernst Weiss
Rose Weitzen
Joseph Wiener
Herbert Winter
Lili Winter
Ida Wise
Nachemia Wurman
Max Wyszogrodzki
Helen Yermus
Lucy S. Zaifman
Mark Zaifman
Frances Zaks
S. Z. Zaks
William Zelon
Etty Zigler
Sheva Zilberberg
Hadasa Zytaner

Chapter 1

INTRODUCTION

This work is a study of reactions to the Holocaust by a number of its surviving victims, all with a fifty-year perspective on their tragic experience. What meaning and implications has the Final Solution had for these aging men and women? What evidence is there that the severity of their trials still shapes their attitudes half a century after the fact? To what extent are survivor opinions a function of personal, socioeconomic, and cultural backgrounds? In the most abstract sense, this work is a meeting and testing ground between the particular perceptions of the victims and the general premise of the author—that the Holocaust is as much a reflection of the pathology of humanity itself as it is a reflection of its most vicious subspecies: the pathology of Nazis and Nazism.

Unlike some earlier efforts, the interest here is not with the private travails of the victims during the Second World War. It is not with the details of how people managed to get through the Nazi Final Solution—how or why they endured their own personal catastrophes and narrow escapes.[1] These are not the stories of relatives and friends. The subject explored here is largely public and sociopolitical. We have sought to elicit the opinions of Holocaust survivors with respect to Nazi policies toward Jews in the 1940s and the survivors' perceptions of various relevant actors at the time, including, in Raul Hilberg's terminology, the perpetrators (i.e., Germans and Nazis), the victims (i.e., Jews), and the bystanders or various segments of the non-Jewish society of the time in Europe and also people living outside the Nazi-dominated world, Jews included.[2]

What led to the launching of this project was the perception by its author—himself a Holocaust survivor and Warsaw ghetto inmate in the period 1940–42—that the "big issues" of the Holocaust were largely the domain of an intellectual academic elite, for the most part physically unconnected to the experience of the Holocaust itself. While the philosophers, journalists, historians, and political scientists wrote books and articles about the major facets of the Holocaust, the surviving victims usually did little more than catalogue their individual sufferings and adventures in the larger tragedy. The initial purpose in this study, therefore, was to provide a significant "voice" to the victims themselves, so that the judgments of posterity with respect to the Holocaust in all subsequent time—when no more survivors are to be found alive—could be, at least in part, those of the victims themselves. After all, these are the people who lived through the "real experience," not people who merely read about it in American or European libraries or who may have heard about it from relatives and friends.

This is not to say, of course, that the opinions of any individual or group, even survivors, can resolve the mysteries and controversies of a phenomenon so monstrous and overwhelming as Hitler's Final Solution of the Jewish Question. An ultimate judgment on all the issues of the Holocaust universally convincing to all human beings is unlikely. Admittedly, if history is, in a larger sense, a court of world public opinion, all the witnesses before it may, and indeed must, be scrutinized critically and appropriately discounted for whatever self-interests and biases they are likely to inject into their testimony. But all these considerations notwithstanding, it is still the case that the judgment of eyewitnesses and victims of Hitler's murderous policies constitutes a very important element in the larger meaning of what happened. Something interesting is to be learned by questioning eyewitnesses—even long after the fact. The Holocaust was an event of immense impact in the life of the Jewish people. It was probably one of the four most memorable occurrences in Jewish history, which otherwise include the thirteenth-century B.C.E. flight of Moses and the Jews from Egypt; the first-century C.E. extinction of Jewish statehood by the Romans, and the consequent Diaspora of the Jewish people; and, finally, the resurrection of Jewish statehood in 1948. Given the magnitude of the murder of the Jews—more than one out of every three Jews alive in the world in 1939 was dead by 1945—one could be forgiven for advancing the audacious hypothesis, as we do in this work, that the shadow of the Holocaust would still be strongly discernible among its victims half a century after its passing, even if only with some overlays accumulated in later time.

The principal author of this study was initially, and a little naïvely, interested in a survey of survivor opinion around the world, with respondents from all the major survivor communities around the globe. What thwarted this lofty project in the last several years was the gradual realization that enormous resources, human and financial, would be required for its completion. Also, it became apparent in the course of a trial run of the questionnaire with a small group of survivors that there was considerable reticence on the part of the survivors about sharing their views with the world at large. Several factors were probably at work: the pain of having to think once more and at length about some very terrible experiences; the challenges of a long, multi-item, English-language questionnaire; and, to a degree, suspicion of the motives of the researcher and hence, anxiety about the way information or opinions given out might be ultimately used, or misused. The present study is a much more modest and manageable undertaking.

Our information was obtained from a mail questionnaire sent out in 1996, 1997, and 1998 to over seven hundred survivors, most residing in the United States and Canada, and a handful in Israel. Two hundred fifty-one people responded to this survey, or about 36 percent. Although these respondents do not constitute a sample of Holocaust survivors in a statistical sense—something that is probably unobtainable—our analysis of the survey returns shows that they are a fairly representative group. We have here a virtually equal distribution between men and women. The group includes a variety of occupations and social and cultural backgrounds, blue-collar, business, and professional; those with little formal education, and those with college and postgraduate training; assimilated and non-assimilated Jews; believers and atheists.

Country of residence is an important variable with respect to the experience of the Holocaust. More Jews lived in Eastern Europe on the eve of the Second World War than in Western Europe—by a large margin. Poland alone contained a Jewish population of at least 10 times the size of its equivalent in France. There were at least 14 times as many Jews living in Poland as in Germany in the latter part of 1939. The Jewish population of Rumania was nearly 6 times as large as that of Holland; Hungary was inhabited by more than 5 times as many Jews as was Italy.

German extermination camps were located principally in Eastern Europe, especially in Poland. For diplomatic and political reasons, with a view to the sensibilities of local opinion, Nazi policies toward Jews in Western Europe tended to be outwardly somewhat more restrained. The deportations, and particularly the killings, were more frequently done out of sight of the inhabitants there than was the case in places such as Poland, Ukraine, Lithuania, Hungary, Rumania, or Yugoslavia.

Some of the Western European countries, such as Denmark, Norway, and Luxembourg, effectively contained only a few thousand Jews. The Jews of Western Europe tended to be more assimilated, more integrated into their respective societies, than their counterparts in the East. Anti-Semitism was stronger and more prevalent in Eastern Europe. In general, a larger share of the Jewish population perished in the East than in the West. For all these reasons, the Holocaust as a powerful destructive force had a certain geography attached to it—generally more virulent in the East, somewhat weaker in the West.

Our group of survivors therefore reflects the preponderance of Eastern Europeans in the Jewish catastrophe. Its principal component consists of Polish Jews—57 percent of the total. This figure is very close to the share of deaths in the Holocaust attributed to Polish Jewry by various scholars, including Martin Gilbert,[3] Israel Gutman, and Raul Hilberg. The former Czechoslovakia, Yugoslavia, and Rumania, as places of residence among our survivor respondents, are also close to most scholarly estimates of these countries' share in Holocaust losses. Residents of Hungary are somewhat overrepresented, whereas residents of Germany, France, and Holland are within a reasonable range of most such estimates. None of our respondents hail from Norway, Denmark, Italy, Bulgaria, or Greece. Given that some of our Rumanian respondents may have lived on Soviet territory in 1941, the most seriously underrepresented country here is probably Russia within the USSR. However, given the many respondents from eastern Poland, Ukraine, Belarus, and Lithuania, we are probably well within the averages attributed to the USSR. Given the deviations, the total pool of our survivors from the twelve countries suffering the bulk of Holocaust deaths—Poland, the former Soviet Union, Germany, Austria, the former Czechoslovakia, Hungary, Rumania, Lithuania, the Netherlands, Belgium, Luxembourg, and France— adds up to 96.6 percent of the whole group. This figure corresponds closely to the estimates of most scholars for these countries' share of deaths in the Holocaust. (See Figs. 1.1–1.5 and Tables 1–2 for demographics.)

We did not include in our survey a number of persons who were *not* actually residing in the relevant countries at the outbreak of the war. A few such persons, some residing in the United States and some in Britain, for example, sent us responses, which we certainly appreciate and acknowledge. But we did not include here for the purposes of analysis anyone who

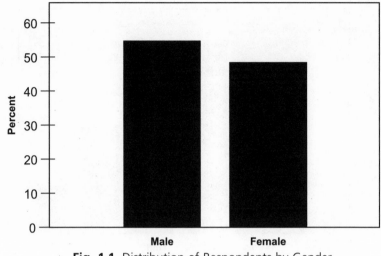

Fig. 1.1. Distribution of Respondents by Gender

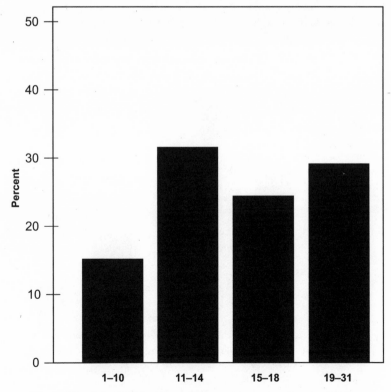

Fig. 1.2. Distribution of Respondents by Age in 1939

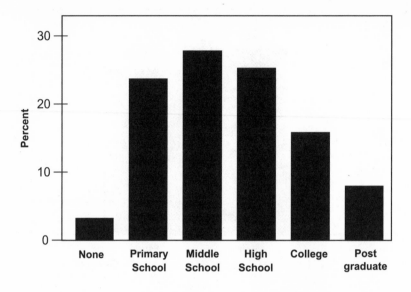

Fig. 1.3. Distribution of Respondents by Level of Education Attained

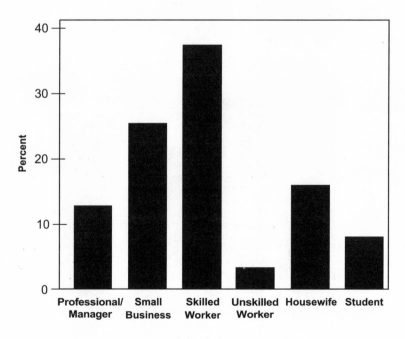

Fig. 1.4. Distribution of Respondents by Recent/Current Occupation

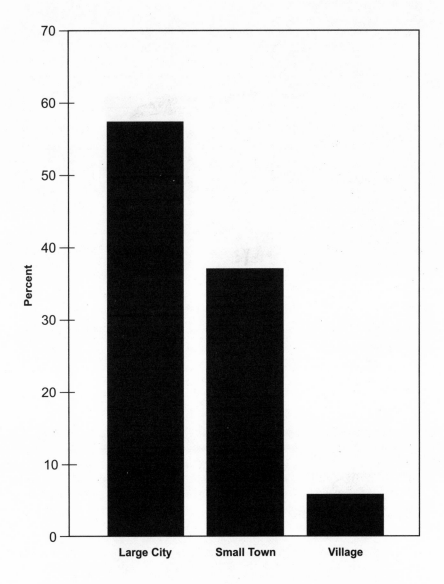

Fig. 1.5. Distribution of Respondents by Residence before Holocaust

Table 1. Respondent Country Distribution in Relation to the Distribution of Holocaust Deaths According to Various Sources

	Gilbert	Hilberg	Gutman	Robinson	Our Data
Poland*	52.8%	58.8%	51.5%	78.0%**	57.2%
Hungary	3.5	3.5	9.8	6.9	13.4
Rumania*	8.3	5.3	4.9	0.7	7.0
Czechoslovakia	3.8	5.1	2.6	4.8	5.0
Germany	2.8	2.4	2.4	2.1	4.0
The Netherlands	1.9	2.0	1.7	1.8	2.5
Lithuania*	2.4	2.5	2.5	—	2.0
France	1.5	1.5	1.3	1.4	1.5
Austria	1.1	1.0	0.8	1.1	1.0
USSR	17.6	13.7	18.3	—	1.0
Yugoslavia	1.0	1.2	1.0	1.0	1.0
Belgium	0.4	0.5	0.5	0.4	0.5
Luxembourg	0.0	0.0	0.0	0.0	0.5
TOTAL	97.1	97.5	97.3	98.3	96.6

*   To at least some degree these locations overlapped with the USSR in 1941.

** Includes Poland and the USSR.

See Martin Gilbert, "Final Solution," in *The Oxford Companion to World War II*, ed. I. C. B. Dear and M. R. D. Foot (New York: Oxford University Press), pp. 364–71, esp. Table 31, p. 365; Raul Hilberg, *The Destruction of the European Jews* (New York: Holmes and Meier, 1985), Table B-2, p. 339; Israel Gutman and Robert Rozett, Appendix Table 1, in *Encyclopedia of the Holocaust*, ed. Israel Gutman, vol. 4 (New York: Macmillan, 1990), p. 1799 (note also pp. 1797–1802); Jacob Robinson, "Holocaust," *Encyclopedia Judaica*, vol. 8 (Jerusalem: Keter Publishing House, 1972), pp. 828–905, esp. Table 1, p. 889.

Table 2. Jewish Population in Europe c. 1939*

Country	Population	% in Nazi-occupied or dominated Europe outside USSR
Poland	3,400,000	54.2
Rumania	850,000	13.5
Hungary	445,000	7.0
Czechoslovakia	357,000	5.7
France	260,000	4.1
Germany	234,000	3.8
Lithuania	155,000	2.5
The Netherlands	112,000	1.8
Latvia	95,000	1.5
Greece	73,000	1.2
Yugoslavia	68,000	1.1
Austria	66,000	1.0
Belgium	60,000	1.0
Bulgaria	48,200	0.8
Italy	35,000	0.6
Denmark	6,500	less than 0.1
Estonia	4,560	less than 0.1
Norway	1,700	less than 0.1
Finland	1,000	less than 0.1
Luxembourg	300	less than 0.1
Albania	200	less than 0.1

*Figures represent data available in 1939 or a period closest to it, according to Salo W. Baron, *Encyclopedia Judaica*, vol. 13, Table 3, pp. 890–91. The last six cases are supplied from other *Encyclopedia Judaica* articles. (*Encyclopedia Judaica* copyright © 1972, Gale Group. Reprinted by permission of The Gale Group.) Baron's figure of the Jewish population in Poland appears to be underestimated.

spent the whole period 1939–45 outside the perimeter of Nazi control, domination, and predation.

Our respondents are divided into two groups. The larger, principal group of 203 persons consists of those who survived the Final Solution and the Second World War in areas under Nazi control or under regimes allied with the Nazis. A smaller group of survivors—35 persons—consists of those who experienced Nazi occupation only briefly at the beginning of the war and who managed to escape Hitler's rule, in most cases by flight into Soviet-occupied Polish territory in 1939 and 1940. (In the comparisons of these two groups in chapter 7, we refer to the first group as "full-term" survivors, in contrast to the "part-term" survivors.)

Given the time of our survey (i.e., the late 1990s), the principal respondent group features a fairly impressive, bell-shaped age distribution, with 61.5 percent of our survivors aged at least 14 at the beginning of the Second World War, and therefore at least 20 at its conclusion. Only about 3 percent were less than 10 years old in 1945, and these respondents were presumably so young that their personal memories of the Holocaust period could be assumed to be at least somewhat indistinct.[4] Over 90 percent of the respondents were at or above the bar or bat mitzvah age when the war ended. The average age of our respondents in 1996 was 74. Our respondents constitute a diverse and fairly representative group of survivors, not confined to one point of origin, one particular profession, or a single social class. Most of our respondents had had prolonged exposure to the cultural environments of Canada and the United States, a few others in Israel—in many cases something on the order of a half-century. Moreover, these respondents reflect a variety of routes to survival: some in camps, some in hiding, some under false (Gentile) identities, and some in partisan groups.

There is one—unmeasurable—sense in which our respondents are *not* a representative group: specifically those Jews, or persons of Jewish origin, who in the aftermath of the Second World War completely abandoned their Jewish identities. How many survivors of the Holocaust fit this category is not really known, but as individuals they are obviously encountered. They may be people who were brought up as Christians by families of rescuers— with varying degrees of knowledge of their Jewish backgrounds. They may also be people who independently concluded, in the aftermath and even in the precise consequence of the Holocaust, that they were "tired" of maintaining an identity that had brought them, one might think, so much grief, suffering, and endangerment. In any case, such persons are *not* included in our survey because all of our respondents either were identified from lists of various Jewish community organizations—such as, for example, Toronto's Holocaust Education and Memorial Centre—or else, having heard of our survey, made themselves known to the researchers as Jewish survivors. It should be pointed out, however, that none of our respondents belonged to or participated in Jewish entities that imposed any political, philosophical, or organizational behavioral tests upon them. In most cases "belonging" meant being on a mailing list and also perhaps attending occasionally some idiosyncratically chosen (although at least in some sense Jewish) social or cultural events. A prime example of this sort of entity was the American Congress of Jewish Survivors of Concentration Camps of Los Angeles, many of whose members participated in our survey.

What is of particular relevance, however, is that given the considerable diversity of our respondent group, with some much greater and some much lesser Jewish identifications, it has been possible for us to identify background characteristics that all but certainly have implications even for those survivors whose Jewishness has been abandoned.

Larger and more frequent studies would be needed to see just how "typical" and "timeproof" our respondent group was in relation to the hundreds of thousands of survivors still living around the world on the eve of the twenty-first century. In the physical and biological sciences, replication of experiments and the progression from smaller to larger studies is routine. To be sure, those still alive in 2000 are not necessarily representative of those who were alive in 1945. The continuity of views among survivors over the last half-century is also clearly a matter of conjecture. Our effort here is premised on the modest proposition recalled some years ago by the late Adlai Stevenson, namely, that it is better to light a candle than to curse the darkness.

A number of intellectual themes guided the direction of our research. One of our concerns is cognitive. A question, historically made famous in another connection, is very applicable here: what did the Holocaust survivors know, and when did they know it? In the perspective of Holocaust history, it seems important to have some sense of the victims' awareness of the fate that was being prepared for and inflicted upon them. To what degree did the victims realize (or perceive) just what the Nazis had in store for them? And could this perception—or as the case might be, the lack of it—be related to some underlying characteristics of the respondents? How did the victims see their situations at the beginning of the Final Solution and during its course, and, again, what factors figured in the differences among our respondents?

Another important aspect is the apparent "learning experience" derived by the survivors from the Holocaust. Given the grim realities of the 1940s in the lives of Jews inhabiting Hitler-dominated Europe, the enormous scale of the horrors and sufferings of a whole people, it would seem all but inevitable that there would be a significant impact among the survivors on some very fundamental perceptions of the human experience. These include the classic question about "the nature of man," to wit, are people basically good? It would also presumably include some reflections and perspectives on the subject of anti-Semitism, which, after all, exhibited its ultimate form in the Nazi Final Solution. In general, it would seem that many expectations and anticipations of the contemporary world all around them would be influenced by the survivors' traumatic memories and implicit "lessons" of wartime experience.

A third concern here is in the relationship of the Holocaust experience to the cultivation of a Jewish identity. How did the Holocaust affect the sense of Jewishness among people who had suffered and lived through it? What Holocaust experiences, judgments, or attributes of the survivors seem to have been supportive of the maintenance of a Jewish identity, either in its religious or secular form, or indeed in both? What judgments, experiences, or attributes seem to have been conducive to the abandonment, or perhaps at least the attenuation, of such identities?

Our fourth focus of inquiry is evaluative. What balance sheet do the survivors draw with respect to their Holocaust experience? How do they see its heroes and its villains, if any? What elements of blame and praise do they retrospectively attach to the roles of the various participants, victims, and bystanders?

The last theme addressed in our research involves comparisons by the survivors in relation to the more recent, that is, post–Second World War, sufferings, killings, and persecutions inflicted at various times and places upon non-Jews. What inferences do the Jewish victims of the Holocaust make from their own particular experiences to the tragic sufferings of other peoples? In this, it would seem, there is much to learn about the victims' perceptions of their own problems as well as the problems of others, and, more broadly still, about the links between suffering and empathy among human beings.

Our questionnaire was designed to facilitate the analysis of these intellectual themes. It contained a total of eighty-four questions, a few of which elicited factual or demographic information, but the great majority of items probed, through variously worded multiple-choice questions, the attitudes, opinions, feelings, and evaluations of the survivors. One of the important characteristics of our survey was that many of our questions allowed, and indeed invited, respondents to supply their own answers or to provide combinations of answers either from alternatives presented in the questionnaire or initiated by themselves. Such open-endedness has its problems for people trying to measure public opinion. It is obviously more manageable for the investigator to "force" responses by limiting the respondents to some clear-cut, easily defined, and presumably readily "scalable" answers. Our view here, however, was that the nature of the subject matter, its complexity and its importance in history, should discourage any methodological "purity," no matter how much it might simplify the job of the researcher. Given the unique background of our survivor respondents, we are gratified and honored by the comments of so many of them validating the general significance and usefulness of our questionnaire.

Among many positive comments of our respondents, a few may be quoted:

> I think it is an important topic that should be front and center at all time.
> Very good both the questions and topic. I tried my best to answer them.
> Excellent questionnaire.
> This questionnaire was structured very well.
> The questions covered the most important parts.
> A very important topic and an excellent format of questionnaire.
> I appreciate the broad, inclusive generality of questions and opinions.
>   Thank you.
> I hope it will do some good.
> Excellent questions.
> Very important to keep it alive.
> I trust that your effort and published data will make a difference.
> Generally comprehensive and I have added some comments.
> Very well prepared. Took me only half an hour to fill out.
> Good! Please make sure to mention in your book that there were decent
>   people who helped Jews in Hungary, Slovakia, Poland.
> I can only congratulate you on this idea. Many thanks.
> Relevant.
> It's a good idea.
> Very well put together.
> Very relevant and finally interested in our opinions for which I want to
>   thank you.
> Interesting questions.
> It was thorough and well drafted.

> Very genuine. Should have been asked much sooner. Many have passed
> away.

Of course, not everyone approved, or approved completely. Among the
more skeptical comments we drew were the following:

> What is the relevance of the data collected? What will all this prove?
> I had some difficulty in answering certain questions as the answers lay
> somewhere in between.
> Good questionnaire but to some of the questions there is no, there cannot
> be, a definite "yes" or "no" answer.
> Too late, too little.

Only about 15 percent of our respondents commented about the questionnaire itself, but the margin of approval in those comments was about 10 to 1.

Many individual questions in our survey schedule were scalable. In
other words, the alternative choices offered our respondents fell along a
single continuum that could be ranked in some order and assigned numer-
ical values. In these cases, it was possible to analyze and compare individuals and groups based on these data. However, in order to explore some of
the broader intellectual themes, which lay at the heart of this research, we
had to deal with a number of interrelated questions that probed different
features of these more complex concepts. In order to get at these broader
issues, we had to create a measure that combined the responses from several questions into a single scale that would allow us to measure variations
in survivor attitudes along these issue dimensions. The multiple-choice
alternatives to the questions associated with an issue dimension were classified into simple, dichotomous categories such as strong or weak, positive
or negative, approve or disapprove, like or dislike, and so on. Positive
responses were assigned a value of 1, negative responses a value of 2, and
neutral or no responses were coded as 0. These values were then added
together, resulting in a single score that roughly measured the intensity of
the feelings, attitudes, opinions, or evaluations of the survivors on these
issue dimensions.

Following these procedures we constructed several scales:

- **Cognition scale**: Awareness or perception of hostile actions or intentions against Jews during the Holocaust emanating from the external
  environment, i.e., from Nazis, Germans, or other non-Jews. The
  scale combines the responses to several questions exploring different

aspects of the survivor's awareness, understanding, or feelings about the behaviors and actions of others during the Holocaust. The larger the scale numbers, the more negative or pessimistic the perceptions of the individual.

- **Learning scale**: Responses that, one may assume reasonably, are bound to be influenced by the Holocaust experience. They actually constitute part of an individual's "worldview"; that is, they are ideas that people might have developed independently of the Holocaust, but which, by their nature, likely relate to reflections upon that experience. An example is the respondent's view of human nature: is mankind good? What are the prospects of humanity in the aftermath of the Holocaust? Responses range from positive, relatively optimistic ones on one end to negative, relatively pessimistic ones on the other.
- **Identity scale**: The sense of identification with and involvement in activities cultivating or promoting "Jewishness" in various possible guises, ranging from interest in and support of Israel to involvement in Jewish charitable or cultural activities, Jewish marriages, and the perpetuation of the memory of the Holocaust, among others.
- **Blame scale**: Degree of culpability attributed to all sorts of relevant actors, including Nazis, Germans, Jews, non-Jews, Allies, and the world at large, for their actions or nonactions in the phenomenon of the Holocaust. This is an evaluative index. Questions probe feelings of blame attached to contemporaneous participants in the tragedy. Views of Pope Pius XII are illustrative. Is he perceived as one who did what he could on behalf of Jews? One who either did not know about the fate of the Jews or was unable to act to help? Or one who did not want to help because of a variety of possible considerations including personal antipathy toward Jews?
- **Comparison scale**: A measure of "empathy" in relation to postwar events, from least sympathetic to most sympathetic. This scale is based on a single question: "Some people compare tragic events in Bosnia, Rwanda, and Cambodia with the Holocaust. Do you see some or any equivalence to the Holocaust in these events?"

In order to probe the "Holocaust effect" upon present-day survivors, we have employed several variables, each presumed to have some potential explanatory power on social and political issues, Holocaust-related or otherwise. These variables embody different elements of the respondents' personal backgrounds, some reflecting characteristics exhibited or possessed before the Holocaust, some reflecting characteristics associated with the Holocaust itself, some associated with the post-Holocaust period, and, finally, also the transtemporal gender and personality traits.

Among our independent variables we have included these basic situational and demographic characteristics: gender; age; country of residence in 1939; urban versus small-town or rural domicile; current material welfare; degree of satisfaction in life; level of education attained; profession; prewar family wealth; family background in terms of assimilation and also in terms of religious practice; portion of family lost in the Holocaust; assistance by non-Jews; and manner of ultimate survival as in deportation to a camp or going into hiding. We also employed optimism, belief in God, and degree of Jewish identity as sometimes dependent and sometimes independent variables.

We have also employed four compound independent variables, i.e., combinations of variables. The first of these is *socioeconomic status*. It consists of three elements: level of education attained, level of current material welfare, and the occupational status of the respondent. Those in the "upper tier" would typically be respondents who have had some college education or better, who profess themselves to be well-off or very well-off, and who classify themselves as businesspeople or white-collar professionals, such as lawyers and doctors. The "lower tier" would typically include those with a high school education or less, who profess to make ends meet or who are facing financial hardship, and who may be described as blue-collar or lower-level clericals in their occupations.

Through this socioeconomic model we can presumably judge how the perceptions and evaluations of the Holocaust and related matters have been filtered. This model corresponds to most social science understandings of class, which has always been regarded as a very important determinant of political and social attitudes and behavior, including voting and party affiliations.

Might one expect that the lion's share of attitudinal differences among our Holocaust survivors is determined by how well they have done in life as reflected in class status? Perhaps this would be the case, *regardless* of what these people experienced in the Holocaust, *if* what has happened to the survivors *since the war* is really more important that what had happened to them some fifty years ago. For some, presumably, the patina of material well-being may have covered or even erased the memory of old sufferings.[6]

What might we expect from the well-to-do as opposed to the poor, in relation to the several indices we described above? Hypothetically, material success might predispose people to moderate or soften their feelings about past events, which would result in lower scores on the cognition and blame scales. It might move them, given presumably more resources and skills, to greater activism in Jewish affairs, or it might tend to promote more optimistic attitudes in terms of the learning scale and similarly more universalist attitudes about analogizing between the Holocaust and other, more recent murderous events of this century.

As mentioned above, we also employ an education variable dividing our respondents into two substantial groups: those with more formal education and those with less. Among our respondents, 152 reported completing only a high school education or less; 42 reported college-level and/or postgraduate studies. Since education is one of the elements of our definition of class, there is a certain amount of overlap here. Even if we were to define "class" without recourse to education, there would undoubtedly still be a considerable overlap between "high" income and higher levels of educational attainment. In fact, the correlation between the level of formal education attained and the level of "current material welfare" enjoyed among our respondents was a positive .21.

Like socioeconomic status, education is a variable that for most survivors represents the post-Holocaust period of their lives. In 1939, 80 percent of our respondents were nineteen years old or younger. Since Nazi rule in Europe effectively abolished education for Jewish children and youth, most of our respondents could attend college and obtain graduate training only in the years following 1945. For a majority, this was true even with respect to completing a high school education.

Our hypothetical expectations of education were quite similar to expectations of class. However, it seemed to us that knowledge, information, and the ability to process information are all sufficiently important in and of themselves to warrant separate analysis. One might presumably expect more informed, balanced, and nuanced judgments from the more educated as opposed to the less educated. If this were so, there could be significant differences between the more and the less educated on issues where "information" and the "facts of the case" could theoretically be seen as especially constraining. This would apply particularly to the cognition scale, the learning scale, and especially the comparison scale.

As Almond and Verba suggested in their pioneering study *The Civic Culture*, higher levels of education might also predispose people to more social activism, with possibly more positive consequences among the educated for the Jewish identity index. In any case, regardless of the directions that they might follow, we felt that it was important to trace the interpretations of the more and the less educated among the Holocaust survivors.[7] After all, education represents the closest proxy for the presumed power of "information" and of "rational thinking."

Our second compound variable is based on *personality characteristics*. These we assume are likely to have characterized their possessors over the course of their lifetime, although we inferred them from answers that were supplied recently and that refer to present-day circumstances. This model divides our respondents into two groups: one comprising "positive personalities," people who could be described as happy and optimistic, and the other made up of people who could be described as unhappy and pessimistic, or, in larger numbers, simply much less happy and much less optimistic. The variable derives from answers to the following two questions in our survey:

Looking back on your life at this point, would you say that you feel—all things considered:

    a. Highly satisfied
    b. Moderately satisfied
    c. Somewhat disappointed
    d. Seriously disappointed

How would you describe your current feelings with respect to the future of the world?

    a. Optimistic about chances for peace, prosperity and progress for all people
    b. Unsure about peace, prosperity and progress
    c. Pessimistic about peace, prosperity and progress
    d. Don't know; cannot say

Among our "positive" respondents, 52 percent reported that at no time during the period of the Holocaust did they believe that Nazi Germany would actually win the Second World War. On the other hand, among our more "negative" types, this obviously optimistic point of view was reported by only 35 percent of the respondents.

Our assumption, aided by discussions in the relevant literature, is that happy and optimistic personalities are likely to be positive and open-minded in their social attitudes, less given to harsh and blanket judgments of others, all of which might imply lower cognition, blame, and learning scores as well as higher (more empathetic) comparison levels.[8]

Our last two compound variables involve respondent characteristics that are likely to be associated with significantly negative attitudes on the cognition, blame, and learning indices as well as the comparison index, although high with respect to Jewish identity. First, the *culture variable* derives from the survivors' pre-Holocaust backgrounds. One of the most important distinctions among European Jews on the eve of the Holocaust, especially in central and eastern parts of the continent, was between the assimilated and the nonassimilated Jews. We refer to this distinction as cultural, since it usually entailed issues of language, religion, social customs, diet, often even dress and appearance, degree of integration in the local non-Jewish community, and also important questions of self-identification. The assimilated were more likely to speak at home the language of the country in which they lived; their religious beliefs and practices were less likely to be fervent or central to their lives; their customs and personal appearance would usually mirror those of the Gentile world around them. They were more likely to think of themselves in dual terms, that is, "we are Germans *and* Jews," or even "we are Germans first and Jews second." Some would even attempt to reject their Jewish roots and connections, although Nazi racial anti-Semitism would deny them this right in the 1940s. The assimilated would likely have many non-Jewish associates at work, as well as non-Jewish acquaintances and friends, and be more attuned to non-Jewish media of information and entertainment than the nonassimilated.

Indeed, among assimilated Jews, nearly 39 percent reported receiving the assistance of Gentiles during the Holocaust, whereas only 30 percent of the nonassimilated gave an indication of receiving any such help. What was even more important, however, was the fact that the nonassimilated Jewish survivors of the Holocaust were far more likely to have spent the war in Nazi-run camps compared with the assimilated, who were *much* more likely to have survived by hiding among Gentiles, living under a false Gentile identity, or perhaps through membership in a partisan group.

We hypothesized that for people who described themselves as coming from nonassimilated families, the Holocaust was psychologically a more painful wound, partly because of the greater isolation of such individuals from the larger society of the time, and partly because of its clear-cut assault upon the central elements of their identity as individuals—their Jewishness. This presumably would express itself in higher scores on all of the indices of our study, that is, more overall negativity in responses, but with a significantly higher, compensatory sense of Jewish identity and participation after the Holocaust.

The final compound variable was designed to measure the effects of individual suffering in the Holocaust. This we termed the *exposure variable*, based upon certain inferences from information supplied by the respondents. It consisted of several elements, relating to age, time spent in Nazi concentration and/or liquidation camps, and residence in Poland during the 1940s, as well as origin in nonassimilated families for reasons explained above. Individuals classified as having had high exposure to suffering were those who tended to be from nonassimilated homes, who were adults during the period of the Holocaust, who survived the Holocaust in Nazi concentration camps, and who lived in Poland at the beginning of the Second World War. Individuals with lower exposure were those who came from assimilated homes, who were very young, who survived the war by means other than incarceration in Nazi-run camps, and who did not live in Poland. The effect of this variable in terms of the difference between high-exposure and lower-exposure attitudes was anticipated to be analogous to the cultural model. In fact, it proved to be the strongest of all our explanatory variables.

An explanation of our interpretation of "suffering" is in order. Age in relation to the memory of suffering seems important for several reasons. People who were relatively mature at the time of the Holocaust would be more likely to have had both vivid and detailed recollections of various events, as opposed to the more vague, perhaps even blurry memories of the very young. Mature memories would also reflect the ability of the survivors to put events and occurrences into a more coherent and concrete context. The more mature people were more likely to understand why particular occurrences were frightening and threatening, and also, by their fuller appreciation of recent contrary conditions, why they may have been revolting and demeaning. Even family losses would likely be seen differently by older versus younger respondents. Losing a relative one knew well was obviously different from losing one who was really unknown; thus to have lost one's uncle or grandparent at the age of eighteen would probably have been a traumatic and haunting experience, whereas an equivalent loss at the age of three might be little more than a mark in a genealogy table.

As to our third variable, granted the possibility of some individual exceptions, the survival in a concentration camp was most likely, in our view, to be connected to a vivid sense of suffering on the part of the respondent. The camp, whether a concentration camp or a combination of destruction and incarceration with a forced-labor facility, was a more likely setting in which the survivor would have been exposed, on a daily basis, in a continuous fashion, to the experience of atrocities and brutalities inflicted upon others as well as upon himself. On the other hand, persons who had survived the war in other settings, such as in hiding or in partisan groups, very likely experienced great stress, deprivation, and anxiety, and may well have suffered and witnessed trauma on *some* occasions, but they were much less likely to be exposed on a daily, hour-by-hour, minute-by-minute basis to the brutal mistreatment of Jews by Nazi operatives. People who survived under assumed Gentile identities lived relatively "normal" lives, although they were subject to the ever-present anxiety of discovery and death and also, to be sure, within the less-than-ideal conditions of Nazi occupation.

With respect to the last variable, residence in Poland was connected with two important factors enhancing an individual's sense of suffering. Poland was the principal site of Hitler's Final Solution. It was the focus in terms of the number and kinds of camps built and operated by the Nazis for the purpose of exterminating the Jewish people, not only from Poland itself but from other parts of Europe as well. The names of Auschwitz, Majdanek, Treblinka, Belzec, and Sobibor, not to mention the ghettos of Warsaw, Lodz, Krakow, Bialystok, and Wilno are irrevocably linked with Poland. Secondly, and some might argue relatedly, the social environment of Poland was generally very hostile to Jews.

In the 1940s, the atmosphere of life in Poland for most Jews was likely to combine many negatives generated by frequent and nearby Nazi depredations and the sense of overwhelming isolation and abandonment due to the antipathy of the local population. The latter condition constituted a huge difference between the circumstances of Jews in such countries as Denmark, Holland, Italy, France, Belgium, Greece, and Bulgaria—perhaps even Germany itself—and those in Poland. In all probability, only the Jews from the Baltic states, Slovakia, Croatia, and the Ukraine, of whom not many were left, and possibly Rumania would have been closely comparable in this respect to the Jews of Poland.

Significant "internal" evidence supports our hypothesis with respect to the traumatic effects of residence in Poland. Among Polish Jews the perception that anti-Semitism in the surrounding society was a *very* important factor in the execution of the Holocaust was shared by many more respondents than was the case among non-Polish Jews. This view of the role of anti-Semitism was weaker in the West and stronger in the East.

Among Polish Jews, the perception that non-Jews "cooperated with and supported" the Nazi extermination of the Jewish people was much more characteristic (frequent) than among their non-Polish counterparts. When asked to give reasons why assistance may not have been given to

Jews by non-Jews during the Holocaust, most Polish survivors attributed it to anti-Semitism. Among non-Polish survivors, that opinion was much less common, with a larger balance of more benign motives attributed to Gentiles such as "indifference," "fear of Nazis," and "lack of information."

Perhaps most telling was the issue of awareness of the horrors that were descending, and about to descend, upon the Jewish people in the Second World War. When asked, "Would you say that by the summer of 1942, you were aware of a Nazi attempt to exterminate all Jews?" 48 percent of the respondents from Poland answered "definitely yes," whereas only 24 percent of the respondents outside Poland gave the same answer.

The exposure model (or compound variable), embodying most directly the experience of the Holocaust itself, actually has greater explanatory power in terms of the attitudinal indices of this study than any of the others. Moreover, it is literally by several magnitudes more powerful as an apparent attitude-shaper than the two models that rely either exclusively or largely upon the respondents' postwar experiences and current socioeconomic criteria. In the most general sense, the study validates the powerful hold of the past upon the present among those who had lived through the trauma of Hitler's Final Solution. (See appendix B for a list of variables in the analysis.)

Naturally, our findings here have all sorts of implications for propositions about the Holocaust in the extant literature. A few examples may suffice. Illustratively, we find the late political philosopher, Hannah Arendt, who was never near the scene when Nazi *Einsatzgruppen* began their mass murders and the trains began to roll toward the gas chambers, claim that Jewish victims had a major share of responsibility in the Final Solution. In her well-known book, *Eichmann in Jerusalem: A Report on the Banality of Evil*, Arendt's account of the activities of Jewish communal leaders would reasonably lead one to believe that the evil inflicted by Jews upon Jews was actually even worse than what the Nazis themselves had done to Jews.

We find Arendt saying, for example: "To a Jew this role of the Jewish leaders in the destruction of their own people is undoubtedly the darkest chapter [!] of the whole dark story."[9] Or, "in fact [Jewish policemen] were, of course [?!] more brutal and less corruptible [than Germans] since so much more was at stake for them."[10] "Without Jewish help in administrative and police work—there would have been either complete chaos or an impossibly [!] severe drain on German manpower."[11] Arendt claims that if Jews were "unorganized" and "leaderless," but not "cooperative" with Nazis, there would have been "plenty of misery" but hardly as many victims in the Holocaust as there actually were, and she points to Holland, where among the Jews who simply fled into the surrounding environs, "forty to fifty percent" survived.[12] An amazingly defective example, one would think, in the European context!

What was perhaps most interesting in Hannah Arendt's account was that it was fundamentally a two-party account of the Holocaust. The Holocaust, to Arendt, was something that occurred between the Jews and the Germans. It may have happened in many countries, but it was basically a two-party problem between the victims and their oppressors. The question of the "environment" in which the Final Solution took place, especially, of course, in Poland, where most of the killings took place, was never even touched upon by the highly judgmental Arendt. Were there really any reasonable prospects of such things as food, shelter, work, or medical assistance for Jews escaping in large numbers into areas inhabited by Poles? Arendt did not seem to know much about Polish or other Eastern European anti-Semitism.

There were literally only three references in Arendt's book to Churchill, Roosevelt, and Stalin—one each. In only one case, that of Roosevelt, was there any *connection* suggested between the particular leader and the Holocaust. In the case of Roosevelt, Arendt referred briefly to his attempts to put pressure on the Hungarian government to stop the deportation of Jews from Hungary to the gas chambers in July 1944.[13] There was no mention here, of course, of the fact that by July 1944 most of the Jews of Europe had already been killed by the Nazis. There was no mention that neither Roosevelt nor Churchill nor Stalin showed any interest whatsoever in the fate of European Jewry—even when, and even after, they publicly acknowledged the Final Solution on December 17, 1942, in a statement made by British Foreign Secretary Anthony Eden to the House of Commons in London on behalf of eleven Allied governments. Of course, the Allies knew a great deal about the treatment of the Jews by the Nazis in Europe long before that particular statement—but without any consequence. Between them, Churchill and Roosevelt did not even devote one radio broadcast to the fate of European Jews: not even one appeal to the peoples of Europe on behalf of the Jews—not in 1941, 1942, or 1943. A couple of passing notes were made in a statement by Roosevelt in late March 1944; none by Churchill or Stalin.

Unlike the members of Jewish communal councils, who were found so wanting by Hannah Arendt, these Allied leaders did not live in fear of the Gestapo, had access to all sorts of information, and possessed means of action at their disposal that were far more formidable than anything located in European ghettos during Nazi rule.[14] Would the testimony of Holocaust survivors support Arendt's account, or would it perhaps contradict it? That seemed to us an eminently worthwhile topic of inquiry.

As it turned out, the Arendt view that the conduct of Jewish community leaders and policemen was even *worse* than that of the Nazis themselves received literally no support.[15] For the Holocaust survivors, the course of the Final Solution was distinctly a three-party problem, not one with two parties. Their judgment of the world external to both Jews and Nazis is a very severe one—and it deserves to be remembered.

Given the centrality of this issue, i.e., Allied indifference, to the Holocaust, and to the perception of the Holocaust by the survivors, a brief explanation of the Allied declaration of December 17, 1942, seems well warranted. It was delivered on behalf of the governments of Belgium, Czechoslovakia, Greece, Luxembourg, the Netherlands, Norway, Poland, the United States, the United Kingdom, the Soviet Union, and Yugoslavia and the French National Committee.

The statement, made public by Anthony Eden, included the phrase that the attention of the above-named parties

> has been drawn to numerous reports from Europe that the German authorities, not content with denying to persons of Jewish race in all the territories over which their barbarous rule has been extended the most elementary human rights, are now carrying into effect Hitler's oft repeated intention to exterminate the Jewish people in Europe. From all the occupied countries Jews are being transported, in conditions of appalling horror and brutality, to Eastern Europe. In Poland, which has been made the principal Nazi slaughterhouse, the ghettoes established by the German invaders are being systematically emptied of all Jews. . . . None of those taken away are ever heard of again. . . . The number of victims of these bloody cruelties is reckoned in many hundreds of thousands of entirely innocent men, women and children.

The British foreign secretary prefaced his remarks by declaring that the reports upon which the Allied declaration was based were "reliable," and that they had reached the British government "recently." In the conclusion of the official declaration, Eden said that the Allied governments (1) condemned the "bestial policy of cold-blooded extermination," (2) were strengthened in their resolve to "overthrow the barbarous Hitlerite tyranny," and (3) resolved to ensure that "those responsible for these crimes shall not escape retribution."[16] He said nothing about any possible assistance to the victims.

In the ensuing discussion Eden was asked by one M.P., "May we take it from the right honorable Gentleman's statement that any persons who can escape from any of these occupied territories will be welcomed and given every assistance in the territories of the United Nations?"

Eden replied: "Certainly we should like to do all we possibly can. There are, obviously, certain security formalities which have to be considered. It would clearly be the desire of the United Nations to do everything they could to provide wherever possible an asylum for these people, but the House will understand that there are immense geographical and other difficulties in the matter."[17]

To say that this misrepresented British policy toward Jewish exiles seeking entry into Palestine, for example, would be an understatement. Eden also volunteered a remark that exceeded exaggeration: "I may also say that all the information we have from the occupied countries is that the peoples there, despite their many sufferings, trials and tribulations, are doing everything in their power to give assistance and charity to their Jewish fellow subjects."[18]

However Eden may have misrepresented his own attitude and that of the British government, the fact of the Nazi Holocaust was now, at last, publicly declared on behalf of all the major Allied powers as well as several governments-in-exile. Henceforth, any official pretending not to know what was happening to the Jews of Europe was blatantly in denial.

But that, in fact, became the prevalent practice after December 17, 1942. It was even appropriately capped by Winston Churchill's multivolume *History of the Second World War*, published in the 1950s, which made no reference whatsoever to the 1942 declaration and no mention of the Holocaust itself in the text of the work. (It seems that one endnote reference to events in Hungary "got away" from the Prime Minister in volume 6.) In fact, in August of 1946, Churchill actually claimed that he "had no idea when the war came to an end of the horrible massacres [to which Jews were subjected]."[19]

In December 1942, Franklin Roosevelt told several representatives of American Jewish organizations visiting him at the White House that "we shall do all in our power to be of service to your people in this tragic moment."[20] But in fact, as Michael Marrus writes, "Although periodically informed about mass killings, FDR was prepared to run no risks for the Jews [and] thought that action on their behalf meant trouble politically."[21]

Indeed, it was remarkable, but hardly surprising, that one finds the following observation in the obviously authoritative diaries of Joseph

Goebbels just four days before the Eden declaration: "The question of Jewish persecution in Europe is being given top news priority by the English and the Americans. . . . At bottom, however, I believe that both the English and the Americans are happy that we are exterminating the Jewish riff-raff."[22] Nothing in the Goebbels diaries subsequent to the December 13, 1942, entry suggests that he, after the Allied declaration, had the least cause to change his mind about this rather fundamental appraisal of Allied attitudes toward the Final Solution.

No amount of analysis and discussion can bridge the factual gap between actually killing people and passively watching it happen—or even between killing and in some ways facilitating or indirectly enabling the killings to occur. But the moral or even legal gap between these phenomena is quite another matter. One of the more remarkable discoveries of our study is that Holocaust survivors attach not merely a very high degree of blame to the so-called bystanders, but that the severity of their collective judgments of the bystanders is analogous in its harshness to the judgment of the perpetrators. In practical terms, this means that, given choices about interpreting the behavior of the various actors, the survivors tend to choose the most negative interpretation of the designs and actions of the perpetrators, and they also tend to choose the most negative and guilt-bearing alternatives for the bystanders. In this latter sense, there is virtually *no* difference between the evaluations of the killers and the evaluations of the witnesses and observers of the killings.

An interesting recent claim about the Holocaust is found in the work of American political scientist Daniel Jonah Goldhagen. Goldhagen has suggested that German anti-Semitism prior to Hitler's time and during his rule was so virulent that it furnished voluntary mass support by virtually the whole German people for the Final Solution. Says Goldhagen: "The cultural cognitive model of Jews was the property of Nazis and non-Nazis alike."[23] Since no one ever "excelled" Adolf Hitler in anti-Semitic policies, it would seem reasonable to infer from Goldhagen's analysis that the anti-Semitism of most Germans was also historically "unexcelled." In fact, Goldhagen makes this claim explicitly (p. 419).

Interestingly, however, that does not seem to be the view of the Jewish survivors of the Holocaust—certainly not among most of the people we have interviewed. In the perception of our respondents, anti-Semitism was *most* virulent not among Germans but among Poles. Actually, among the Jewish survivors from Poland, first place in attributed anti-Semitic attitudes went to Poles over Germans by a margin of nearly 2 to 1. As discussed more fully in chapter 5, Ukrainians and Poles jointly exceeded Germans and Austrians on this unenviable scale.[24]

It is of considerable significance to note that if the Holocaust is seen as a three-party phenomenon, rather than a two-party phenomenon, Daniel Goldhagen's sweeping condemnation of most Germans, if not actually all Germans, is in effect undermined. Goldhagen does not argue that every German man, woman, or child actively participated in the murder of the Jews. What he says, reasonably enough, is that the overwhelming majority of Germans were silent when Hitler and the Nazis proceeded to slaughter the Jews. From this proposition, which is factually quite persuasive, he goes on to a more problematic one, namely, that most Germans actually shared Hitler's "eliminationist anti-Semitism." But did Winston Churchill and Franklin Roosevelt also share this belief?

There is little question that these Allied leaders had much more access to information about the fate of European Jews (especially from the Polish government-in-exile in London) than, let us say, a streetcar conductor or a plumber or a flower shop clerk in the city of Hamburg in, say, 1943. The so-called ordinary German may have noticed that Jews were gone from Hamburg, and he may have heard rumors about what was happening to the Jews in the East, but that was certainly less than receiving authoritative briefings from Polish officials and diplomatic and intelligence reports over a substantial period of time.

Moreover, Allied leaders were not constrained by the Nazi police apparatus, and they also had capabilities—diplomatic, political, economic, intelligence, and military—far in excess of any "ordinary Germans." Why did they not act and why did they, for the most part, remain silent? Were they, too, eliminationist anti-Semites? Was Pope Pius XII an "eliminationist anti-Semite"?[25] Were the United States Congress and the British House of Commons made up of eliminationist anti-Semites? We do not propose to address these questions here but simply point out that victim testimony has implications for all sorts of more general issues surrounding the great tragedy of the European Jews.

There is, to be sure, a large scholarly literature in the postwar period on the issue of what the Nazis intended to do to the Jews before the *Einsatzgruppen* of 1941 went into action. There are disputes between the so-called intentionalists and functionalists: those who see an initial design for the Final Solution, especially with Hitler personally, and those for whom the whole process was something that developed incrementally among contradictory initiatives and interests of various Nazi agents: something that the Nazis almost stumbled upon. There was, for example, Arno Mayer's *Why Did the Heavens*

Not Darken? The "Final Solution" in History (New York: Pantheon Books, 1989) suggesting the "stumbling process" or a by-product interpretation of the Final Solution as a consequence of Hitler's war with the Soviet Union, his anti-Bolshevik crusade.[26] But what were the perceptions of the victims?

Nor can we forget the Australian scholar who argued in a recent book that the course of the Holocaust was so completely controlled by its perpetrators that no actions taken from outside Nazi-occupied Europe could possibly have made any difference. This was the theme of William D. Rubenstein in *The Myth of Rescue: Why the Democracies Could Not Have Saved More Jews from the Nazis* (New York: Routledge, 1997), with a sentence worth quoting: "Not one plan or proposal, made anywhere in the democracies by either Jews or non-Jewish champions of the Jews once the mass murder of the Jews had begun, could have rescued one single Jew [!] who perished in the Nazi Holocaust" (p. 84).

(Not even one or two radio broadcasts by Allied leaders at the time could have done that much? Perhaps there were not enough plans, and above all, not enough will to do anything about them.) In any case, the victims, years after the fact, do not agree with the Rubenstein perception of events. These are, of course, but a few of the relevant examples.

At this juncture, we may appropriately turn to the specific topics of our inquiry, the evidence of survivor observations concerning cognition, learning, identity, blame, and comparison.[27]

NOTES

1. In alphabetical order, several such works of individual memory follow: Thomas Geve, *Guns and Barbed Wire* (Chicago: Academy Chicago, 1987); Vera Laska, ed., *Women in the Resistance and in the Holocaust* (Westport, Conn.: Greenwood Press, 1983); Isabella Leitner, *Fragments of Isabella: A Memoir of Auschwitz* (New York: Crowell, 1978); Hanna Levy-Hass, *Inside Belsen* (Totowa, N.J.: Harvester Press, 1982); William R. Perl, *Operation Action* (New York: F. Ungar, 1983); Samuel Pizar, *Of Blood and Hope* (Boston: Little, Brown, 1980); Sylvia Rothchild, ed., *Voices From The Holocaust* (New York: New American Library, 1981); Eva Schloss, *Eva's Story: A Survivor's Tale* (London: W. H. Allen, 1988); Ruth Schwertfeger, *The Women in Theresienstadt* (New York: St. Martin's Press, 1989); Peter Silverman, David Smushkovitz, and Peter Smuszkowicz, *From Victims to Victors* (Quebec: The Canadian Society for Yad Vashem, 1992); Michael Zylberberg, *A Warsaw Diary, 1939–1945* (London: Vallentine, Mitchell, 1969).

2. Note Raul Hilberg, *Perpetrators, Victims, Bystanders: The Jewish Catastrophe 1933–1945* (New York: Harper Collins, 1992).

3. Martin Gilbert, "Final Solution," in *The Oxford Companion to Second World War*, ed. I. C. B. Dear and M. R. D. Foot (New York: Oxford University Press, 1995), p. 365.

4. However, the principal author of this study was seven years old in 1939 and testifies to the fact that even for the very young, the Holocaust was an overwhelming experience, not likely to be ever forgotten.

5. I.e., are the perceptions and judgments of the Holocaust survivors significantly different between males and females? Recent literature on women and on gender differences suggests such possibilities. Perhaps the nurturing roles of women have contributed to different attitudes among them. Perhaps a different, somewhat lesser propensity to express anger and violence on the part of women might mitigate their Holocaust judgments with respect to various actors more so than in the case of males. Perhaps among Jewish women, given the historical legacy, there might be a stronger propensity to cultivate cultural and religious Jewish traditions than would be the case with males. There are many different views about what gender differences in perception and expression are, or might be, including the view that psychology and biology have little to offer—that "differences" are basically a function of "social expectations about women." See Naomi Weinstein, "Psychology Constructs the Female," in *Female Psychology: The Emerging Self*, ed. Sue Cox (Chicago: Science Research Associates, 1976), pp. 91–103. Note the view that women in "Western society" are more likely to express emotions or feelings than men. Cf. Nancy Henley and Jo Freeman, "The Sexual Politics of Interpersonal Behavior," Ibid., pp. 174–75. Would that suggest stronger female reactions to the experiences of the Holocaust? More, or stronger, blame-related attitudes? See also Aguenta Fischer, "Emotion," in *Gender and Psychology*, ed. Karen Trew and John Kremer (London: Arnold, 1998), pp. 82–94, suggesting a greater degree of emotional expressiveness among women. Whether socially conditioned, and/or to whatever degree biologically conditioned, is it possible that, given various presumed nurturing orientations, women have more empathetic impulses than men? See Mary J. Larrabee, ed., *An Ethic of Care: Feminist and Interdisciplinary Perspectives* (New York: Routledge, 1993), and especially the discussion by Marilyn Friedman, "Beyond Caring: The De-Moralization of Gender," pp. 258–73. See also Margaret W. Matlin, *The Psychology of Women* (New York: Hold, Rinehart and Winston, 1987), esp. pp. 485–86, and Eliyahu Kitov, *The Jew and His Home*, trans. Nathan Bulman, 12th ed. (New York: Shengold, 1982), p. 59: "Jewish tradition relates that it was the righteous women who enabled our forefathers to be redeemed and brought forth out of Egypt. . . . The women were always more loyal to God than were the men." P. 63: "The origin of everything good that one finds in the world and amongst Jews is women. . . . Show me a great man and I will show you a great mother." Finally, see also Francine Klagsburn, *Voices of Wisdom* (New York: Pantheon Books, 1980), who says that

"within the framework of Jewish law, women were and, in many respects, continue to be second-class citizens. . . . [But] within their accepted roles, and in everyday life, women received great honor and respect, and often much power" (p. 90).

6. See Charles H. Page, *Class and American Sociology* (New York: Shodeen Books, 1969), p. xvii: "By the middle 1950s few sociologists . . . would have challenged the assumption that 'class' is a strategic variable in the shaping of most social patterns."

7. See G. A. Almond and Sidney Verba, *The Civic Culture* (Boston: Little, Brown, 1965), p. 277, for linkage between class and education in their study. Note also: "Our data have shown education to be the most important determinant of political attitudes" p. 370.

8. See Leona E. Tyler, *The Psychology of Human Differences*, 3d ed. (New York: Appleton-Century Crofts, 1965), pp. 179–82, on substantial research suggesting that various personal attributes relating to attitudes and behavior show significant stability over individual lifetimes. Note also class *and* personality differences, with, e.g., more "broad-minded" opinions among upper classes and dogmatic views on religious and moral issues among lower classes. The differences might vary among ethnic groups (p. 357). See also an earlier study by Henry A. Murray et al., *Exploration in Personality* (New York: Oxford University Press, 1938), p. 501. Henry P. David and J. C. Brengelmann, eds., *Perspectives in Personality Research* (New York: Springer, 1960), pp. 249–50, support the consistency or constancy of various personality traits, but with a recognition that, in a world of many attributes, there is also a process of constant change. See also Leona E. Tyler, *Individual Differences, Abilities and Motivational Directions* (Englewood Cliffs, N.J.: Prentice Hall, 1975) p. 194: "Orientation(s) favorable or unfavorable to intellectual development . . . persist tenaciously throughout the years from early childhood to maturity." See also pp. 207–208.

Given some uncertainty over the lifelong nature of "optimism" versus "pessimism," as of any personality trait, we still assume that those whom we classify as "optimists" at the time of this inquiry would likely "filter" or "repress" negative perceptions or judgments more than would the "pessimists." We assume a certain degree of congruence between the respondent's personality and stance toward the world. See Margaret W. Matlin and David J. Strang, *The Pollyanna Principle: Selectivity in Language, Memory and Thought* (Cambridge, Mass.: Schenkman, 1978). These authors suggest that "optimism" is an important survival-management concept for people, and that in subjective terms, most people are "happy" and "optimistic" most of the time. Note especially the generalizations pp. 1–2. Our most optimistic survivor respondents only partially fit this model—certainly with some serious reservations.

See also Avner Ziv, *Personality and Sense of Humor* (New York: Springer, 1984), p. 174: "Intuitively most people know that humor can contribute to better human relations." A positive outlook is seen here as reinforcing health and presumably various personally preservative and enhancing characteristics (pp. 2–3).

9. Hannah Arendt, *Eichmann in Jerusalem: A Report on the Banality of Evil,* rev. ed. (New York: Viking Press, 1964), p. 117.

10. Ibid., p. 119.

11. Ibid., p. 117.

12. Ibid., p. 125.

13. Ibid., p. 201.

14. For a scholarly rebuttal, see Jacob Robinson, *And the Crooked Shall Be Made Straight: The Eichmann Trial, The Jewish Catastrophe, and Hannah Arendt's Narrative* (Philadelphia: The Jewish Publication Society, 1965).

15. Among our 203 respondents, 47 elected to answer the following open-ended query: "An important question about the Holocaust which I feel has never been addressed is: _____." Among the 47 persons replying to this question, *one* wrote that "the leadership of the Rabbis and the fanaticism of the Jewish people helped the Nazis to exterminate us." However, even this singular opinion falls short of the Arendt thesis.

16. *Parliamentary Debates*, Commons, 5th ser., vol. 385 (1942), p. 2083.

17. Ibid., p. 2086.

18. Ibid., p. 2085.

19. See Michael J. Cohen, *Churchill and the Jews* (London: Frank Cass, 1985), pp. 266–67.

20. Monty Noam Penkower, *The Jews Were Expendable: Free World Diplomacy and the Holocaust* (Urbana: University of Illinois Press, 1983), p. 86.

21. See M. R. Marrus, "Bystanders to the Holocaust," in *FDR and the Holocaust*, ed. Verne W. Newton (New York: St. Martin's Press, 1996), p. 155. Roosevelt's personal attitude was probably more accurately reflected in private remarks he had made at Casablanca on January 17, 1943, three months before the Warsaw ghetto rising. He was speaking with Vichy French General Charles Nogues and his own political representative in North Africa, Robert Murphy:

Mr. Murphy remarked that the Jews in North Africa were very much disappointed that 'the war for liberation' had not immediately resulted in their being given their complete freedom. The President stated that he felt the whole Jewish problem should be studied very carefully and that progress should be definitely planned. In other words, the number of Jews engaged in the practice of the professions (law, medicine, etc.) should be definitely limited to the percentage that the Jewish population in North Africa bears to the whole of the North African population. Such a plan would therefore permit the Jews to engage in the professions, at the same time would not permit them to overcrowd the professions, and would represent an unanswerable argument that they were being given their full rights. To the foregoing, General Nogues agreed generally, stating at the same time that it would be a sad thing for the French to win the war merely to open the way for the Jews to control the professions and the business world of North

Africa. The President stated that his plan would further eliminate the specific and understandable complaints which the Germans bore towards the
Jews in Germany, namely, that while they represented a small part of the
population, over fifty percent [*sic*] of the lawyers, doctors, school teachers,
college professors, etc., in Germany, were Jews.

See Department of State, *Foreign Relations of the United States: The Conferences
at Washington 1941–1942, and Casablanca, 1943*, Publication 8414 (Washington,
D.C.: U.S. Government Printing Office, 1968), p. 608. The president's figures
reflected some wild anti-Semitic stereotypes. At the beginning of 1933, Jewish
physicians constituted about 11 percent of all German physicians; Jewish lawyers
were 16 percent of the German total. See Saul Friedlander, *Nazi Germany and the
Jews*, vol. 1, *The Years of Persecution* (New York: Harper Collins, 1997), pp.
29–30. A perusal of FDR's wartime speeches and statements reveals only one occa-
sion, in late March 1944, when the president mentioned, very briefly, the plight of
the Jews and appealed for the world's sympathy and help on their behalf. By that
time, however, most of Hitler's Jewish victims were already dead. Churchill made
no such speeches at all.

22. *The Goebbels Diaries, 1942–1943*, ed. Louis P. Loehner (Garden City,
N. Y.: Doubleday, 1948), p. 241 [December 13, 1942].

23. Daniel Goldhagen, *Hitler's Willing Executioners: Ordinary Germans and
the Holocaust* (New York: A. A. Knopf, 1996), p. 116. See also p. 460: "Germany
during the Nazi period was a society . . . fundamentally different from ours today
. . . inhabited by people . . . not 'ordinary' by our standards."

24. Goldhagen, *Hitler's Willing Executioners*, p. 119: "Only once was there
large-scale protest by Germans on behalf of Jews, namely when German women
massed in Berlin and demonstrated for three days [!] for the release of their
recently incarcerated Jewish husbands. How did the regime respond in the face of
this popular opposition? It backed down. The six thousand Jewish men were freed.
The women suffered no disabilities." Interestingly, however, *no* such demonstra-
tions—for example, no church masses—were ever held in Poland during the years
1939–45 on behalf of, or in explicit sympathy with, the Jews—or, indeed, analogously, among numerous Polish exiles throughout the world during the same
period, to the author's knowledge.

25. See especially the recent work by John Cornwell, *Hitler's Pope: The
Secret History of Pius XII* (New York: Viking, 1999); also see the provocative
work, in English translation, by Rolf Hochhuth, *The Deputy* (New York: Grove
Press, 1964); Saul Friedlander, *Pius XII and the Third Reich: A Documentation*
(New York: Knopf, 1966); among defenses, Michael O'Carroll, *Pius XII: Great-
ness Dishonoured* (Chicago: Franciscan Herald Press, 1980); also John F. Morley,
Vatican Diplomacy and the Jews during the Holocaust, 1939–1943 (New York:
KTAV Publishing, 1980), esp. p. 209: "Vatican diplomacy failed the Jews during
the Holocaust by not doing all that was possible for it to do. . . . It betrayed the

ideals that it had set for itself." See also Michael Phayer, "Pope Pius XII, the Holocaust, and the Cold War," *Holocaust and Genocide Studies* 12, no. 2 (1998): pp. 233–56, esp. p. 248: "Pius XII's focus on Communism as a threat to the Christian West led him to relate Catholic spirituality to international affairs rather than to the Holocaust."

26. See Christopher R. Browning, *The Path to Genocide: Essays on Launching the Final Solution* (New York: Cambridge University Press, 1992), esp. chap. 4, pp. 77–121. Browning tries to straddle the gap between the functionalists and the intentionalists, without a single reference to Hitler's *Mein Kampf*, which, after all is said and done, could easily have convinced any reasonably intelligent and attentive reader that Hitler personally envisioned the murder of the Jews as the optimum solution of the "Jewish Problem." See also Alexander J. Groth, *Democracies against Hitler: Myth, Reality and Prologue* (Aldershot, U.K.: Ashgate, 1999), pp. 20–27.

27. We wish to share this methodological note with our readers. The purpose of our study is to bring some light to a subject of enormous complexity and human sensitivity. We have chosen to employ a methodology of very basic statistics and common sense. Our findings should be accessible to any person who can simply appreciate the difference between "more" and "less" and between "frequently" and "infrequently." We are waiving the laurels of advanced calculus and cutting-edge statistical wizardry in a spirit of humility; we do not expect to have the "last word" on this great subject. We also do so in the spirit of the Aristotelian injunction that attempting excessive rigor on matters inherently somewhat imprecise is a grave mistake. It is our impression that this is a mistake frequently committed by statistical zealots. We do, however, refer the reader to a brief discussion of multiple regression results in chapter 8 and also to the appendices.

Chapter 2

COGNITION

Although cognition and evaluation are closely related, in this chapter we focus mainly on the cognitive dimension: the personal knowledge, awareness, and understanding that survivors had of the events and the conditions leading to and preceding the Holocaust. Did they, by and large, realize that Nazi rule would bring them systematic and pitiless extermination? How did they view their environment and their prospects on the eve of the war and during the years culminating in the Final Solution? How did the survivors see the choices confronting them before the start of the deportations to the gas chambers? What perceptions did they have of their Gentile neighbors?

Although the line may not always be easily drawn, our purpose here is to elicit those survivor opinions most closely linked to personal experience. This would involve judgments about occurrences or situations that were either witnessed or experienced by the survivors or that were likely witnessed and discussed by the survivor's family, neighbors, friends, and acquaintances during the Holocaust period.

Our questionnaire contained eight individual items that related in various ways to the survivors' awareness and understanding of their environment. Our data, of course, are recall data; we were asking our respondents for a reconstruction of their understanding of events that occurred over fifty years ago. However, given the catastrophic effect of these events on the survivors' lives, some powerful memories were likely to be invoked (see cognition scale, Fig. 2.1).

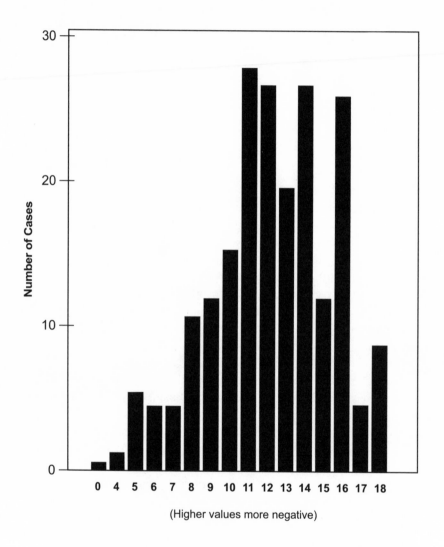

Fig. 2.1. Distribution of Values on Cognitive Scale

The first part of our chapter derives from survivor responses to the following three questions, linked to the victims' perceptions of German intentions regarding the Jews in the early 1940s:

How did you estimate Nazi intentions toward Jews at the start of the war?
  a. I did not think that *in practice* the Nazis would be any worse in their treatment of Jews than anybody else.
  b. I did not know what to expect.
  c. They planned severe measures against Jews but not mass killings of innocent persons.
  d. They planned the total extermination of the Jews.
  e. Cannot recall.

In terms of the above expectations, do you think most *other* Jews in the country where you lived believed at the outset of the war that:
  a. *In practice* the Nazis would be no worse in their treatment of the Jews than anybody else.
  b. The prospects for Jews were unclear.
  c. Hitler planned severe measures against Jews but not mass killings of innocent persons.
  d. Hitler planned the total extermination of the Jews.
  e. Cannot recall.

Would you say that by the summer of 1942, you were aware of a Nazi attempt to exterminate all Jews?
  a. Did not believe that the Nazis really could have such an intention
  b. Did not really know what to expect
  c. Believed the Nazis would want to kill some Jews, but not all or most
  d. Suspected this, but was not yet sure
  e. Definitely yes
  f. Cannot recall

Our survey reveals that only a relatively small minority, 25 percent of the survivors, believed—by their own subsequent, after-the-fact, testimony—that the Nazis would endeavor to kill all Jews accessible to their control. A much greater number, roughly two-thirds, were evenly divided between those who thought that Nazi intentions were simply unclear, and those who believed that the Nazis would implement some severe measures against Jews but nothing actually approaching total extermination. Nearly 7 percent even believed that the Nazis would not be significantly different in their treatment of Jews from other regimes and other rulers of the contemporary period.

To be sure, expectations of Nazi rule varied by region. Among our relatively few Western European survivors, only 20 percent expected total annihilation. In Poland, on the other hand, 34 percent had that expectation already in 1939. In other Eastern European countries, including places like Hungary, Rumania, and the former Czechoslovakia, the figure was slightly under 25 percent.

A similar pattern of anticipation was reflected in responses to our question about the views of *other* Jews at that time. In Western Europe, 47 percent of our respondents opted for the "severe measures" option as the prevalent Jewish opinion of the time, with less than 12 percent expecting annihilation; 35 percent thought that the issue was unclear for most Jews; and about 6 percent chose the "not worse than anybody else" alternative. But for Poland, the same question elicited an almost 27 percent response predicting annihilation; only 21 percent saw "intentions unclear" as the view of most other Jews; slightly more than 7 percent expected treatment no worse than from anyone else; and 44 percent opted for the "severe measures" alternative. In other Eastern European countries, the views were even more negative than in Poland. Here, actually over 31 percent saw the prevalent Jewish expectation at the time as annihilation; less than 7 percent opted for the "not worse than anybody else" alternative; 26 percent thought that the Jewish perspective was unclear; and over 34 percent believed that "severe measures," but not annihilation, represented the prevalent Jewish anticipation.

In overall terms, only 27 percent of our respondents saw Jewish opinion at the outbreak of the war—distinguished from their own personal views—as anticipating the Final Solution. Some 41 percent thought there was merely a general anticipation of "severe measures"; 24 percent thought the situation was seen by Jews as unclear; and 7 percent effectively dismissed the prospects as probably no worse than under any other regime.

Looked at in retrospect, cognitive perceptions in the East appear to have been more realistic than those in the West. The extermination of the Jews could have been reasonably inferred as Hitler's preferred option, if not quite a fatally inevitable policy, from the text of the Führer's ideological platform, *Mein Kampf.*

In his political "master work" of the 1920s, Hitler set out the premises of the physical destruction of the Jews. He did so both in reviewing the alleged causes of Germany's defeat in the First World War and also in a more general sense. Under the first rubric, he wrote:

If we pass all the causes of the German collapse in review, the ultimate and most decisive remains the failure to recognize the racial problem and especially the Jewish menace.

The defeats on the battlefield in August 1918, would have been child's play to bear. They stood in no proportion to the victories of our people. It was not they that caused our downfall; no, it was brought about by that power which prepared these defeats by systematically over many decades robbing our people of the political and moral instincts and forces which alone make nations capable and hence worthy of existence.

In heedlessly ignoring the question of the preservation of the racial foundations of our nation, the old Reich disregarded the sole right which gives life in this world.[1]

Under the second:

[The Jew] is and remains the typical parasite, a sponger who like a noxious bacillus keeps spreading as soon as a favorable medium invites him. And . . . wherever he appears, the host people dies out after a shorter or longer period.[2]

[The Jew] is [an] adversary of all humanity.[3]

[The Jew] is the eternal blood-sucker.[4]

[The] keenest [Jewish] minds see the dream of world domination tangibly approaching.[5]

From these premises, Hitler arrived at the following explicit conclusion:

Today it is not princes and princes' mistresses who haggle and bargain over state borders; it is the inexorable Jew who struggles for his domination over the nations. No nation can remove this hand from its throat except by the sword. Only the assembled and concentrated might of a national passion rearing up in its strength can defy the international enslavement of peoples. Such a process is and remains a bloody one.[6]

Hitler's public statement in the Reichstag in January 1939 "predicting" the destruction of Jewry as a consequence of any new European war could have been seen as confirming or reinforcing the earlier pronouncements. Since the educational attainments among Jews and communication networks in Western Europe were generally more advanced than those in the East, one might find the contrast in these Jewish views somewhat surprising. But given the greater and certainly more prolonged exposure of

Eastern European Jews to the actual physical as well as political and social ravages of anti-Semitism, it is perhaps not surprising that Hitler's threats were taken more seriously in the East than they were in the West. Perhaps also the traditions of the Enlightenment, stronger in Western Europe, tended to influence the Jews of that region much more strongly toward an ultimately mistaken, but understandable, discounting of the Nazis. How could such unbelievable barbarism as the *Mein Kampf* scenario occur among civilized people, Germans especially, in the twentieth century? Perhaps it was just unthinkable. In any case, the vision of Jewish annihilation on the eve of the war was a distinctly minority view among the prospective victims in all parts of Europe as reflected in the testimony of the survivors.

What is perhaps more surprising still is that the sense of impending annihilation apparently continued to be a minority view among Jewish victims even as late as the summer of 1942. To be sure, more Jews in all parts of Europe now believed this to be the Nazi agenda. This was especially true in Poland, just as one might have thought, given its importance as the site of the principal Nazi liquidation centers. But even in Poland, in the summer of 1942, as the testimony of our survivor respondents indicates, annihilation was still—albeit just barely—a minority view. Among Polish Jews, 48 percent described their own sense of events in 1942 as definitely based on an annihilation scenario. About 23 percent, however, said that they suspected this, but still were not sure about it. More than 12 percent did not believe it. Eleven percent did not know what to expect, and over 5 percent clung to the hope that only some Jews would be destined for extermination (see Fig. 2.2).

Less certainty prevailed farther from the killing centers. In Eastern Europe outside of Poland, only 22 percent of our survivor respondents reported their full appreciation of the annihilation design in mid-1942; 31 percent said that they suspected it, but weren't sure; almost 30 percent admitted simply to not knowing what to expect, and nearly 16 percent flatly did not believe that the total liquidation of Jewry was an objective of Nazi policy. In Western Europe, 42 percent of respondents declared their certainty about the coming Final Solution, but 16 percent did not believe it, 5 percent did not know what to think, and 37 percent reported themselves still merely suspicious.

Looking at the whole respondent group, we found that even as late as mid-1942, only 39 percent of the survivors, some fifty years after the fact, reported that they were definitely aware of the Final Solution in progress. But 30 percent either did not know what to think or did not believe in total

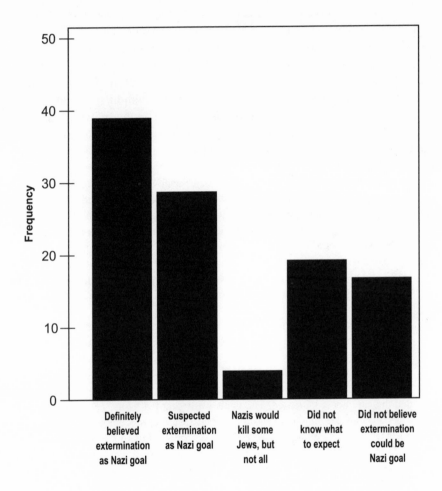

Fig. 2.2. Survivor Awareness of Nazi Intentions toward Jews, Summer 1942

extermination as the Nazi design. Almost 4 percent thought that only some Jews would be actually killed, and 27 percent reported that they suspected this but still were not sure as to what it was that the Nazis were trying to do with or to the Jews of Europe.

And yet, the portents of the Jewish catastrophe were palpably implicit in all sorts of developments, not really new in the latter part of 1942, and all of them already consuming hundreds of thousands of Jewish lives. Some of these portents even antedated the year 1941, which most scholars identify with decisive new Nazi measures leading up to the Wannsee Conference of January 1942 and the full-blown Final Solution.

This is what Jewish historian Emanuel Ringelblum wrote in his Warsaw diary in 1940 about the situation of the nearly five hundred thousand Jews herded by the Nazis into the largest ghetto in Europe:

> Smuggling began at the very moment that the Jewish area of residence was established. . . . It was calculated that the officially supplied rations did not cover even 10 percent of normal requirements. If one had wanted really to restrict oneself to the official rations then the entire population of the ghetto would have had to die of hunger in a very short time. . . .
>
> The German authorities did everything to seal off the ghetto hermetically and not to allow in a single gram of food. A wall was put up around the ghetto on all sides that did not leave a single millimeter of open space. . . .
>
> They fixed barbed wire and broken glass to the top of the wall. When that failed to help, the Judenrat was ordered to make the wall higher, at the expense of the Jews, of course. . . .
>
> Several kinds of guards were appointed for the walls and the passages through them; the categories [of guards] were constantly being changed and their numbers increased. The walls were guarded by the gendarmerie together with the Polish police; at the ghetto wall there were gendarmerie posts, Polish police and Jewish police. . . . The victims of the smuggling were mainly Jews, but they were not lacking either among the Aryans [Poles]. . . . Several times smugglers were shot at the central lock-up on Gesiowka Street. Once there was a veritable slaughter (100 persons were shot near Warsaw). Among the Jewish victims of the smuggling there were tens of Jewish children between 5 and 6 years old, whom the German killers shot in great numbers near the passages and at the walls. . . .
>
> And despite that, without paying attention to the victims, the smuggling never stopped for a moment. When the street was still slippery with the blood that had been spilled, other [smugglers] already set out, as soon as the 'candles' [lookouts] had signalled that the way was clear, to carry on with the work. . . .

The smuggling took place—a) through the walls, b) through the gates, c) through underground tunnels, d) through sewers, and e) through houses on the borders.[7]

What sort of signal were the Nazis sending to the Jews of Europe from the city of Warsaw? Benign neglect and confusion, or aspiration to murder and extermination? Hitler's so-called Commissar Order, issued on June 6, 1941, in anticipation of his attack on Russia, included a phrase about "all Jews" being subject to execution by German forces. It was given the broadest possible interpretation by the Nazis against the Jewish population of formerly Soviet territories (some of which included, of course, prewar Poland). Some three hundred thousand Jewish people are generally believed to have been killed within the first four months of Operation Barbarossa (the German code name for the invasion of the USSR).

As of June 22, 1941, SS commandos followed the regular army, and hundreds of thousands of innocent people were to be murdered in fields, ditches and forests. They were forced to undress under the supervision of the SS policemen or soldiers of the *Wehrmacht*, whips in hand. Many documents describing these mass shootings have been published, including those of German witnesses, such as that of Graebe, on the extermination of Jews in the down of Dubno.

In the occupied territories in Russia, Jews were massacred in ravines and in woods. But this seemed inadequate in the eyes of the murderers: they needed more efficient measures to annihilate millions of Jews. In January, 1942, at the infamous Wannsee conference, it was decided to murder eleven million Jews.[8]

As Lucy Dawidowicz tells us:

[In the] summer of 1941 a new enterprise was launched—the construction of the *Vernichtungslager*—the annihilation camp.

The first death camp to be completed was at Chelmno (Kulmhof in German), sixty kilometers from Lodz, intended for the Jews from the ghetto of Lodz. Chelmno began functioning on December 8, 1941, with mobile vans, using engine exhaust gasses. (Gas trucks turned up at the same time to kill the Jews assembled in a makeshift camp in Semlin, Serbia, where the occupying German army had been embarrassingly efficient in rounding up the Jews for slaughter before annihilation facilities were ready.)

The next death camp to be completed was at Belzec, near Lublin, at the end of 1941; it became operational in February 1942. Construction at

Sobibor began in March 1942. The labor concentration camp Majdanek, near Lublin, which had been set up at the end of 1940, was transformed into an annihilation camp. Similarly, Treblinka, fifty miles from Warsaw, a labor camp since 1941, was turned into a death camp. In the second half of 1941, the technicians of death took over, building camouflaged gassing facilities. Different methods of gassing were experimented with—in mobile or permanent installations, using exhaust engine gasses or Zyklon B. In the first half of 1942 both Majdanek and Treblinka joined the roster of functioning killing camps.[9]

Following the rough chronology of Samuel Willenberg:

On 8 December 1941 killing[s] began in the first extermination camp, Chelmno (Kulmhof) situated in the part of Poland incorporated in the Reich. This camp was to claim 360,000 Jewish victims.

In March 1942 the camp at Belzec and in April of that year the camp at Sobibor were opened. Belzec would claim 600,000 and Sobibor 250,000 Jewish lives.

In May–June 1942 the construction of Treblinka extermination camp began.

On 22 July 1942 the leader of the Jewish Council in Warsaw, Adam Czerniakow, was informed by the Germans that all Jews in the ghetto were to be resettled in the east.

The first transport from Warsaw arrived in Treblinka on 23 July 1942.

By mid-August, as many as 12,000 Jews were arriving daily in Treblinka.

Between 23 July and 28 August 1942, 200,000 Jews from Warsaw and over 112,000 others were murdered there.

By mid-November 1942, 438,600 Jews had been killed in Treblinka.[10] It may be recalled, of course, that until the Allied declaration of December 17, 1942, in London by Foreign Secretary Eden, no national or international agencies of any authoritative character had ever publicly "certified," that is, officially and explicitly confirmed, the Final Solution as a Nazi policy in progress. The Third Reich obviously never admitted it. For practical purposes, as far as the Jews of Europe, or anyone else, were concerned it was only a design that during the 1940s could be inferred from various assorted acts occurring within the territories controlled by Hitler's Germany.

Nevertheless, all these acts, looking into the situation of the summer of

1942, had become quite numerous, and their scale was massive. Even the reports of them, by word of mouth, and in various media—legal and illegal, internal to Europe and external to it—were by then clearly very frequent, alarming, and mutually reinforcing. It was more than a year since the *Einsatzgruppen* had begun murdering the Jews of the western Soviet Union en masse. Deportations to the gas chambers and ovens of Treblinka and Majdanek were proceeding apace, from the principal European ghetto of Warsaw as well as from other destinations.

Was anyone receiving letters, telegrams, and telephone calls from those deported to all those locations testifying to their continued existence, let alone their well-being? And, apart from the massive killings themselves, were there not many collateral indications, in terms of the behavior of Nazi authorities toward Jews, that strongly suggested that extermination and destruction of the Jewish people were the goals of Nazi policy? In what manner were Jews being rounded up and deported? Did Nazi methods generally suggest concern with the biological-physical preservation of the Jewish people? Or did they, in fact, suggest the very opposite? Why would Jews escaping the ghettos, for example, be subject to the death penalty? Why would non-Jews giving aid and shelter to Jews be subject to the same penalty, and frequently summary execution? What was being done with Jewish property and Jewish cultural and religious institutions and artifacts when Jews were being "moved" or "resettled"? Indeed, going back to 1940–41, long before the Wannsee Conference, and without going into anybody's "secrets," what food rations were being officially accorded to the half-million Jews inhabiting the Warsaw ghetto? What was the meaning of 184 calories per day? Was there not a clear message here, among many others, to be sure?

Although many Jewish victims—subsequently survivors—did not *know* what was in store for the Jews of Europe, many of them, especially in 1942, appear to have also engaged in blatant denial. If it was not clear— even in Poland—in June, July, August, and September of 1942 exactly what Nazi policy toward the Jews was, it had to be very nearly clear. With all but virtual certainty, *some* denial—i.e., an unwillingness to fully acknowledge the Nazi design—has to be attributed to people's understandable reluctance to face the unfaceable—certain extinction by state fiat in the short run. Not to have known, or in the case of a significant portion of respondents, not to have even strongly suspected what the Nazis were attempting, is in one sense astonishing, and yet in another quite understandable.[11] In any case, regardless of the mix involved here—how many victims really did not know, and how many simply, and desperately, did not want to know or acknowledge the horrible truth—our finding highlights an important aspect of the Holocaust.

The Nazi policy of never publicly and precisely revealing the aims of all the various measures that, in the aggregate, constituted the Final Solution was highly effective. For one thing, it helped to disorient the victims— induce a state of uncertainty and confusion—always helpful in inhibiting any possible counteraction or resistance. For another, this policy ensured a significantly more bountiful "crop" for the Nazi executioners than might have been possible otherwise.

The most compelling illustration of this confusion was within the largest concentration of Jewish population in prewar Europe, i.e., Poland. When the Soviet forces occupied eastern Poland on September 17, 1939, in pursuance of the Stalin-Hitler pact, the border between the two occupation zones—Nazi and Soviet—remained open and porous for many months after the initial partition. Many thousands of Jews fled from west to east during that period, and of those who were fortunate to either emigrate into the further recesses of the Soviet Union, or, indeed, be forcibly deported there, the great majority survived the war. Many, however, were sufficiently confused about their situation so as to either return from the Soviet to the Nazi zone before Hitler's launch of Operation Barbarossa in 1941, or, with equal futility, made no effort to flee eastern Poland in advance of the occupying Nazi forces in June 1941. In either case, these actions sealed their doom. Literally hundreds of thousands of Jews who died in the Holocaust could have been saved during this early period of the war if they had simply known what to expect from the Nazi conquerors.

Many could have been saved through emigration—certainly in 1940 and 1941, but probably also in 1942 and in places like Hungary and Rumania, even 1943. Although restrictions on Jewish immigration to the United States, Britain, Canada, and other Western countries—as well as Palestine, under British mandate—were a well-known story of the period, there were, nevertheless, still some countries willing to accept Jewish immigrants. This was especially true for those Jews who had significant material means to pay their way. In the case of Switzerland, for example, people capable of making very large donations to the particular cantons in that country could purchase Swiss citizenship and, thereby, naturally, gain the right of residence. Much more accessible to what may be termed the mainstream Jewish middle class were various countries in Latin America, such as Paraguay, Bolivia, and the Dominican Republic. Naturally enough, given the seeming risks and discomforts of such long-range removals into a veritable unknown, most Jews were reluctant to part with familiar social and physical surroundings to migrate to such destinations. But, given the certain choice between murder and life in Paraguay or Bolivia, most people would probably opt for the latter.

Following the Nazi conquest of Poland in September 1939, most foreign embassies and consulates continued to function in Warsaw for some time after the occupation. There were still neutral and nonbelligerent countries through which one could travel out of Nazi Europe. Even as late as 1942, when Nazi designs were much clearer, and more restrictions had been placed by the Nazis on Jewish emigration, there were still Latin American and various other diplomatic missions in places such as Hungary, Rumania, and Vichy France, to which Jews might have had access—had they been willing to seek it. Granted, the opportunities available to middle-class Jews were not really there for the millions of poor and very poor Jews of Europe.[12] But even if 5 to 10 percent of the Jewish population had escaped the gas chambers, this would have meant saving perhaps between three hundred and six hundred thousand people. Of course, if even much smaller numbers had been saved, it would still have been meaningful.

Official secrecy and international silence—from all quarters—surrounding the Final Solution had many highly favorable consequences from the Nazi perspective. Among the perpetrators, it made operations easier. Quite a few people who had helped in the killing process, or even simply witnessed it, could psychologically evade the consequences of their own actions and inactions. The Nazis were, as Adolf Eichmann later argued before the court in Jerusalem, simply *transporting* the Jews, moving them from one place to another. What did this have to do with murder? The fiction could be maintained, for themselves and for others, that no crime was being committed. Among the Gentile bystanders the magnitude of what was being done to the Jews, and of what was being witnessed, could be significantly lessened—thereby also lessening the challenge to everyone's own sense of moral responsibility and awareness.[13] The Jews were being rounded up and sent away, but who was to say for what purpose and why? Even the Führer's enemies and various highly respected, public "neutral parties" had nothing to say about this subject. Why should private persons be unduly disturbed about all this? How important was it to help Jews escape capture and to hide them from their Nazi pursuers or otherwise assist them? One did not hear much about this sort of thing even from the BBC or the Voice of America, or the Vatican radio, or the Red Cross, or whatever was left of the old League of Nations in Geneva. Private consciences were left to private reflections and private devices. As for the victims, unaware of the Nazi grand design, they were more likely to submit than to flee or revolt.

Given the responses of our survivors with respect to their own knowledge, or lack of it, regarding Nazi intentions toward Jews in the summer of 1942, we found a surprising, one might think, and certainly credulity-straining, contrast in their answers to the following question:

> What is your opinion of the claim sometimes made that most people in Germany did not know what was happening to the Jews of Europe, even as late as 1943 or 1944? You actually:
> a. Believe it
> b. Feel uncertain about it
> c. Do not believe it
> d. Have no opinion
> e. Other—explain: _____

Fully 88 percent of all those answering this question, and 85 percent of all our respondents, said that they did not believe this claim (see Fig. 2.3). Overwhelmingly, the survivors supported the proposition that the German people knew what was happening to the Jews of Europe. In the West, almost 90 percent of our respondents believed this; in Poland, 87 percent; and in the rest of Eastern Europe, the figure was 89 percent.

With due allowance for the fact that 1943 and 1944 placed the situation in a later, and thus even clearer, perspective than the summer of 1942, this was an astonishing response. After all, the so-called ordinary German could only know with certainty that all the Jews in his or her town, village, or neighborhood were gone and that they had been officially "deported to the East." Beyond that, one could certainly learn virtually nothing of the fate of the Jews from Germany's official media. Even if one listened—at considerable personal risk—to the broadcasts by BBC and the Voice of America, one would learn very little in any general sense, as noted earlier, about the fate of the Jews. What many Germans might have heard, and were perhaps even likely to hear from time to time, were rumors, whispered reports by soldiers and officials, and those who may have come into contact with such soldiers and officials, about some of the atrocities being perpetrated against Jews in various places.

Naturally, Germans, like everyone else, were in a position to "put things together," making inferences from the tenor of Nazi rules, pro-

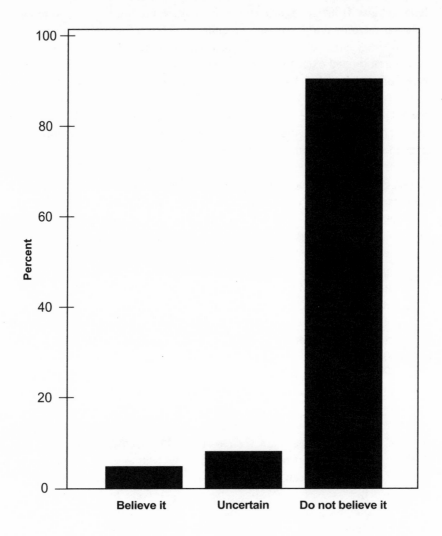

Fig. 2.3. Survivor Opinion on the View That the German People Didn't
Know about the Holocaust, 1943–44

nouncements, and propaganda; the disappearance of the Jews; the fact that people in Germany were not hearing any reports from those Jews who had left; and also from the reports and stories about the killings that were circulating to some degree in various quarters. After all, members of the SS and of the Wehrmacht; people who designed, manned, and operated the concentration and extermination camps; and people who operated the railroads of the Third Reich—all these people were part of German society.

At the same time, however, against all these factors must be balanced the fact that there were no public admissions to the population by the Nazi state, and that neither the Western Allies nor the Soviet Union virtually ever mentioned the Final Solution in their broadcasts aimed at Germany (the declaration of December 17, 1942, being one of a truly few exceptions to this general rule)—nor did the pope, for that matter, whatever the explanations, justifications, or rationalizations that one might choose to employ in discussing this quite indubitable fact. Not a word was heard from the International Red Cross.

The silence of "those in authority," both at home and abroad, was bound to stimulate German public opinion in the direction of mass denial, analogous (although adopted for different reasons) to the denials of the survivors. If German authorities were engaged, in their official capacities and in the name of the German Reich and the German people, in the systematic, mass murder of innocent men, women, and children, then this was a very ugly business. Many people, if not all, to be sure, would feel distinctly uncomfortable being in some way part of such an enterprise and contributing to it either directly or indirectly. For all such people, therefore, there would be an enormous psychological incentive to wring every ounce of reassurance (however dubious) from the absence of "authoritative confirmations of rumors" in order to maintain their own personal sense of rectitude and freedom from any oppressive sense of guilt, as well as to be able to maintain the belief that the cause of German victory on the eastern front, and the war as a whole, was a good thing. After all, their sons, husbands, brothers, uncles, and cousins were all fighting for that victory day in and day out. They themselves were probably contributing, too, through industrial and economic efforts on behalf of the Fatherland. It would indeed be only human to go a very long way in order to avoid accepting devastatingly unpleasant and dangerous conclusions. If one wanted to maintain loyalty to the Führer and to the Reich, and if one wanted to avoid the dangerous imperative of opposing the regime, it would have made all the sense in the world to say, "Rumors are rumors. I am better off not thinking about this."[14]

Interestingly, however, within about three weeks of the Wannsee Conference of February 14, 1942, Nazi Propaganda Minister Joseph Goebbels was paraphrasing Hitler in his diaries as follows:

World Jewry will suffer a great catastrophe at the same time as Bolshevism. The Führer once more expressed his determination to clean up the Jews in Europe pitilessly. There must be no squeamish sentimentalism about it. The Jews have deserved the catastrophe that has now overtaken them. Their destruction will go hand in hand with the destruction of our enemies. We must hasten this process with cold ruthlessness. We shall thereby render an inestimable service to a humanity tormented for thousands of years by the Jews. This uncompromising antisemitic attitude must prevail among our own people despite all objectors. The Führer expressed this idea vigorously and repeated it afterward to a group of officers who can put that in their pipes and smoke it.

The Führer realizes the full implications of the great opportunities offered by this war. He is conscious of the fact that he is fighting a battle of gigantic dimensions and that the fate of the entire civilized world depends upon its issue.[15]

If many Jews, and many Germans—for quite different reasons, to be sure—resorted to denial about the reality of the Holocaust, they were not alone. Among many parties to this tragedy, belligerent and neutral, were also the governments of Great Britain and the United States, eager to keep their own costs low; not to antagonize their Middle East, oil-rich, and strategically important connections by opening up any floodgates for Jewish escape to Palestine; and not to offend various shades of anti-Semitic opinion at home and abroad.[16]

Jan Ciechanowski, the Ambassador of the London-based Polish government-in-exile to the United States for most of the war, made some highly relevant observations—especially with reference to the summer of 1942:

The incredible details of the system of human extermination started by Hitler's gang were as yet unknown to Americans at large. But the Polish Government was being fully informed about all these happenings owing to the perfect system of daily contact which it had successfully set up with the Polish Underground.

From information I was receiving and constantly communicating to the American Government and to the press, and describing in my numerous speeches in many American cities, the monstrous pattern of

Hitler's mass extermination of Polish Jews and of Jews brought to Poland
from other countries was becoming clearly evident. The Polish Underground insistently demanded that our government present these facts to
our allies and especially to the American Government.

General Sikorski was working on it overtime in London and I was
following up his requests to the President, the State Department and the
Combined Chiefs of Staff.[17]

Ciechanowski notes that as early as 1942 he went to Roosevelt to ask
for retaliatory measures and a protest by the Great Powers against the atrocities: "The general lack of understanding of German barbarity and a certain
basic kindheartedness toward the Germans were most striking at the time.
They appeared suddenly in some of my contacts with American officials
and representatives of American public opinion. . . . The average American, and even officials who had every means of being fully informed, practically refused to believe the Germans capable of the horrors which they
were committing."[18] How did the ambassador explain all this? "As victory
was becoming more and more certain, the natural sporting instinct of the
American people was beginning to reassert itself. . . . The elections were
approaching. The numerically strong and well-organized group of Americans of German descent constituted an influential body in the electorate.
. . . Because of increasing fear of Russia and of Communism, the idea was
spreading that Germany, after having been purged of Nazism, might be
used as a convenient barrier against Soviet expansion."[19]

When German diplomat Albrecht von Kessel was interrogated as a witness at the Nuremberg trial, the prosecutor put the following query to him:

> *Question*: Since you worked for a considerable time both with the
> International Red Cross and at the Vatican, I should like to ask you to sum
> up your testimony by stating your opinion on two questions. Have these
> two great humanitarian organizations ever protested on principle to Hitler
> against the anti-Jewish measures?
> *Answer:* No, neither of them.[20]

Finally, a very important aspect of the Holocaust reflected in our
survey was that which tended to make Jews vulnerable, to isolate them and
to expose them to persecution: local, residual anti-Semitism. This was a
force characterized by both active and passive elements. In its active
aspect, anti-Semitism encouraged people to help the Nazis find out who
were Jews and where they might be found. It encouraged people to turn in

Jews who were in hiding or under assumed identities and to denounce to the Nazis non-Jews who were helping them. It even encouraged overt cooperation with the Nazi killers.

In its passive aspect, anti-Semitism was the popular sentiment that sanctioned the refusal to help Jews, to speak on their behalf, and to maintain a sense of solidarity with them. It encouraged a silently indifferent acceptance of whatever measures the Nazis might impose on individual Jews or upon Jewish communities—all in the spirit of social estrangement. Through the prism of anti-Semitism, Jews, though fellow citizens, were often seen as hostile aliens, outside the national community, and therefore as not deserving of the sympathy and support of their Christian neighbors.

As Figure 2.4 illustrates, the attitudes of the Nazi perpetrators of the Final Solution—as seen by the survivors—were not those of mindless robots. The executioners manifested perverse delight in the killing of the Jews. This was anti-Semitism at its most deadly nadir. (To be sure, prevalent attitudes, important as they were, were not everybody's attitudes everywhere.)

In her study of the Final Solution in Denmark, Leni Yahil reports the story of two Gestapo officials who had physically attacked a couple of pedestrians in Copenhagen because these individuals seemed to them to be Jewish. "A crowd at once gathered and became so angry that the Germans escaped only with the greatest difficulty to the nearest subway station." In Denmark, she points out, unlike many other European countries, the whole population consciously identified with the Jews.[21] Critically, however, and probably influenced by Danish attitudes, the German military and civil authorities themselves were tacitly sympathetic to the escape of Jews from Denmark to Sweden. "It was an open secret that the Germans deliberately abstained from interfering with the flight of the Jews."[22]

In this section, our focus was upon the general importance of anti-Semitism in the country of respondents' residence in making it possible, or at least more feasible, for the Nazis to carry out the extermination of the Jews as effectively as they did.[23]

On the issue of the strength of anti-Semitism in the respondents' country of origin, 79 percent of our survivor respondents viewed it as very strong, 17 percent saw it as moderately strong, and only 3 percent identified anti-Semitism in their country of origin as fairly weak. Once again, the perception of anti-Semitism was strongest in Poland, with 90 percent of respondents describing it as very strong and 8 percent as moderately strong. In Western Europe, fewer than half of our respondents (47 percent)

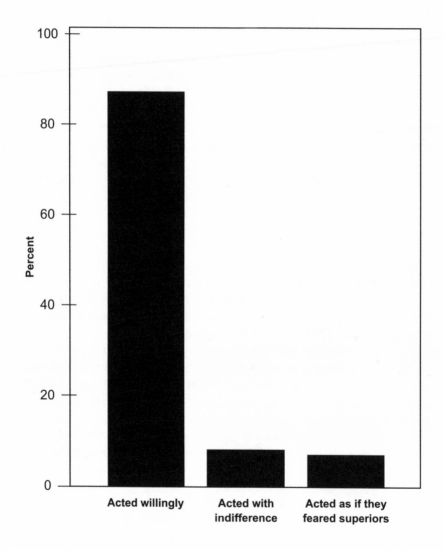

Fig. 2.4. Survivors' Impression of Germans Active in the Holocaust

described anti-Semitism of their countries as very strong, 41 percent as moderately strong, and 12 percent as fairly weak. In Eastern European states outside of Poland, 69 percent of respondents saw anti-Semitism as very strong, 28 percent as moderately strong, and 3 percent as fairly weak.

Although it is evident from this analysis of the responses to individual questions that cognitive awareness and wartime countries of residence are interrelated, our cognitive scale offers a fuller and more detailed understanding of cognitive differences. Using the responses to all eight questions, we coded the less pessimistic or less negative answers as 1, the more pessimistic responses as 2, and neutral or no responses as 0. When these values were added together, the total number provided a cognitive score for each respondent. The aggregate scores ranged from the least pessimistic with a figure of 4 to the most pessimistic with a figure of 18 and an average score of 12.1. As expected with such a high mean, the scale tilts toward the upper range of values. The lowest quartile of respondents scored 10 or less and a score of 15 and higher placed an individual in the top quartile (refer back to Fig. 2.2).

It is not surprising, of course, from our earlier discussion, that the average score for survivors from Poland was 12.9, while those from Western Europe averaged a much lower score of 9.4, and those living in Eastern Europe outside Poland scored in between, with an average of 11.7. Moreover, 25 percent of our Polish respondents fell in the top quartile of the scale, while only 5 percent of the Western Europeans did. For the other countries of Eastern Europe, 14 percent scored in the top quartile.

The level of education, age in 1939, and gender are other variables that we have related to individuals' ability to comprehend what was happening in the world around them. Since education and age are continuous variables ranging from low to high, they can be correlated with the level of cognitive awareness as measured by our scale. The correlation for age is quite small (.10) and is not statistically significant, but the correlation for education is almost twice as large (–.18) and is statistically significant. Education therefore is associated with cognitive awareness. But contrary to what we would predict, the relationship is a negative one, which means that the higher the level of education, the less the cognitive awareness of the respondent. It should be noted, of course, that the formal education of most of our respondents was not completed until after the horrifying experience of the Holocaust. As for gender, there is little difference, a meager 1 percent, between the average cognitive score of women (12.2) and men (12.0).

Assimilation and family material welfare are other factors that could potentially influence the way individuals perceive and interpret German actions. A well-to-do, highly assimilated Jewish family might have been less capable, or less willing, to accept the reality of what was going to happen to it than the more vulnerable poor.[24] Differences in family prewar wealth, however, are only slightly associated with cognitive awareness. Individuals who came from very or moderately well-off families had a score of 12.3, a bit higher than the 11.9 score for those from families who were making ends meet or were poor. On the other hand, a comparison of the cognitive mean score of assimilated and nonassimilated Jewish families is much more striking: nonassimilated Jews had a mean score of 12.6 in comparison with a 10.6 average for assimilated Jews, a robust difference of 19 percent. Clearly the nonassimilated were much more apprehensive and negative in their perceptions.

Looking at the larger picture, might not our multidimensional models capture even larger differences in survivor perceptions? In chapter 1 we outlined four such models, the first three being socioeconomic status, an index combining education, occupation, and current material welfare; a personality model based upon the individual's feelings about the future of the world and the degree of satisfaction with one's life, dividing our survivors into pessimists and optimists; and a culture model based on the degree of assimilation, the religious background of one's household, and the extent of one's personal religious beliefs. This third model enabled us to divide respondents into traditional and modern categories. Exposure to suffering represents the fourth model, consisting of four variables we thought especially relevant to the trauma of the Holocaust: age in 1939, degree of family assimilation, country of residence, and whether the responded survived the Holocaust in a concentration camp or somewhere else. Table 3 summarizes the comparative mean scores for each of these models.

The personality model demonstrated practically no difference between the average cognitive scores of optimists and pessimists, with a net difference of 0.12. Socioeconomic status (SES) offered a little better explanation of cognitive differences. Those who ranked lower on the SES scale had a higher average cognitive score of 12.82, while those who ranked higher had an average score of 11.95—a 7.5 percent difference between the two groups.

By contrast, the culture model accounted for a larger difference in victims' awareness and perceptions of various actors involved in the Holocaust. With respect to the first of these, traditionalists (i.e., people from religious and nonassimilated homes who professed themselves religious believers)

Table 3. Explanatory Models and Cognitive Scores

Models	Mean Scores
Personality	
Optimist	11.84
Pessimist	11.96
SES	
Low	12.82
High	11.95
Culture	
Traditional	13.12
Modern	11.00
Exposure	
Low	9.91
High	13.11

Note: Higher scores denote more negative perceptions

were 16 percent more negative in their perceptions of the Nazi-German-Gentile environments of the Holocaust era than were the modernists. The latter, of course, were people who came from nonreligious and assimilated families and who classified themselves as nonbelievers or doubters.

The largest difference in perceptions was apparent between people who, according to our definition, had the greatest exposure to suffering in the Holocaust and those who, relatively speaking, had the least. The low-exposure group had an average score of about 9.9, as opposed to the higher group, which had a score of about 13.1—a very large difference of 24 percent. The former group consisted of inmates of Nazi camps, domiciled in Poland, relatively mature in age at the time of the Holocaust, and descended from nonassimilated families. Their opposites were relatively younger people who lived outside Poland, came from assimilated homes, and, most importantly, survived the Final Solution not as inmates of Nazi concentration and extermination camps but with some degree of help from the Gentile society, whether in hiding, under assumed identities, or in partisan detachments. Those survivors whose personal sufferings were more intense tended to be more aware of the grim realities of the Holocaust.

NOTES

1. Adolf Hitler, *Mein Kampf*, trans. Ralph Manheim, Sentry ed. (Boston: Houghton Mifflin, 1943), p. 651.

2. Ibid., p. 305.

3. Ibid., p. 307.

4. Ibid., p. 310.

5. Ibid., p. 313.

6. Ibid., p. 651.

7. Ringelblum entry included in the collection edited by Yitzak Arad, Yisrael Gutman, and Abraham Margaliot, *Documents on the Holocaust: Selected Sources on the Destruction of the Jews of Germany and Austria, Poland and the Soviet Union* (Jerusalem: Yad Vashem, 1981), pp. 228–29.

8. See Miriam Novitch, *Sobibor, Martyrdom and Revolt* (New York: Holocaust Library, 1980), on the activities of the *Einsatzgruppen* at the commencement of Operation Barbarossa, p. 19.

9. Lucy S. Dawidowicz, *The War Against the Jews 1933–1945* (New York: Holt, Rinehart, and Winston, 1975), p. 135.

10. Samuel Willenberg, *Surviving Treblinka*, ed. Wladyslaw T. Bartoszewski (London: Basil Blackwell, 1989), pp. 7, 9, 11, 12. See also Jean Francois Steiner, *Treblinka* (New York: New American Library, 1979), esp. p. ix: "The boast of Treblinka was 'from door to door in forty-five minutes'—from opening the cattle cars to slamming shut the gas chambers." See p. xv on the camp's beginnings. Its operations ended in August 1943.

See Franciszek Piper in *The Holocaust and History, The Known, the Unknown, the Disputed, and the Reexamined*, ed. Michael Berenbaum and Abraham J. Peck (Bloomington: Indiana University Press, 1998), pp. 372–73.

In Birkenau, the first half of 1942, two provisional gas chambers with a capacity of 800 and 1,200 people were put into operation in two houses taken from expelled peasants. Until September 1942 the bodies of the gas victims were buried in mass graves; subsequently, corpses were burned in the open air. . . . From 1942 onward, the majority of Auschwitz victims died in the gas chambers. Most were Jews gassed as families—men, women, and children. Upon their arrival, Jews were subjected to selections, conducted mainly by SS doctors. At first these selections were conducted sporadically; after July 4, 1942, they became routine. Young and healthy people were chosen for labor from the new arrivals; the rest, including almost all the children, were sent directly to the gas chambers. Prisoners able to work were placed in barracks and then registered. After a period of quarantine they were put to work maintaining the camp or in industrial enterprises such as mines, armament factories, and other plants. The prisoners so employed outside Oswiecim were moved to subcamps located close to their work sites. If they became seriously ill, they were returned to Auschwitz-Birkenau.

Non-Jewish prisoners were not subject to preliminary selection; as a rule all of them were registered. Between July 1941 and April 1943, after registration, they underwent selections as did the Jews, and those who were weak or otherwise unfit for work were killed by phenol injection or in the gas chambers. Selections of non-Jews, however, were less frequent and less strict.

See also Robert Jan van Pelt and Deborah Dwork, *Auschwitz: 1270 to the Present* (New Haven, Conn.: Yale University Press, 1996), pp. 298–302 on the start-up of the killing operations against Jews in the spring of 1942.

11. Among other sources, see Don Levin, *The Lesser of Two Evils: East European Jewry under Soviet Rule 1939–1941* (Philadelphia: Jewish Publication Society, 1995); Lucjan Dobroszycki, *Survivors of the Holocaust in Poland* (New York: M. E. Sharpe, 1994); Yehuda Bauer, *The Holocaust in Historical Perspective* (Seattle: University of Washington Press, 1978); Shimon Redlick, ed., *War, Holocausts, and Stalinism: A Documented Study of the Jewish Anti-Fascist Committee in the USSR* (Luxembourg: Harwood Academic Publishers, 1995); Keith Sword, *Deportation and Exile: Poles in the Soviet Union, 1939–1948* (London: St. Martin's Press, 1994); and Jeff Schatz, *The Generation: The Rise and Fall of the Jewish Communists of Poland* (Berkeley and Los Angeles: University of California Press, 1991).

12. In addition to actual destinations allowing immigration in the 1940s, the international passport visa system of the period—and the manner in which it was frequently administered by consular officials around the world—allowed all sorts of avenues of escape to people of means. Those able and willing to pay could frequently obtain a variety of visas, transit or tourist, for example, allowing them to leave one country and travel to another with the right of staying in some locations temporarily but with realistic chances of either extending their stay or traveling to still other destinations.

An article on Jewish immigration to Argentina published in the *Encyclopedia Judaica* contains the following reference: "From 1933 to 1943 between 20,000 and 30,000 Jews entered Argentina by exploiting various loopholes in the law. Between 6,000 and 10,000 of them had to use illegal means to immigrate and their legal status was regulated only after a general amnesty was declared for illegal immigrants in 1948." Haim Avni, "Argentina," *Encyclopedia Judaica* (Jerusalem: Keter Publishing, 1972), 3:415.

An article on immigration to Honduras contains the following interesting reference: "In 1935 the government announced its readiness to accept Jewish scientists and educators from Germany but the offer was not adequately exploited. In 1939 restrictions were imposed on the entry of Jews, Negroes and gypsies. Nevertheless, a considerable number of Jews were saved during the war by Honduran consuls who issued them passports and visas, frequently illegally." Moshe Nes El, "Honduras," *Encyclopedia Judaica*, 8:962.

13. See Zygmunt Bauman, *Modernity and the Holocaust* (Ithaca, N. Y.: Cornell University Press, 1989):

> The technical-administrative success of the Holocaust was due in part to the skilful utilization of "moral sleeping pills" made available by modern bureaucracy and modern technology. The natural invisibility of causal connection in a complex system of interaction, and the "distancing" of the unsightly or morally repelling outcomes of action to the point of rendering them invisible to the actor, were most prominent among them. . . . The experience of the Holocaust brings into relief, however, another social mechanism; one with a much more sinister potential of involving in the perpetration of the genocide a much wider number of people who never in the process face consciously either difficult moral choices or the need to stifle inner resistance of conscience. The struggle over moral issues never takes place, as the moral aspects of actions are not immediately obvious or are deliberately prevented from discovery and discussion. In other words, the moral character of action is either invisible or purposefully concealed. (p. 26)

> To quote [Raul] Hilberg again, "It must be kept in mind that most of the participants [of genocide] did not fire rifles at Jewish children or pour gas into gas chambers. . . . Most bureaucrats composed memoranda, drew up blueprints, talked on the telephone, and participated in conferences. They could destroy a whole people by sitting at their desk. If they were aware of the ultimate product of their ostensibly innocuous bustle—such knowledge would stay, at best, in the remote recesses of their minds. Causal connections between their actions and the mass murder were difficult to spot. Little moral opprobrium was attached to the natural human proclivity to avoid worrying more than necessity required—and thus to abstain from examining the whole length of the casual chain up to its furthest links. To understand how that astounding moral blindness was possible, it is helpful to think of the workers of an armament plant who rejoice in the 'stay of execution' of their factory thanks to big new orders, while at the same time honestly bewailing the massacres visited upon each other by Ethiopians and Eritreans; or to think how it is possible that the 'fall in commodity prices' may be universally welcomed as good news

while 'starvation of African children' is equally universally, and sincerely, lamented." (p. 24)

14. For a discussion of "denial" as an important element in political discourse more generally, see Alexander J. Groth, *Democracies Against Hitler: Myth, Reality and Prologue* (Brookfield, Vt.: Ashgate, 1999), pp. 234–36.

Interestingly, John S. Conway, in an essay titled, "German Churches and the Jewish People since 1945," in *Antisemitism in the Contemporary World*, ed. Michael Curtis (Boulder, Colo.: Westview, 1986), pp. 128–42, says that in the immediate aftermath of the war there was "among Germans . . . a widespread reluctance to examine the implications of their own involvement in the Nazi crimes, which led to a general political amnesia to cover over what became known as 'unbewältigte Vergangenheit' (unmastered past)" (p. 129). Karen Gershon, in her *Postscript: A Collective Account of the Lives of Jews in West Germany since the Second World War* (London: Victor Gollancz, 1969) quotes an anonymous German respondent as follows: "Ordinary Germans between 35 and 60 find it hard to acknowledge that Hitler was a criminal. They feel misunderstood. They demand approval—they don't want to think that everything they fought and suffered for was wrong" (p. 149). Bjorn Krondorfer, in his *Remembrance and Reconciliation: Encounters between Young Jews and Germans* (New Haven, Conn.: Yale University Press, 1995) writes, significantly, "My German upbringing had left me ignorant about Jews and bewildered when I first met them" (p. 9).

Writing about the response of German public opinion to Hitler's anti-Jewish policies during the 1930s, Saul Friedlander writes that "the majority of Germans accepted the steps taken by the regime . . . and looked the other way" (*Nazi Germany and the Jews*, 1:324). Werner Bergman and Rainer Erb, in their recent study *Anti-Semitism in Germany: The Post-Nazi Epoch since 1945* (New Brunswick, N. J.: Transaction Publishers, 1997), investigated German recollections and images of the Holocaust and concluded that "very few interviewees had detailed knowledge of the persecution of the Jews in the 'Third Reich.' . . . Awareness of the magnitude of the crimes and the consequences appeared limited. . . . In addition to the vague ideas in general, doubt about the existence of concentration and death camps was also clearly articulated" (p. 35). Obviously, the acquisition and retention of information by people is not a wholly value-free process.

15. *The Goebbels Diaries, 1942–1943*, ed. Louis P. Lochner (Garden City, N. Y.: Doubleday, 1948), p. 86.

16. It is a matter of great interest, it would seem, that in her study of the Jewish immigrant associations in the United States during the Second World War, Hannah Kliger discovered that "what has been suggested about the general public response by Americans seems true for the *landsmanshaftn* [immigrant associations]. . . . It does not seem that a coordinated plan of action was formulated, nor were these individuals exempt from the inability to recognize the severity of the situation in Europe. Minute books and meeting protocols of the time indicate dis-

cussions of routine affairs." See "A Home Away from Home: Participation in Jewish Immigrant Associations in America," in *Persistence and Flexibility, Anthropological Perspectives on the American Jewish Experience*, ed. Walter P. Zenner (Albany: State University of New York Press, 1988), pp. 143–64 (the quote is from pp. 155–56). The denial of the unthinkable was rather widespread.

17. Jan Ciechanowski, *Defeat in Victory* (Garden City, N. Y.: Doubleday, 1947), p. 117.

18. Ibid., p. 119.

19. Ibid., p. 285.

20. Hochhuth, *The Deputy* (New York: Grove Press, 1964), pp. 317–18.

21. Leni Yahil, *The Rescue of Danish Jewry: Test of a Democracy* (Philadelphia: Jewish Publication Society of America, 1969), p. 393.

22. Ibid., p. 268. Cf. Goldhagen, *Hitler's Willing Executioners: Ordinary Germans and the Holocaust* (New York: A. A. Knopf, 1996), p. 419 for the view that the German people, with very few exceptions, shared Hitler's radical, ultrapathological anti-Semitism. Goldhagen labels it "eliminationist." It is somewhat mystifying that Goldhagen was all but oblivious to the forces of simple indifference, inertia, and subjectively perceived self-interest among the German people— as they might have been to one degree or another anywhere else. Even if every member of the German Wehrmacht, Luftwaffe, and Kriegsmarine was actively implementing the Final Solution—an absurd proposition—that still would have left about 85 percent of Germans on the sidelines, largely silent. Admittedly, silence and passivity could not be taken as evidence of sympathy for the Jews, but did it really require frenzied bloodthirst and hatred to maintain passivity?

On the other hand, Sarah Gordon, in her much more thoughtful *Hitler, Germans and the "Jewish Question"* (Princeton, N. J.: Princeton University Press, 1984) writes that "Germany was a good place for Jews to live during [the] years [1870–1933]. Had the German population been uniquely rabid in its hatred of Jews, it is inconceivable that Jews could have fared so well, especially compared to Jews in other nations" (p. 48). She concludes that "systematic extermination . . . could be carried out only by an extremely powerful government, and probably could have succeeded only under the cover of wartime conditions" (ibid.). Hitler and Himmler were not following German public opinion but were able actually "to ignore public opinion, at least as it would have *likely* manifested itself under conditions of freedom and individual security" (ibid.).

She goes on to say that "knowledge or even rumors of gassings, which were deliberately kept secret were extremely rare outside of eastern Germany. Even though shootings of Russians, Poles and Jews were widely rumored, their extensiveness was not grasped" (p. 301), and "it is utopian to hope that the average human being will risk his security, much less his life for others," especially in wartime (p. 303). She recalls that *Kristallnacht* in 1938 was not really popular in Germany outside the Nazi party itself (p. 309). In Gordon's judgment, "Hitler's central role in the persecution and mass murder of Jews cannot be overestimated" (p. 312).

23. See Michael R. Barrus and Robert Paxton, "The Nazis and the Jews in Occupied Western Europe, 1940–1944," in *Unanswered Questions, Nazi Germany and the Genocide of the Jews*, ed. Francois Furet (New York: Schocken Books, 1989), pp. 172–98, These authors speak of "caution" and of Nazi measures with respect to Jews in Western Europe that could be termed "slow and hesitant," "anxious not to disturb local sensibilities." They also say that "considerable care and diplomacy were necessary" in carrying out the Final Solution, in large measure because "Jews tended to be well integrated in the societies in which they lived" (p. 184).

On the other hand, note Ezra Mandelson's essay, "Relations Between Jews and Non-Jews in Eastern Europe between the Two World Wars," also in *Unanswered Questions*, pp. 71–83. It makes a strong case that "during the interwar period . . . eastern Europe was a uniquely hostile environment for Jews as individuals . . . , [which constituted] a prelude to the Holocaust" (p. 82). Obviously, this state of public opinion in the region was a resource from the Nazi point of view in "solving" the so-called Jewish problem.

24. A parenthetical question at least partially answered by our respondents might be phrased as follows: Was it more important (or useful) for a Jew seeking to survive the Holocaust to be rich or to be assimilated? In terms of assistance from non-Jews, it seems that assimilation was generally much more helpful than was money. The correlation between prewar family wealth and assistance by Gentiles was only .05, but the correlation between such assistance and assimilation was .128. Analogously, the chance of winding up in a death camp or a concentration camp was appreciably less for the assimilated, with a correlation of .08, than it was for the well-to-do, with .09.

Chapter 3

LEARNING from the HOLOCAUST

What did the survivors learn from their Holocaust experience that might be applicable to the contemporary world? Anyone can speculate on the influence of anti-Semitism nowadays, and virtually anyone may ponder the future prospects of mankind half a century after the end of the Second World War. Our assumption here, however, was that the Holocaust experience profoundly affected the survivors' views of many such matters.

What impact of anti-Semitism, in all of human experience, could equal the tragic intensity of the events comprising Hitler's Final Solution of the Jewish Question? What events in human history have ever brought the issues of good and evil, and life and death, into the forefront of ordinary people's everyday lives with the brutal force of the Holocaust? Surely not many. Thus, on the not unreasonable assumption that the Holocaust strongly affected survivor reflections about many political and world issues, we have tried to ascertain some of these views.

We have confined our questions here to themes seemingly connected to the Holocaust experience itself. How do the survivors look upon Germany and Austria in the postwar world? What do they think about relations with these countries? What views do the survivors hold about Israel, a nation-state whose emergence is generally closely associated with Jewish, and international, reactions to the Holocaust? Emerging out of their terrible ordeal, testing all boundaries of faith and reason, how do the survivors reflect upon the nature of human beings and the prospects of mankind?

Using several questions on these themes, we constructed a learning scale intended to measure the general outlook of our respondents. Fundamentally, we wanted to see how positive, or how negative, survivor views and expectations of the contemporary world were. All our questions on the subject of "learning" have been scaled, allowing for relatively more positive (optimistic) to relatively more negative (pessimistic) answers. Examples included such topics as the possibilities of a Nazi revival in Germany: was this likely or unlikely? Another was the influence of anti-Semitism in the postwar world: was it decreasing, increasing, or was it perhaps unchanged from earlier times? Were respondent views of human nature positive, mixed, or negative? In each instance, of course, respondents could avail themselves of alternatives indicating that they were "unsure" or didn't know the answers.

Constructing the scale from most positive to most negative, we were able to place 201 respondents on an 11-point continuum, with a median of 6.1 and with an average score of 6.49. Appropriately, our median figure occurred between the two largest groups of respondents, with 35 individuals at the 6-point level and 32 at the 7-point level on the scale. These findings indicated to us that although there was a substantial distribution of opinions among the survivors along the whole scale, it was, nevertheless, skewed toward the high—more pessimistic or negative—end. In fact, the number of persons with the four most positive scores (0–3) was only 27, but the four most negative scores (8–11) accounted for 71 respondents (see Fig. 3.1).

There was a statistically significant correlation (at the 0.01 level) between "learning" on the one hand and "blame" and "identity" on the other. In essence, those whose views on the contemporary world were relatively bleak also tended to attach relatively high levels of blame to perpetrators and bystanders of the Holocaust, and they also tended to exhibit high levels of Jewish identity (note discussion in chapter 4).

One of the paradoxes revealed by our survey was a remarkable degree of generalized optimism about the world expressed by survivors in response to one specific question, followed, oddly, with many highly pessimistic assessments of specific world conditions. In response to the question, "How would you describe your current feelings with respect to the future of the world?" a plurality of our survivors, 43 percent, declared that they were "optimistic about chances for peace, prosperity, and progress for all people." Only 17 percent described themselves as "pessimistic," and 39 percent said they were unsure (see Fig. 3.2).

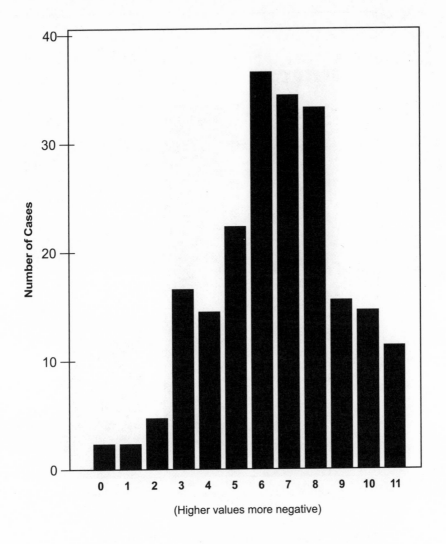

Fig. 3.1. Distribution of Values on the Learning Scale

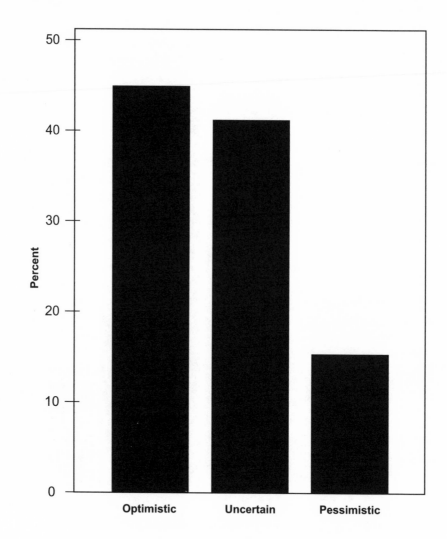

Fig. 3.2. Survivor Opinions about the Future of the World

Though a plurality of our survivor respondents described themselves as optimists with respect to the future of the world, a majority, likely inexorably burdened by the memories and experiences of their earlier lives, exhibited attitudes of anxiety, sadness, and in fact pessimism about the actual goings-on in the contemporary world. This impression was reinforced by responses to numerous other questions.

For example, when asked, "Some say that what happened to the Jews in Second World War could never happen to them again. What is your opinion?" most respondents disagreed: 42 percent said that it might happen again, and 25 percent believed that it was even *probable* that it would happen again. Only 27 percent expressed the view that the repetition of the Holocaust was *unlikely*, whereas a mere 6 percent felt certain that such events would never be repeated (see Fig. 3.3).

When the survivors were asked how they evaluated the strength of anti-Semitism in the current world, only 21 percent expressed the view that it was weakening; 45 percent saw it as actually increasing in strength; and 34 percent saw it as "about the same since the Second World War." Given the centrality of anti-Semitism in the design and execution of Hitler's murderous Final Solution, these were very somber views about the world (see Fig. 3.4).

When asked, "How likely in your opinion is the revival of a dominant new form of Nazism in present-day Germany?" only a slight majority of survivor respondents—52 percent—expressed the view that it was unlikely. A nearly equal number—48 percent—said that it was either "probable" or even that it "was happening already." In response to the question, "Do you think that present-day Germany no longer poses the kind of danger to the world that Nazi Germany did?" only 30 percent thought that it posed no danger, whereas 30 percent thought that it did, and 40 percent expressed uncertainty.

Given an almost fifty-year track record of a democratic and constitutional Germany, ensconced within the framework of NATO and the European Union, this was a remarkably critical judgment. Since 1949, in numerous national elections, no neo-Nazi or extreme-rightist political party has ever surmounted the 5 percent threshold of the popular vote so as to gain even token representation in the parliament of the German Federal Republic. Clearly, the survivor response here was not a mere routine "fact-finding." (We should note also that our questionnaires were collected well before the emergence of Jörg Haider's right-wing Freedom Party as a government coalition partner in Austria.)

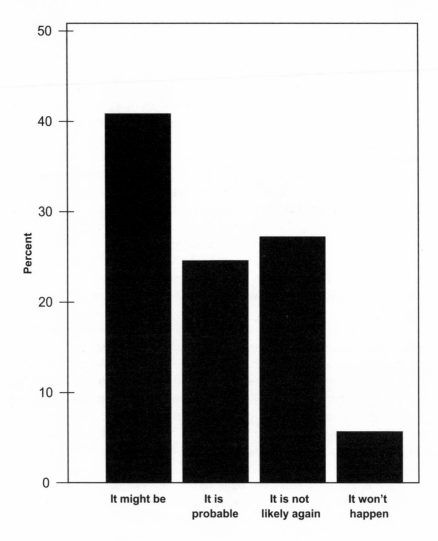

Fig. 3.3. Survivor Views on Whether the Jewish Tragedy Will Be Repeated

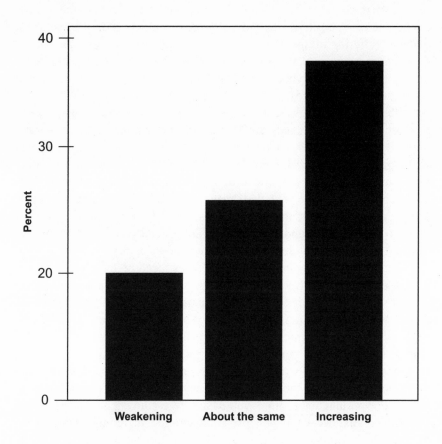

Fig. 3.4. Survivor Opinions on the Strength of Anti-Semitism
in the Postwar World

When asked, "Do you think that the world has really learned something from the experience of the Jewish Holocaust?" the survivors who chose the two most negative interpretations (namely, "No, people hardly know what really happened to the Jews," and "In the case of most people, whatever they learned, very little has changed") constituted 51 percent of the respondents. The most positive alternative, "a great deal has been learned about evil and suffering in this world," was chosen by slightly less than 30 percent. Those replying that "people have learned a little about man's inhumanity to man, at the very least" constituted 19 percent of the total pool responding (see Fig. 3.5).

While relatively few survivors endorsed the view that human nature was generally bad, still only about one-fifth thought that it was generally good. By far the largest number of survivors thought that people, by and large, were capable of being good one minute and evil the next, depending on circumstances. Full 56 percent of our respondents supported this view; 23 percent opted for the view that "man is generally good"; and only 3 percent were willing to say that people were generally bad. Almost a fifth (19 percent) of our respondents felt unable to categorize the nature of humanity; hardly any volunteered their own descriptions.

Considering the nature of the experiences faced by the Holocaust survivors, the depth of suffering, the great personal losses, the horror and the pain of so many years, it was perhaps remarkable that only 3 percent of our respondents were willing to characterize human nature as "bad." Obviously, some human beings inflicted unspeakable trauma on other human beings, systematically and continuously, without seemingly any hesitation or remorse, and indeed with apparent gusto and enthusiasm. That could not be denied. This much the Holocaust survivors themselves admitted. Perhaps to condemn human nature would have been equivalent to condemning oneself and all those whom one loved and admired, including, naturally, the victims. That kind of judgment might seem unpalatable and personally defeatist. Among the remaining alternatives, the response that human nature is basically good was preferred by the survivors over the worst alternative by an overwhelming margin of 8 to 1. On its face, this alternative, given the conduct of the Nazi persecutors, might seem to some a blatant denial of reality. But it has its extenuating elements, given certain possible assumptions. It would make sense under one of two alternative scenarios, at various times invoked by some scholars and commentators. One of these would be to "externalize" the Nazis by seeing them as somehow less than fulfledged humans, as intrinsically marginal, criminal misfits different

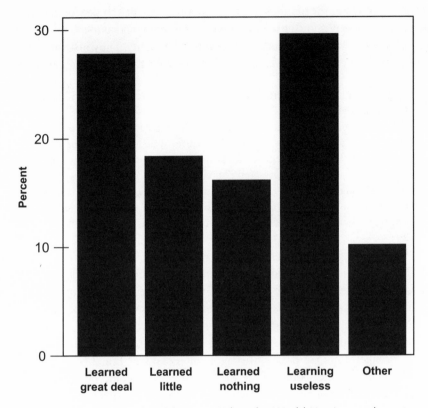

Fig. 3.5. Survivor Views on What the World Has Learned
from the Holocaust

from the good, ordinary, or prevalent human beings. The other alternative would be to externalize them but in a somewhat different, more conditional, way. The Nazis were, or at least could be, good human beings, like everyone else, but because of malevolent circumstances such as exposure to Nazi propaganda, denial of true information, some unusual mindset, coercion, deprivation, a combination of such factors, or other temporary and exceptional distortions, they could be rendered vicious and made to act contrary to the "ordinary" impulses of human nature. This sort of explanation would be very much in line with the liberal tradition of Western culture, for which the assumption of the benignness of mankind is fundamental and justifies democratic self-government.

As Zygmunt Bauman reminds us, the Nazi implementers of the Final Solution, even the camp guards and the actual executioners, were "ordinary men." They were, for the most part, law-abiding citizens in peacetime Germany. They were good husbands, fathers, brothers, and uncles, not some sort of obvious satanic aberrations of ordinary humanity. They just "did their jobs."[1] We can agree with Bauman, as well as with Kren and Rapaport that

> by conventional clinical criteria no more than 10 percent of the SS could be considered "abnormal." This observation fits the general trend of testimony by survivors indicating that in most of the camps, there was usually one, or at most a few, SS men known for their intense outbursts of sadistic cruelty. The others were not always decent persons, but their behaviour was at least considered comprehensible by the prisoners. . . .
>
> Our judgment is that the overwhelming majority of SS men, leaders as well as rank and file, would have easily passed all the psychiatric tests ordinarily given to American army recruits or Kansas City policemen.[2]

The largest group, interestingly, opted for an alternative that could place all, Jews and even Nazis, under one umbrella. In saying that people could be good one minute and bad the next, survivors supported a mixed and changeable concept of human nature. This concept obviously could not explain why the Nazis (and all their presumed collaborators) did what they did. But it was a concept that apparently recognized in a general sense human volatility, the elusive range of human possibilities, good and evil (see Fig. 3.6).

Given these perceptions of the world as it is, what could possibly be the mainsprings of survivors' generalized optimism with respect to mankind's future? One clear, if perhaps only partial, answer stems from the hope and faith engendered in the survivors by the state of Israel. When asked, "How do you personally feel about Israel?" over 81 percent responded that they were "enthusiastically favorable and hopeful of its future." Only less than 7 percent declared themselves skeptical of Israel's future although favorable to its existence. The same number said they were in favor of Israel's existence but were in disagreement with its politics, and a mere 5 percent chose one of two alternatives clearly unsympathetic to the Jewish state, to wit, "opposed to the whole idea of a Jewish state" and "indifferent, Israel has no effect on me." Respondents were then faced with the following questions:

> Do you believe that the existence of the state of Israel will:
> a. Prevent a repetition of the Holocaust of 1939–45
> b. Not affect the future treatment of Jews in the world
> c. Help to encourage future destruction and persecution of Jews
> d. Don't know; cannot say

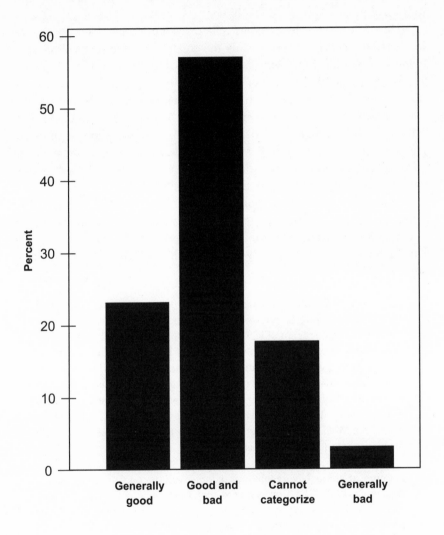

Fig. 3.6. Survivor Views of Human Nature

Eighty-one percent of our respondents opted for the first alternative. Less than 6 percent expressed the view that the state of Israel might somehow facilitate a renewed destruction of Jews, and a roughly equal number refused to pass judgment on this issue.

This, too, was a rather remarkable distribution of opinions given the long history of conflict surrounding the creation and the survival of Israel culminating in the 1948 War of Independence and also in the subsequent 1956, 1967, and 1973 wars, not to mention sundry other forms of opposition, struggle, and disapproval from the Arab and broader Muslim worlds.

Although Israel has won widespread international recognition since its founding, any reasonably dispassionate survey of the public opinion of nations reveals considerable hostility engendered by what is often seen as "Zionist aggression," "oppression," "expansionism," and a plethora of hostile stereotypes associated with the state of Israel.

Apart from perceptions long held within the several Arab states, the opinions of the world community concerning the state of Israel can be not unreasonably inferred from its treatment over many years now by the United Nations. In the summary of Aaron Klieman, worth quoting here at some length,

> UN documents contain an extensive list of declarations charging Israel with acting contrary to international legal norms and conventions and with continued disregard of UN resolutions. All too frequently Israel finds itself described as a primary threat to world peace and security. By the unwritten rules of politics in the United Nations, for all intents and purposes Israel is barred from serving as a rotating nonpermanent member on the Security Council; no Israeli jurist has even been appointed to a term as judge on the fifteen-member International Court of Justice. For many people the Middle East conflict, and Israel in particular, is perceived as a menace to international order and stability.
>
> As an indication . . . consider the wording as well as the lopsided margins of three UN resolutions adopted all in one working day, 7 December 1988. The first declared that Israel was not a peace-loving country and called upon all members to sever diplomatic, trade, and cultural ties with the Jewish state. It was approved by a vote of 83 in favor, 21 against, 45 abstaining. The second condemnation reaffirmed that, contrary to the view of Israel, the question of Palestine was the core of the Middle East conflict. It, too, passed: 103–18–30. The third resolution declared Israeli law null and void in its capital, Jerusalem, and was supported by 143 members, with 7 abstentions. Only El Salvador stood by Israel.[3]

Given the relatively small size of the Jewish state, its lack of natural wealth, its small population, and its geographic vulnerability, the view that its existence would protect world Jewry from the repetition of the Holocaust can hardly seem obvious. Not even the widely presumed nuclear capability of the state of Israel could fully account for such expectations and hopes, especially given the now fairly significant trend toward nuclear proliferation.

The explanation of survivor attachments to Israel is almost certainly rooted in the historical conjunction of two cataclysmic events with enormous impact on Jewish consciousness: the mass murder of the Jews on a scale unprecedented in history was followed within just a few years by occurrences that fulfilled a two-thousand-year longing of the Jewish Diaspora. The Jewish return to Zion and the holy city of Jerusalem, alluded to in all of Judaism's prayer books, the end of bondage and dispersal, the vindication of the sovereign rights of the Jewish state after two millennia of extinction and after so many centuries of persecution—these were events of transcendent joy to most Jews around the world, no matter the obstacles and clouds on the horizon.

To the Holocaust survivors, who in their own persons had paid the price of persecution of Jewry as no other generation before them, the impact of Israel's restoration was in all likelihood simultaneously the most important and positive public event of their lives. It was, to all appearances, a new life for Jewry in the wake of death and destruction as had never been suffered before.[4]

Still, the discrepancy between the respondents' professed optimism about the future of the world and their simultaneous pessimism on so many specific issues suggests that hope and faith in Israel do not fully explain the anomaly. It may be that the assertions of optimism are for many not so much the product of any specific judgments about world conditions as reflections of certain important survivor aspirations, habitually seeking to identify themselves with resilience and affirmation of life despite the perils and the disappointments of the external world.[5] "Optimism" may represent a strongly attractive verbalization of the kind of personal attitude to life that survivors have long cultivated and with which they seek to combat adversity as well as consequent feelings of sadness and anxiety. No fully satisfactory explanation of the contradiction can be offered here.

It is worth noting that a large number of our survivor respondents—42 percent—replied "never" to the question, "At any time during Second World War, did you believe that Hitler and the Nazis would eventually win?" The alternatives offered also included "Yes, throughout the whole war"; "Yes, during the first few years of the war"; "Yes, from time to time"; and "Cannot recall." With respect to this question, one can appreciate that people who were able to mobilize the inner strength to survive the ordeal of the Holocaust would presumably also show considerable fortitude. A response of "Yes, throughout the whole war" would presumably imply the likelihood of a "what's the use" state of mind, not consistent with an individual's determined struggle for survival. Only 5 percent of our respondents were in that category. The attitude represented by a response of never conceding victory to Nazi Germany was perhaps not so much an expression of optimism as it was one of determination and defiance, a kind of psychological "never give in" stance, useful to the individual's quest for survival.

Looking at the aggregate "worldview" responses of our survivors, we find a few questions on which the answers approached consensus. The survivors displayed an almost unanimous opinion about prosecuting people who had taken part in the Final Solution: about 95 percent rejected the idea of a statue of limitations on crimes associated with the Holocaust. Strong consensus prevailed on the usefulness of teaching schoolchildren about the Holocaust, with 86 percent of our respondents in support of this proposition.

Rather surprisingly, especially in light of the so-called Goldhagen thesis, more than 82 percent of our respondents agreed with the view that what the Nazis did to the Jews of Europe might have been done, or could be done, given appropriate circumstances, not just by Germans but possibly by others as well. Clearly and overwhelmingly, the Holocaust survivors were unwilling to attribute the potential for extermination of the Jewish people solely to the actual German perpetrators (see Fig. 3.7).

As noted earlier, two questions related to Israel—its effect on world Jewry and the degree of respondents' personal enthusiasm for the state of Israel—drew, respectively, 82 and 80 percent most favorable answers.

A classic three-way split occurred on the issue of Germany posing a danger in the contemporary world, with 31 percent saying it posed a danger, 32 percent saying it did not, and over 37 percent declaring themselves unsure.

On the issue of how Jews should deal with postwar Germany, only 18 percent agreed with the proposition that Jews should deal with Germans as with anyone else, dealing with each situation separately; 40 percent of our respondents demanded the acknowledgment of guilt by Germans as a prerequisite of normal relations; 24 percent said that Jews should refuse to have anything to do with Germans and boycott their products; 18 percent

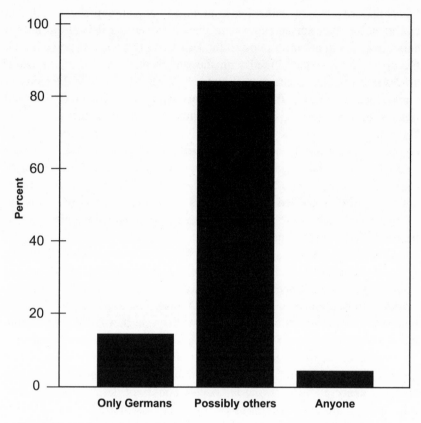

Fig. 3.7. Survivor Views of Who Is Capable of Replicating the Holocaust

advocated "being on guard" against Germans but not shunning them.

On the question of personal contacts, 44 percent declared themselves unwilling to visit Germany, while 43 percent said they would feel "uncomfortable" making such a visit. Less than 6 percent saw travel to Germany as personally "comfortable," and 8 percent felt "ambivalent" about it. Interestingly, an even greater proportion of survivors, 47 percent, declared themselves unwilling to visit Austria, and only 5 percent felt "comfortable" about doing so.

Half a century after the Final Solution, modern-day Germany and Austria still evoked memories of irreparable horror and images of danger and trauma among the survivors. A distinct minority was willing to engage the German and Austrian descendants of the Third Reich without reproach or personal anxiety.

A majority of our respondents, about 56 percent, expressed faith and confidence in God, disagreeing with the statement that if God did indeed exist, God would not have allowed the Holocaust to occur; 44 percent took the opposite view and agreed with the statement. In a number of ways, however, our results confirmed a relatively strong showing by the Deity in the Holocaust. Among those respondents who came from religious and nonassimilated homes, about three-quarters reported themselves as believers. Among people who had survived the war in the most difficult conditions according to our definition—that is, in concentration camps— two-thirds declared themselves believers in God. Interestingly enough, even among people who had said that they came from nonreligious families, one-third described themselves as believers. In overall terms, in response to the straightforward question whether they believed in God, 56 percent of all our survivors said they did.

Given the general strength of secularism in the twentieth-century Western world and, indeed, the view of some people that the Holocaust "proved" the nonexistence of God, these were surprising results.[6] Did the survivors preponderantly believe in God because God saved them? Because they needed God to continue their lives? Because they wished to remain faithful to the traditions of their ancestors and the memories of their beloved?

The latter seems especially implicit in the continuity between past and present among those Jews who came from relatively religious families. For all its violence and horror, the Holocaust could not destroy the bonds of faith that generations worked to establish, at least not among those who survived, and not among those whose religious memories bridged the void of Hitler's murders. There was significant evidence also that belief in God helped the survivors maintain a generally more positive outlook on the prospects of the contemporary world, more so than was the case with the nonbelievers (see data in Tables 4, 5, and 6 for support for this conclusion).

Still, nearly half of all our respondents declared themselves non-believers or doubters. Many of these people had been children of assimilated homes. For them, the Holocaust obviously was not a "turn-around" event. With respect to God, it left most of them where they and their families had been on the eve of the Second World War. Across the great religious and cultural divide of Jewish life in Europe in the 1930s, what the surviving remnants "learned" was substantially conditioned by the legacy of their past. There were dramatic crossovers, but most of the religious kept their faith; most of the secular Jews remained within the realm of their earlier agnosticism or atheism.

One could hardly imagine a more traumatic and jarring social and personal experience than was the Holocaust in the lives of European Jews. But on the issue of faith, the testimonies of the survivors gave renewed proof of the tremendous resilience and durability of culture in people's lives. The combination of cultural legacy and Holocaust experience clearly prevailed over more recent developments in the lives of survivors insofar as their world outlook was concerned (see Table 7).

In a work published in 1976, *Social Indicators in Well-Being: Americans' Perceptions of Life Quality* (New York: Premium Press), Frank M. Andrews and Stephen B. Withey estimated on the basis of national surveys taken at three separate intervals that "close to two-thirds of American adults had feelings about life as a whole that ranged between pleased and mostly satisfied; only between one quarter to possibly one fifth of the population felt less well off than mostly satisfied."[7] Younger people tended to feel somewhat happier than older people, but, above all, as the authors indicate, "Most of our measures showed substantial associations with socio-economic status. As SES increased, feelings of general well being . . . increased, as did reports of satisfaction and happiness. . . . High status people were more optimistic about the progress they would make in the future."[8]

Despite all their past experiences, and despite their generally high family losses, our survivor respondents were quite comparable, at least in

Table 7. Life Satisfaction and Opinion about the Future of the World

	% Optimistic	% Pessimistic, Uncertain
Highly/Moderately Satisfied (*N* – 133)	46	54
Somewhat/ Seriously Disappointed (*N* – 32)	25	75

the aggregate, to the American public in their satisfied-with-life responses. Only about one-quarter of our group reported themselves disappointed, and within this category only 6 percent "seriously disappointed." There was also an analogous evidence of the positive association between SES and satisfaction with life among survivors. Among our low-SES respondents, satisfaction was 11 percent lower than among the high-SES group.

Looking at age, we found that younger survivors tended to be more optimistic about the future of the world. Among those between the ages of one and fourteen in the year 1939, 46 percent described themselves as optimistic; among those between fifteen and thirty-one (our oldest respondents), 42 percent identified themselves as optimistic. Almost twice as many in the older group, 19 percent, professed pessimism as those in the younger group, with only 10 percent. Younger survivors were more likely to believe that the Holocaust would not be repeated, with 41 percent of respondents in that category. Among older survivors, however, this view was expressed by only 26 percent. Those who believed that the Holocaust *might* happen again constituted 32 percent of the younger respondents but 50 percent of the older ones.

Considering age alone, without regard to other social attributes, there was virtually no difference between younger and older respondents in reported satisfaction with life. One likely reason for this difference from the Andrews-Withey American summary is that, basically, all our respondents were fairly old people, so that our age distinctions did not discriminate between people who might have been thirty or forty as opposed to those who might have been seventy or older; they distinguished between people who were either in their sixties or perhaps in their seventies and eighties. Among persons of low-SES, older respondents actually reported themselves more satisfied than younger ones by a margin of about 4 percent. But among the high-SES group, age seemed to make a much more dramatic difference in the opposite direction: a sixteen-point difference in favor of (meaning greater satisfaction among) the younger respondents.

The relationship between optimism and satisfaction with life was similar to the patterns evident in past American surveys. People who had reported themselves highly satisfied were about 15 percent more optimistic about the future than were those who had described themselves as disappointed or only moderately satisfied (refer to Table 7). It is of considerable interest, however, as an indicator of the importance of intangible and nonmaterial factors, that our low-SES respondents who had declared themselves highly satisfied with their lives were actually much more optimistic about the future of the world than high-SES respondents who said they were only moderately satisfied or even disappointed—by over 25 percent. Within the high-SES group, the difference in optimism between the professedly satisfied and the professedly less satisfied was a substantial 16 percent in favor of the more satisfied.

Satisfaction with life was generally greater among those of our respondents who declared themselves believers in God than among nonbelievers. The association between belief in God and satisfaction in life and optimism about the future of the world was stronger than the association between the respondent's material welfare and the attitudes of satisfaction and optimism. People who reported belief in God tended to be less successful financially and professionally in the postwar world than nonbelievers or doubters, who tended to come from assimilated nonreligious or less religious households. The assimilated were also more likely to have received help from non-Jews during the Holocaust, as one might expect, given their presumably greater integration into the surrounding prewar Gentile societies of their time. The attitudes of the nonbelievers were generally more empathetic toward the Gentile world on a host of issues ranging from the importance of anti-Semitism to the Final Solution to the linkage between the Holocaust and other twentieth-century massacres.

On the other hand, although poorer and less financially successful, the believers tended to be happier and more optimistic about the world. Among low-SES respondents, believers outscored nonbelievers by about 6 percent in life satisfaction; among high-SES persons, believers outscored nonbelievers by about 8 percent. The overall difference between the two categories—believers and nonbelievers—was about 7 percent of greater satisfaction with life among believers.

In considering the impact of each of our six explanatory models, we need to take note first of what may be termed the larger picture. What the Holocaust survivors appear to have "learned," their responses to a variety of postwar issues concretely reflected in our nineteen questions, was conditioned primarily by factors connecting them to their pre-Holocaust backgrounds and by personal experiences during the Holocaust itself. The more immediate and recent experiences of their lives, reflected in such indicators as money, socioeconomic status, and, for the most part, education were much less important. All this reflected the primacy of the past over the present in the lives of the survivors. The three most powerful explanatory models were exposure to suffering, culture, and personality. The three weakest models were socioeconomic status, education, and gender—a result that is perhaps surprising in view of the canons of modern sociology.

Beginning with the weakest model, we discovered that on seven out of the sixteen questions, gender made hardly any difference in respondent attitudes. (We considered a 4 percent difference or less to be "hardly any.") There was genuine male-female unanimity on the issue of a statute of limitations for Holocaust-related crimes; there was virtual unanimity on postwar attitudes toward Germany, on visiting Germany, on human nature, on who might be capable of committing mass murder of the Jews, and on the effect of the state of Israel on the fate of world Jewry. Slightly larger differences, in the range of 4 to 7 percent, characterized responses to several other questions: whether the Holocaust could occur again; on revival of Nazism in Germany; feelings about the future of the world, about Israel, and about the existence of God and the occurrence of the Holocaust; about teaching Holocaust subject matter to schoolchildren; and about visiting Austria (but not Germany). Only in three cases out of the sixteen were gender differences greater than 7 percent. Moreover, the pattern of differences was not entirely consistent. For example, on the issue of feelings about Israel, men were more positive than women by a margin of 5 percent. But on the anticipated effect of Israel on the fate of world Jewry, women were more positive than men by 3 percent.

Nevertheless, granted relatively narrow differences in most cases, women appeared more wary, essentially more pessimistic, on issues related to Germany and to anti-Semitism, as if the memories of all the past sufferings were more vivid and firmly fixed in their minds. This was manifested most clearly with respect to the question about the strength of anti-Semitism today—16 percent more women than men judged it stronger—and also with respect to the danger of Germany today, with 13 percent more women than men expressing greater concern. Women were also more pessimistic than men with regard to what it was, if anything, that the world had learned about, and from, the Holocaust—by 8 percent. In line with our expectations, but only by a narrow margin of 6 percent, women were more frequently "believers" as compared with men. Across all seventeen questions, gender contributed a 5.5 percent difference in responses.

A genuine surprise was the relative weakness of education as an influence on the attitudes of the survivors. Although in most instances the gaps between the more and the less educated were fairly narrow, there was some tendency toward less anxiety and more moderate views of the contemporary world by the better-educated respondents. The most dramatic example of this was the question concerning postwar attitudes toward Germany. On this issue, the less-educated respondents were much more likely to favor harsh treatment or no contact with Germans, and the more-educated far more likely to favor unrestricted, case-by-case dealings. The magnitude of the difference was 25 percent. The less-educated were appreciably more likely to believe that a revival of Nazism in Germany was either imminent or even underway already. The more-educated were also somewhat, though by a small margin, less likely to support the existence of God. They more frequently agreed with the proposition that if God existed, God would not have permitted the Holocaust to occur. All in all, differences attributable to the effects of education were generally quite modest. Across all sixteen questions, the average difference in responses was about 7 percent.

An even greater surprise, however, was generated by the attempt to differentiate survivors' attitudes on the basis of socioeconomic status. Here at last, one might have thought, we would encounter a force that might well sweep all before it. Would it not seem reasonable, especially with all the background of contemporary social-science research, that affluence and material well-being, aided by professional and educational attainments conferring high social status, would sharply differentiate their possessors from those situated on the other side of the great material divide? Perhaps if the here-and-now—or perhaps the "now-and-recently"—were more important in people's lives than whatever it is that happened to them long ago, the socioeconomic factor would prove the best possible differentiator of attitudes—especially, one would think, because many of the questions discussed in this chapter constitute a kind of world outlook that is fairly universal and not inextricably linked to the Holocaust. But these anticipations did not materialize.

In about half the cases, attitudinal differences between high-SES and low-SES respondents were all but trivial, that is, below 4 percent. And in only six of the seventeen did the differences reach or cross the 10 percent threshold. Considering all the issues explored in this chapter, SES was not a strong predictor. It failed to identify consistent tendencies of interpretation. Higher-SES respondents surprisingly evidenced less confidence in teaching schoolchildren about the Holocaust than did their low-end counterparts. They were somewhat less positive in their feelings about Israel, but they were more positive in their assessments of the effect of Israel on the future of world Jewry. They were as willing to visit Germany as the others, but they were more likely to confine the potential Holocaust perpetrators to Germans alone. They were more negative in their assessments of what the world had learned from the Holocaust experience, but they were also more skeptical about any possible revival of Nazism in Germany.

Across all questions, SES yielded a difference of 7 percent between high and low respondents. The more powerful explanatory forces proved to be those of culture, personality, and individual experience—even though undergone some fifty years earlier.

The culture model provided us with the most robust attitudinal discriminators. In twelve of seventeen questions there were double-digit point differences between respondents classified as "traditionalists" as opposed to "modernists." In only three instances were attitudinal differences of less than 4 percent. In six cases, attitudinal differences attributable to the culture model exceeded all the rest. The average difference in opinions on all the questions was 20 percent, almost three times greater than that produced by SES or education, and almost four times greater than the average difference attributable to gender. Beyond sheer numbers, there were more consistent tendencies here.

The most obvious, ideologically coherent differences between "modernists" and "traditionalists" were reflected in responses to the question about the existence of God and the fact of the Holocaust. What the modernists in effect denied, the traditionalists affirmed by a very large margin. They asserted God's existence despite the Holocaust, whereas the modernists saw in the tragedy a reason to doubt or disbelieve the existence of God. There were substantial differences also with respect to feelings about Israel, and the anticipated effects of Israel on Jewry, both far more favorable among the traditionalists. A number of questions—and answers—seemed to reflect the traditionalists' faith in God's providence, and therefore, it would appear, a greater optimism about the future of the world; greater optimism about what the world learned from the Holocaust; more confidence that the Holocaust would not recur; more positive feelings about human nature; and, concomitantly, it would appear, a tendency to compartmentalize the Holocaust experience with the Germans.

Although simultaneously more positive about the world, the traditionalists were also more concerned than the modernists about the possible danger of a resurgent Germany and more likely to have hardened their attitudes toward Germany in the postwar years. The traditionalists, with an almost obvious respect for the words of the Torah, expressed far greater faith in the effectiveness of teaching schoolchildren about the Holocaust than did their modernist counterparts. Since two of the three components of "traditionalism"—religious family background and nonassimilated origins—represented factors that influenced respondents before the Holocaust, the strength of the culture model was a powerful testimonial to the continuing significance of the past in survivor attitudes toward the present and the future.[9]

Another strong determinant of survivor opinions with a likely anchor in the past was personality. Based on the criteria of satisfaction with life and anticipations of the future, this model proved to be a powerful differentiator of survivor orientations in the post-Holocaust world. This model produced twelve double-digit percentage differences between the optimists and the pessimists. It was also the strongest discriminator in seven cases, and the average difference attributable to the personality factor was a robust 16 percent (excluding the two questions that involved some degree of tautology between the model and the dependent variable, to wit, feelings about the future of the world and feelings about human nature).

Once again, as in the case of the culture model, we find here not only a substantial magnitude of difference but also a remarkable consistency of direction. Positive personality types were likely to see anti-Semitism as less powerful in the postwar world than did their more negative or pessimistic counterparts. They were more likely to have softened their feelings with respect to the Germans and less likely to believe in a revival of Nazism in Germany. They saw less danger of a future threat emanating from Germany. They were more favorably disposed to unrestricted, unprejudiced dealings with postwar Germans. They were much more positive in their assessments of Israel and the effects of Israel's existence upon the fate of Jewry. They were overwhelmingly more positive in their estimates of what the world had learned about, and from, the Holocaust. They were also more likely to see Germans as the only people capable of carrying out the Holocaust.

What was nevertheless quite striking about the responses of this most personally positive group of respondents was that, even among them, the attitude toward *visiting* Germany or Austria was, in effect, no different from their more negative and pessimistic counterparts. Their anxieties with respect to a repetition of the Holocaust—all their other opinions notwithstanding—were also virtually the same as those of the pessimists. Their view on the statute-of-limitations issue was no different.

Our final explanatory model—exposure to suffering—partook of some of the attributes of culture, of course, with respect to religious and non-assimilated backgrounds of our respondents, but it also included residence in Poland, survival in concentration camps, and relative maturity in terms of age at the time of the Holocaust for the so-called high-exposure cases. This model ranked second behind culture in its explanatory power, with a 17 percent average difference on all questions between our groups of "high-exposure" and "low-exposure" respondents. It also yielded double-digit differentials in fourteen of the seventeen questions discussed in this chapter. Apart from the essentially consensual response about a possible statute of limitations for Holocaust-related crimes, there was only one question here where the attitudinal difference between high- and low-exposure cases was as low as 4 percent.

The pattern of responses by people classified in terms of exposure had a good deal in common with the culture and personality models. People who could be classified as modernists and optimists under the two previous models were similar in outlook to the low-exposure cases of our last model. People who were classified as traditionalists and pessimists were broadly analogous in orientation to the high-exposure respondents of the last model, but there were also some significant differences. People with high exposure were much more enthusiastic with respect to teaching children about the Holocaust. The high-exposure cases also expressed more confidence in what the world may have learned from the Holocaust, whereas their presumed analogues in the culture and personality models, the traditionalists and the pessimists, expressed less confidence.

There was virtually no difference between optimists and pessimists in the personality model with respect to the likelihood of the Holocaust being repeated. In the exposure model, however, there was a substantial difference, with more negative expectations or anticipations maintained by respondents who had had a high degree of exposure to suffering. In contrast, there was a much wider gap in attitudes with respect to human nature within the culture model than there was within the exposure model.

In general terms, the exposure model differentiated attitudes of concern and anxiety in the postwar world with respect to anti-Semitism, a renewed threat of Germany and Nazism, the persecution of Jews, and feelings about Israel. High-exposure cases generally expressed more concern and anxiety than low-exposure cases, but they also evidenced greater faith in God, and, in comparison with low-exposure cases, considerable equanimity with respect to the future of the world and the character of human nature. Together with the traditionalists, the high-exposure respondents were more likely to see the Holocaust as a distinctly German operation, with less likelihood of other national or social entities being involved in acts of such heinous nature.

Looking at the larger picture of the Holocaust survivor world outlook, it is clear that cultural determinism far outweighed material and economic determinism. The legacy of the past, the cultural and personal backgrounds of respondents even before the Holocaust occurred, was extremely important with respect to what survivors thought about the contemporary world. This legacy was more important than various recent experiences of survivors' lives—including material success or failure, or the amount of information and intellectual-cultural training acquired in the aftermath of the Holocaust. The influence of Jewish history in Europe before 1939 still dominated the intellectual horizon of the survivors half a century after the Holocaust (see Table 8).

As to the substance of the victims' worldviews, there were seemingly inescapable tensions between the wish for, and the aspiration to, optimism and hope for the future on the one hand, and deep concern and anxiety about issues that underlay the Holocaust itself—anti-Semitism and the capacity of mankind to learn from its past foremost among these—on the other.

Table 8. Learning Index Correlations with Fifteen Continuous Independent Variables

Family losses in Holocaust	.180
Mode of Holocaust survival	.153
Life satisfaction	−.136
Belief in God	.121
Exposure to suffering	.107
Wartime residence by country	.106
Personality	−.104
Current material welfare	.073
Family religious background	−.063
Outlook on future	.061
Residence before Holocaust (urban versus rural)	−.036
Family prewar wealth	.027
Education	.018
Socioeconomic status	.007
Age in 1939	.004

NOTES

1. Zygmunt Bauman, *Modernity and the Holocaust* (Ithaca, N. Y.: Cornell University Press, 1989), p. 19.

2. George M. Kren and Leon Rapaport, *The Holocaust and the Crisis of Human Behavior* (New York: Holmes and Meier, 1980), p. 70.

3. Aaron S. Klieman, *Israel and the World after 40 Years* (New York: Pergamon-Brassey's International Defense, 1990), p. 32. See also Harry B. Ellis, *The Dilemma of Israel* (Washington, D. C.: American Enterprise Institute, 1970), who says, "Over the years many Israelis have become increasingly disillusioned with the United Nations because of a voting pattern that has developed within the world body . . . frequently [voting] censure of the Jewish state" (p. 83).

See also Avi Beker, *The United Nations and Israel: From Recognition to Reprehension* (Lexington, Mass.: Lexington Books, 1988). He recalls that in October 1982 Iran offered a resolution calling on the UN General Assembly to expel Israel as a "false and illegitimate state." The resolution was not voted on by the General Assembly, only because U.S. Secretary of State George Shultz threatened American withdrawal from the body as well as the withdrawal of crucial American financial support should it be enacted. Apparently, the discussion of this ultimately abortive measure was favored by 79 member states and opposed by only 9, with 31 states abstaining (p. 1). Interestingly, Beker concludes that "the existence of the State of Israel [has] added a new dimension to Anti-Semitism, which sometimes attempts to conceal itself in a certain amount of obscurity while exploiting various disputes in international politics for its parochial purposes" (p. 91). Symbolically perhaps, Beker titled the last chapter of his book "The Shattering of the United Nations Dream" (p. 121).

Daniel Patrick Moynihan, who was at the time the U.S. Permanent Representative to the UN, noted that when on November 19, 1975, a resolution was put forward in the General Assembly that "Zionism is a form of racism and social discrimination," it was defeated by a vote of 67 to 55 with 15 abstentions. "Chaim Herzog, then the Israeli Permanent Representative and now President of Israel, later commented that this had been the highest pro-Israeli vote in a decade. It may prove the highest, ever after" (Daniel Patrick Moynihan, *Loyalties* [New York: Harcourt Brace Jovanovich, 1989], p. 36).

4. As David Biale says in *Power and Powerlessness in Jewish History* (New York: Schocken Books, 1986), "No single event has so concentrated the attention of Jews on the question of power as the creation of the modern state of Israel. Just as the Holocaust has come to represent the powerlessness of the Diaspora, so the return to political sovereignty symbolizes for many the negation of the Diaspora and the first real embodiment of Jewish power in two thousand years. That the same generation experienced the extremes of power and powerlessness has had a profound effect on the ways Jews regard political sovereignty" (p. 145).

See also Enid L. Fackenheim, *The Jewish Return into History: Reflections in the Age of Auschwitz and a New Jerusalem* (New York: Schocken Books, 1978); Roberta S. Feuerlicht, *The Fate of the Jews: A People Torn between Israeli Power and Jewish Ethics* (New York: Times Books, 1983); and Simon Rawidowicz, *Israel: The Ever Dying People and Other Essays* (Cranbury, N. J.: Associated University Presses, 1986).

5. Note the conclusions of Anton Gill, *The Journey Back from Hell: Conversations with Concentration Camp Survivors* (London: Grafton Books, 1988). Gill interviewed 120 concentration camp victims, many but not all Jewish, and concluded that, above all, "most survivors suffer more than they show" (p. 458).

6. Note Abraham E. Millgram, *Jewish Worship* (Philadelphia: Jewish Publication Society of America, 1971), who says that "before the advent of modernity the Jew wanted to know *how* to pray; now he wants to know *why* to pray. While waiting for an answer he has lost the habit of praying; then he forgot how to pray; and by now he does not know to whom to pray. To be sure, there are Jews who adhere to the tradition of daily prayer, but these Jews are only a small minority within the American Jewish community" (p. 598).

7. Quoted in Millgram, *Jewish Worship*, p. 311.

8. Ibid., p. 335.

9. Given the importance of assimilation in this model, we note parenthetically that only 20 percent of the nonassimilated thought that a repetition of the Holocaust was actually probable in the future, but among the assimilated 34 percent thought so. Among the nonassimilated, the percentage of respondents who thought that another Holocaust was either unlikely or even certain not to occur again was 36 percent. Among the assimilated, such positive views were expressed by 29 percent.

Among the nonassimilated, 47 percent professed themselves optimistic about the future of the world, while among the assimilated only 38 percent expressed optimism. Pessimists constituted 14 percent of the nonassimilated but 18 percent of the assimilated respondents.

Chapter 4

JEWISH IDENTITY

What effect did the Holocaust have upon its victims in terms of their Jewishness? Did it enhance their sense of ethnic identity, or did it dilute it? Was there perhaps a differentiated impact upon the survivors depending on their pre-Holocaust backgrounds and their Holocaust experiences? What was the impact of current socioeconomic factors? How did the survivors compare with "mainstream" American Jews?

In order to deal with these questions, we have constructed a Jewish identity scale made up of eight attitudinal and behavioral variables. In the attitudinal category, we probed respondents' feelings about such subjects as religion, Zionism, and Israel. In the behavioral, we sought responses with respect to community activities, discussions of the Holocaust with children, issues of intermarriage, and also visits to Israel. The distribution of values on this scale proved to be fairly continuous and normal with a couple of exceptionally large concentrations on the high side of the mean (see Fig. 4.1).

The inquiry here is, of course, subject to certain limitations mentioned in chapter 1. All our subjects had made some, at least minimal and formal, commitment to Jewish identification by the very act of membership in the organizations whose lists supplied us with the names of our interviewees. We have not obtained any data from people, probably considerable in number, who did not subjectively identify themselves as Jewish but who had suffered persecution at the hands of the Nazis in the Second World War because they were born Jewish and the Nazis classified them as Jews

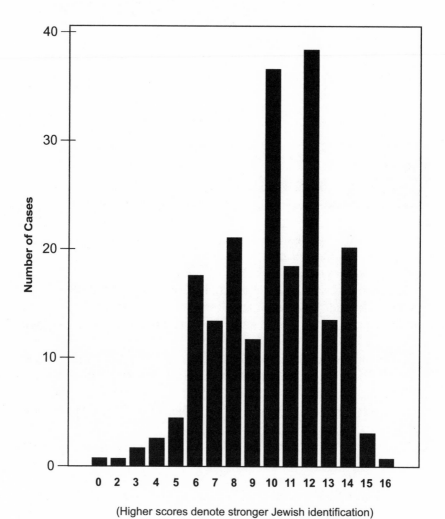

(Higher scores denote stronger Jewish identification)

Fig. 4.1. Values on the Identity Scale

according to their racial laws. Nor did we gather information from people who, for whatever reasons, had abandoned all Jewish identity after the war. Nevertheless, the levels of organizational involvement among our respondents could, and in fact did, differ very widely. Some people had simply signed on to mailing lists; others were busy participants. Given the differentiated nature of our questionnaire, we believe that much could be learned in this survey from our respondents about attitudes toward Jewishness. Here, indeed, one finds different allegiances, intensities, and levels of involvement with respect to all things Jewish. These, in turn, seem to be related to different backgrounds, experiences, and orientations on the part of the survivors. Ultimately, by inference from "more" to "less" in attitudes and backgrounds, some idea might be gleaned here of the attitudes of the unrepresented absentees—the Jewish "rejectionists," as it were.

In the first category of questions, those dealing with affect, we asked for respondent self-assessment as Jews and about their attitudes toward Israel. Did the survivors think that the Holocaust affected their own sense of being Jewish, and if so, how? How did they perceive the state of Israel and its effect on the fortunes of world Jewry? Had they ever considered settling in Israel (aliyah)?

On the issue of behavior, we sought answers with respect to the frequency of the survivors' Jewish contributions and activities; visits to Israel, if any; respondent discussions of the Holocaust with children; and questions about intermarriage among children of the respondents.

The last set of questions—those concerning the marriage of respondents' children to non-Jews—was premised on the proposition that marriage itself could well be a sudden and spontaneous act but that, generally speaking, through the progeny, it was likely to reflect upon the life of many years within the respondents' families. (This assumption appears to be vindicated by our findings.)

The following are two subsidiary questions posed to respondents on the issue of marriage:

If any of your children who married did not marry Jewish, did any of their spouses convert to Judaism later?

    a. Yes

    b. No

    c. Not applicable

If any of your children married non-Jews who did not convert to Judaism, did they maintain anything that might be termed "a Jewish home"?

a. Yes
b. Some did, some did not
c. No
d. Not applicable

These questions also turned out to be supportive of our general assumption with respect to intermarriage. All sorts of differences among the respondents became readily apparent. For most, the Holocaust seemed to strengthen at least some aspects of their Jewish identity. Making an aliyah to the state of Israel seemed in itself a significant divider in determining the intensity of people's Jewish preoccupations. There were clear distinctions in terms of organizational or community activities of survivors; in frequency of visits to Israel; in family discussions of the Holocaust, and also in the degree to which survivors with children managed to transmit Jewish identification to their progeny, a process implicitly suggesting a very prolonged, virtually lifelong period of orientations and activities within families.

In aggregate terms, two-thirds of our respondents saw their sense of Jewish identity as enhanced by the Holocaust in some form, whether religious, Zionist, or simply more generally Jewish (see Fig. 4.2). However, a quarter of the respondents saw the Holocaust as having no effect at all on their Jewishness. Did these more "marginal" Jews provide us with some clues as to the identity of those who were lost to Judaism in the aftermath of the Holocaust? Nearly three-fourths of our respondents reported that all of their children married Jews; in roughly one of five cases, however, some did and some did not. Only 7 percent of our respondents said that none of their children married Jews.

An impressive 70 percent of our survivor pool declared itself regular and frequent contributors to Jewish causes, personally, financially, or both. For practical purposes, all the rest reported themselves as contributors "from time to time." Only 1 percent of those responding to this question (184 persons total)—in fact, just two individuals—declared that they contributed only "rarely."

Of our ten elements of Jewish identity in the postwar world, the two most important were personal feelings about Israel and contributions to Jewish causes. Those who described themselves as enthusiastic about Israel or as regular and frequent contributors to Jewish activities and institutions exhibited overall identity scores 31 percent higher (in each case) than those who said that they had reservations or questions about Israel and those who contributed occasionally, rarely, or never. None of the other eight elements

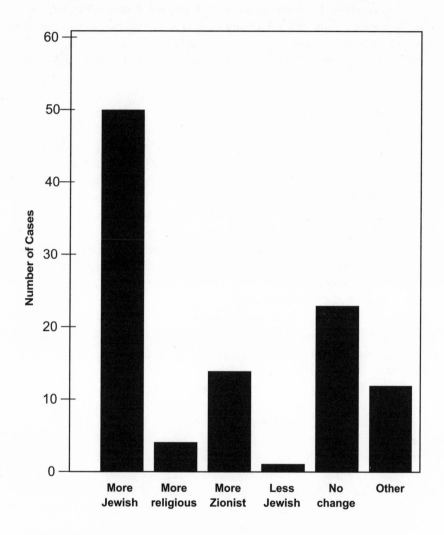

Fig. 4.2. Effect of the Holocaust on Survivors' Sense of Jewish Identity

was quite as critical in differentiating people on the Jewish identity scale as these two variables.[1]

Considerable divisions prevailed with respect to family discussions of the Holocaust. Fifty percent of our respondents reported discussing this subject with their children occasionally, and only 37 percent said they discussed it frequently. About 11 percent said that they had discussed the Holocaust rarely, and 2 percent reported that they never discussed it.

The scores of favorability toward Israel were simply overwhelming, in excess of 80 percent on both of our Israel-related questions: general approval and expectations of favorable consequences for Jews.[2]

An obviously critical issue about Jewish identity in the aftermath of the Holocaust is what personal attributes differentiate between those who identify as Jews more and those who identify less. Our data indicate that the least significant factors were precisely those attributes that the survivors accumulated largely, if not entirely, *after* the Holocaust. These are, respectively, education and socioeconomic status. Differences between those with more education and those with less education accounted for only a 1.2 percent gap in Jewish identity scores, with a fairly slight advantage, that is, more Jewish identity, for the more educated. Dividing our respondents into three categories of Jewish identity—high, middle, and low—we found 43 percent of the college-educated among the high identifiers, as compared with 35 percent among those with only a high school education or less. On the other hand, 26 percent of the college-educated were in the low identifier category, whereas only 20 percent of the less educated fell into this essentially least allegiant and/or affiliated group.

Socioeconomic status accounted for only a 2.7 percent difference in identity scores, with a slight advantage to the higher-status persons. Looking at current affluence alone, there was relatively little difference between those who were well-off or better and those who merely made ends meet or faced financial difficulties—4.2 percent. The well-off ranked slightly higher on the identity scale. In a threefold division of high, middle, and low, among the more affluent 38 percent were high identifiers, and among the less affluent respondents 35 percent.

Gender differences were also relatively modest with, as we had anticipated, a small advantage for women, with an average of 4.6 percent higher Jewish identity scores among females. When we divided our respondents into three parts on the identity scale—high, medium, and low—40 percent of women were in the high-identity group, as compared with only 32 percent among men.

Age was a more significant discriminator, showing a 5.7 percent difference in Jewish identity scores. The difference was in favor of the older people, that is, those who were fourteen to thirty-one years old in 1939, as compared with those one to thirteen years old at the outbreak of the Second World War. In a threefold division of high, middle, and low identity scores, 40 percent of older people were classified as high identifiers, but among the younger group only 29 percent identified in this category. Among the younger respondents, 26 percent were low identifiers, but among the older group only 18 percent were.

Overall, residence in Poland during the conflict was associated with Jewish identity scores 8.8 percent higher than residence outside of Poland. Among those who lived in Poland at the beginning of the war, 40 percent belonged to the high category of Jewish identifiers in a threefold division, but only 28 percent of those who had lived outside of Poland in 1939 did. On the other end of the scale, among the people from Poland, only 18 percent were low identifiers, whereas 26 percent of those from other countries were in that category.

Incarceration in a concentration camp was linked to greater Jewish identification by 5.8 percent. Among concentration camp survivors, 39 percent were in the high identifier category; among those who survived outside of camps, only 29 percent were. Only 17 percent of camp inmates were in the low identifier category, but 29 percent of those who survived outside camps were found in this category.

Very much in line with the suffering syndrome, among people who had lost all or most of their family in the Holocaust, Jewish identity scores were on average 10.6 percent higher than among those who had only lost some or none. Once again dividing respondents into high, medium, and low identifiers, we found that among those who had lost almost everyone, 38 percent were in the high identity group, compared with only 20 percent for those in the "some or none" category.

An obviously significant factor was personality. Among people whom we have classified as having more positive personalities, based on their views of the future and their satisfaction with life, there was an average Jewish identity score 10 percent higher than among those whom we have classified as more negative. Looking at the factor of satisfaction with life alone, we found the more satisfied to have an average Jewish identity score 7.3 percent higher than the more disappointed. Using our high, medium, and low categories, we found that among the more satisfied, 49 percent were high identifiers, whereas among the disappointed, only 32 percent fell into this category.

Clearly, however, the most important difference and predictor was culture. This factor accounted for a 20 percent difference in Jewish identity scores, with much higher levels of identification among people who came from nonassimilated, religious families and those who also professed themselves believers in God. Among religious believers, Jewish identity scores were 10.6 percent higher than among the doubters and the nonbelievers. Among believers, 43 percent were high identifiers, but among the agnostics and atheists the figure was only 28 percent. Identity scores were nearly 8 percent higher on average among those who came from nonassimilated families. In this case, however, the major difference was on the lower end of the identity scale. We found that among the nonassimilated, 40 percent were in the high identifier category, whereas among the assimilated, only 33 percent were. On the other hand, only 18 percent of the nonassimilated were to be found in the low identifier category, whereas nearly 30 percent of the assimilated were in this bottom group.

The way in which people survived the Holocaust was consistently, and predictably from our point of view, related both to their cultural backgrounds and to their sense of Jewish identity after the war. Among survivors who had *not* been assisted by Gentiles during the Holocaust, representing presumably the more traditional, isolated Jewish culture of prewar Europe, Jewish identity scores were on average 4 percent higher in the post–Second World War era as compared with those who had been so assisted.

Actually, even the pattern of past residence, however slightly, fit the apparently traditional requirements of stronger Jewish identity. People who had come from small towns and villages—the historical *shtetl*—rather than from the larger towns and cities of Europe averaged identity scores about 2 percent higher in the aftermath of the Holocaust. Once again, we have evidence here of the greater importance of cultural and historic factors, rather than of material and current ones, in shaping the social attitudes and the behavior of the Holocaust survivors in the wake of their catastrophic experience (see Table 9).

In this study, we found that Jewish identity scores were somewhat negatively related to empathy (–.070), as discussed in the chapter on comparing the Holocaust. They were, however, positively and significantly related to the cognition and learning scales, with indices of .155 and .235, respectively. Given our coding, this meant that greater Jewish identity was associated with more negative perceptions of Holocaust circumstances and more negative views of world prospects and tendencies. It also involved

Table 9. Correlations between Jewish Idenfication and Seventeen
Independent Variables in Order of Magnitude

Family religious background	.187*
Wartime residence by country	.168*
Exposure to suffering	.158
Cultural background (Family's religion, assimilation and own belief)	.153**
Prewar assimilation of family	.131
Family losses in Holocaust	.107
Age in 1939	.105
Mode of Holocaust survival	.103
Family prewar wealth	−.096[†]
Belief in God	.086
Life satisfaction	−.068[†]
Current material welfare	−.052[†]
Socioeconomic status	.033
Residence before Holocaust (urban versus rural)	−.032
Personality	−.013[†]
Outlook on future	−.013[†]
Education	−.004

* Significant at .001 level

** Significant at .005 level

[†] Note that because of the coding of our questions, these relationships are actually positive, i.e., for example, higher levels of material welfare are associated with higher levels of Jewish identification.

somewhat higher (.106) blame feelings with respect to the roles of various Holocaust actors.

Background differences among our respondents suggest that, from the standpoint of cultivating a Jewish identification, the Holocaust was an unequally energizing experience. It appears to have inspired more Jewish identification, zest, and commitment from those people who already had a certain predisposition for it in terms of their social backgrounds before the Holocaust. Whatever impact the tragedy may have had in people's lives, it did not seem to reverse past trends. The more marginal Jews in terms of their own identities do not appear to have drastically changed course. There was no powerful compensatory trend to more ardent Jewish identities on the part of those who were assimilated in 1939.

Looking at aggregate figures, 50 percent of our respondents described themselves as "more aware of their Jewish identity" in consequence of the Holocaust experience. Nearly 13 percent described themselves as "more Zionist." But only 3 percent said that they were more religious, whereas 22 percent said that their feelings had not changed, and 1 percent were actually less concerned about their Jewish identity.

A common characteristic among the survivors that suggests a strong Holocaust impact on their private lives seemed to be an almost startling degree of social cohesion manifested in a very high marriage rate and very low divorce rate among our respondents. Nearly 80 percent reported being married. Between 14 and 15 percent were widowed. The number of single persons and those divorced was, in each case, only about 3 percent. Over 80 percent of our respondents were parents.[3] According to U.S. Census Bureau demographic data, involving on average much younger persons, 56 percent of American adults in 1998 were married and lived with their spouse. Some 24 percent had never been married; the divorced constituted 10 percent of the population, and the widowed 7 percent.[4]

Aggregate data, to be sure, demonstrated some differences between the more superficial and the more profound commitments among respondents. For example, enthusiastic attitudes about Israel as a force in world affairs were virtually consensual among the survivors. But the same was less true with respect to the consideration of aliyah, a more formidable test of loyalties both to a Jewish existence and the Jewish state. Among all our respondents, 21 percent never considered aliyah as a personal alternative, but 9 percent actually tried it and gave up on the attempt within a short period of time. A remarkable 52 percent of our survivors did seriously consider immigration to Israel, and nearly 16 percent were either permanent residents or at least longtime residents of Israel in the course of their lives.[5]

Among American Jews, according to recent William Helmreich data, fewer than 16 percent had visited Israel twice or more. Among our survivor respondents, however, the equivalent figure was 79 percent. In fact, 43 percent of our survivors had visited Israel five times or more. Looking for some comparability, we took the 16 percent of our respondents who had traveled most frequently to Israel and we found that they went ten or more times.[6]

From both attitudinal and behavioral data, it is apparent that attachment to Israel represents a powerful emotional value for the survivors. Metaphorically speaking, it is the transition from death (Holocaust) to life (Israel) and from utter powerlessness to respected strength and self-determination. Israel is an implicit promise, if not a guarantee, that the Holocaust "will never happen again." Indeed, that was the frequently delivered, explicit message of Israel's notable prime minister Menachem Begin, whose father perished during the Holocaust in Poland.[7] For the surviving Jews, the delight of Israel's resurrection in modern times was greatly magnified by the background of the Holocaust disaster.

A critically important emotional bond between Holocaust survivors on the one hand and the state of Israel on the other derives, quite logically, we believe, from the main premise of the survivors' understanding of their own experience in Nazi-occupied Europe. From that perspective, when the Jews were being led to their deaths, there was seemingly no one in sight to stand up for them, no one to defend them, no one to take any risks on their behalf. When the Polish underground movement staged its famed uprising against the Nazis in Warsaw in August and September of 1944, Allied planes repeatedly flew risky supply missions over the city and took significant casualties in the process. Allied leaders, Roosevelt and Churchill personally, made diplomatic appeals to Stalin for even more help. When, at last, exhausted Warsaw freedom fighters surrendered, British Foreign Secretary Anthony Eden issued a declaration warning the Nazis that the Allies expected the surrendering Polish insurgents to be accorded all the rights of combatants protected by the long-standing international conventions. But nothing remotely equivalent was done when Jewish freedom fighters in the Warsaw ghetto fought, died, and were murdered in its ruins in April and May of 1943. Allied capitals were silent. Allied leaders were not even publicly cognizant of the events taking place in the Polish capital.

Few things could explain better the difference that Israel made for surviving Jews in the international environment than the events of late June and early July 1976. On June 27 of that year, an Air France plane flying from Tel Aviv to Paris, with many Jewish passengers on board, was hijacked by Middle Eastern terrorists on its stopover in Athens. It was then taken to Libya and then to Uganda. On July 4, 1976, six large Israeli planes flew 2500 miles across the Red Sea and the horn of Africa carrying 150 commandos and 33 medical personnel to the airport at Entebbe in order to free the hostages. The mission, though obviously risky, was spectacularly successful. To be sure, then UN Secretary-General Kurt Waldheim harshly denounced the Israeli operation; it was also condemned by a subsequent meeting of the Organization of African Unity. To the Jewish survivors of the Holocaust, however, the symbolism of July 4, 1976, in juxtaposition to what had happened to them in wartime Europe, could not have been clearer.

When Prime Minister Begin visited the White House at the time of the Camp David Accords of 1978, he told President Carter, "Mr. President, I want to tell you that I have taken an oath in the name of the Jewish people that another such tragic episode [the Holocaust] in the history of the Jewish people will never happen again—never again."[8]

The emotional linkage between Israel and the Holocaust is also vividly recalled in the text of a remarkable speech made in Poland one year before the outbreak of the Second World War by Menachem Begin's political leader and mentor, Vladimir (Zeev) Jabotinsky:

> For three years I have been pleading with you, the Jews of Poland, the cream of world Jewry. I have warned you again and again that the catastrophe is approaching. My hair has turned white and I have aged during these years because my heart bleeds that you, my dear brothers and sisters, cannot see the volcano which has started to spew out the fire of extermination. I see a terrible sight. Time is short, but it is still possible to be saved. I know that you cannot see it because of your daily problems. But I demand faith of you. After all, you have learned that my prognoses always come true. If you think otherwise, then drive me out of the Jewish community. But if you believe me, then listen to my eleventh-hour cry. In the name of God, let each and every one save his soul while he still can. And I want to tell you one more thing. Those who succeed in getting away will be privileged to witness a moment of great Jewish rejoicing: the rebirth of a Jewish State. I do not know whether I myself will do so. My son—yes! I am as sure of this as I am that the sun will rise tomorrow morning.[9]

What appears to be of particular importance from the standpoint of our study is a remarkable *consistency* in attributes associated with *all* aspects of Jewish identity among the survivors. Culture, generally reinforced by the individual's exposure to suffering during the period of the Holocaust, seems to be the strongest element in all these identifications.

A few illustrations may suffice. Beginning with the ten-item Jewish identity scale, the people with high exposure to Holocaust suffering exceeded the low-exposure group by 26 percentage points. Regular and frequent contributors to Jewish causes averaged exposure scores 15 percent higher than those who were "occasional" and "rare or never" contributors. They also exceeded the latter by 20 percent on the culture scale; i.e., they represented much more traditional Jewish background orientations. It may be recalled that the overall difference between regular and rare contributors on the Jewish identity scale was 31 percent, in favor of the regular.

Respondents who reported discussing the Holocaust with their children "frequently" averaged 13 percent higher exposure and 19 percent higher culture scores than among those who reported talking about it "rarely" or "never." Those respondents who were "in the middle" on this question—they discussed the Holocaust with their children "occasionally"—were predictably also midway between these two above-mentioned categories with respect to exposure and culture scores. The overall Jewish identity scores of the "frequent" discussants were 18 percent higher than those of the "rare" discussants of the Holocaust.

Among those respondents who thought about making aliyah, there was a 5 percent higher overall Jewish identity score than among those who said they had never considered it. There was also a 17 percent difference on the exposure scale and a 23 percent difference on the culture scale—in favor of those who had considered immigration—among this group.

Interestingly, and appropriately it would seem, among people who *tried* aliyah unsuccessfully and those who, relatively speaking, succeeded, the Jewish identity scores were actually *higher* than among those who merely thought about doing it. In terms of culture scores, all the people who did go to Israel were very close, virtually identical, with those who thought about it but did not go. Among those who tried aliyah but failed, exposure scores were actually significantly lower—by 21 percent. Among those who succeeded, exposure scores were 14 percent higher than among those who had given up on Israel and 10 percent higher than among respondents who had never given Israel a thought. (The latter group had a culture score 20 percent lower than those who had been considering aliyah.)

If—or to the extent that—Jewish interests might be measured by actual travel to Israel, the Holocaust survivors as a whole were a very impressive group. Only about 5 percent of our survivors who responded to the question said that they had never visited Israel. Among 187 respondents answering this question, the average number of visits was 5.6, and the median 4.0. Once again, what was of special interest here was the impact of the cultural and personal experience factors identified earlier. The largest difference, that is, most trips versus fewer trips on the basis of any particular variable, was supplied by our exposure model. There was a 46 percent difference between the (more frequent) high-exposure visitors to Israel and the (much less frequent) low-exposure visitors.

Given the obvious financial constraints involved in travel to Israel, it was not surprising that socioeconomic status was an important discriminant. There was a 28 percent difference between high-SES persons and those of low SES; the former averaged 6.3 trips to Israel, whereas the latter only 4.5. Based on money alone (current material welfare), the well-off traveled 11 percent more often than those merely making ends meet or experiencing financial difficulties. Although 11 percent was obviously a significant difference, it was perhaps less than one might have expected given the all but inescapable financial hardships of such travel. Clearly, many people for whom such a trip was not easily affordable made an extraordinary effort to go to Israel, financial difficulties and sacrifices notwithstanding. Predictably, in terms of traditional affiliations, women averaged about 26 percent more trips to Israel than men. Those with a completed college education or better averaged about 23 percent more trips than those who were less educated.

All of the intermarriage issues explored in our survey also conformed to the pattern evident in the other areas of Jewish identity. Approximately 73 percent of our respondents reported that all of their children (if indeed they had children) married Jews. About 7 percent reported that none of their children married Jews, and 19 percent said that at least some of their children married Jews. When we divided the respondents into two groups, those whose children all married Jews versus those whose progeny married, all or partly, out of the faith, the first group exceeded the second by 19 percent on the overall Jewish identity scale. The first group was more traditional in background, 9.5 percent higher on the culture scale. In addition, more of its members came from homes where Yiddish was spoken. It exceeded the second group on the exposure scale by about 3 percent.

When we asked our relevant respondents—48 cases—if the spouses of their children's non-Jewish partners converted to Judaism, 29 survivors responded yes and 19 no. Among those responding yes, we found the average culture score to be 21 percent more traditional than among those who answered no. We also found a difference of 11 percent in the expected direction among those two groups of people with respect to exposure.

An appropriate summary of the Jewish identity issue among Holocaust survivors must acknowledge an achievement. The achievement belongs, above all, to generations of relatively observant and pious Jewish families of Eastern Europe, who, over many years, managed to inculcate a powerful cultural heritage in their sons and daughters. Even the brutality and horror of Hitler's Holocaust, clearly one of the most traumatic events in human history, could not destroy or erode this legacy. Indeed, our evidence suggests that the experience of the Holocaust at its worst—in Poland and in concentration/extermination camps—in many, even most, cases served the very opposite purpose. It increased the sense of Jewish identity and the commitment of the survivors to a Jewish life and a sense of solidarity with fellow Jews. From this perspective, in light of this renewed or strengthened commitment to Jewish identity, the Holocaust may be seen as a singular Nazi failure. Far from achieving the destruction of Jewry, Hitler's Final Solution seems to have energized and strengthened a substantial portion of the European Jewish remnant, with obviously important consequences for the future. If the Nazi aim for the Jews was eventual extinction, the actual effect seems to have been a renewal providing another strong leaven for development both in Israel and around the world.[10]

Despite all of Hitler's murderous efforts, and the veritable sea of Jewish blood spilled in the process, the moral and social power of Jewish tradition had had its victory. For those who perished, it was victory from beyond the grave. The accumulated years of parental love, care, and dedication and the disciplines of learning and observance had not been spent in vain. In the language of modern commerce, these years yielded a very substantial payoff.[11] Some enduring values survived within the Holocaust remnant as a legacy of the traditional, close-knit, and relatively insular Jewish home.

Our analysis suggests that the effects of the Holocaust among the survivors—the consequences of the interaction between suffering and cultural heritage—have been substantially independent of the material, economic, and intellectual influences of the survivors' post-Holocaust life. The legacy has proved highly resilient: to all appearances capable of withstanding the vicissitudes of material fortune and of cultural/intellectual innovation experienced by survivors since the war.

Returning to the question of Jewish defections resulting from, or at any rate occurring in, the years following the Holocaust, a few conclusions are clearly implicit in the data of this chapter. Whereas the Holocaust strengthened the ethnic resolve of those people who had significant Jewish roots before the outbreak of the Second World War, its effect upon Jewish "marginals" was palpably less powerful.

In virtually all areas of Jewish identification, whether related to affect or behavior, people who came from assimilated homes, nonreligious backgrounds, and families where Yiddish was not spoken were significantly less "allegiant" in a Jewish sense than their nonassimilated opposites. Such people often came from large cities rather than small towns or villages.

Because they were better integrated into the non-Jewish society than the more religious, traditionalist Jews, they were also more likely to have received the help of Gentiles in their efforts to escape the verdict of the Final Solution. They were also more likely to have survived the war by hiding among Gentile neighbors, or hiding under a false identity within the larger, non-Jewish society.

Although there are significant differences in Jewish involvements and identifications between these two groups of survivors, they occur within certain limits. The Jewish identity scores of our respondents with the more secular and assimilated backgrounds are obviously less than those of people with more traditional backgrounds. But they are still about two-thirds as substantial as those of the more ardent or involved. This means that many of our secular/assimilated respondents are also persons who have supported a variety of Jewish organizations and activities, donated their money and time to Jewish community activities, visited Israel, identified as Jews and also identified with Jews, found a Jewish meaning in the events of the Holocaust, and are deeply concerned with anti-Semitism and the persecution of Jews at home and abroad. On the whole, the Holocaust survivors in our respondent group were a very impressive collectivity of committed and involved Jews.[12]

In pondering their involvements, one must take account of the evolving nature of "Jewishness" in modern times, and particularly in North America. One is especially reminded here of the work of Marshall Sklare and Joseph Greenbaum, which provides an interesting "new" model of what it means (or at least meant in 1979) to be a "good Jew." In their so-called Lakeville study, they identified eight factors considered important to a Jewish identity by their (Jewish) respondents. Among these, only two had anything to do, explicitly at least, with being "Jewish." The authors' respondents agreed that it was important for people to "accept being a Jew and not try to hide it" and also to "know the fundamentals of Judaism." The other elements of the definition of the "good Jew" consisted of leading an ethical and moral life, supporting humanitarian causes, promoting civic betterment and improvement in the community, gaining the respect of Christian neighbors, helping the underprivileged improve their lot, and working for the equality of African Americans. As the authors comment, "This list of essential qualities for being considered a good Jew is indicative of how far [the new] conceptions deviate from past models of Jewish religious piety."[13]

Qualities found among the interviewed community members to be "desirable" rather than "essential" included the following:

1. Being well versed in Jewish history and culture—73 percent
2. Marrying within the Jewish faith—51 percent.
3. Contributing to Jewish philanthropies—49 percent
4. Knowing the fundamentals of Judaism—48 percent
5. Support of Israel—47 percent

The idea of belonging to a synagogue or temple ranked last, with 44 percent.[14]

With all allowance for the "new Jewishness," however, it seems a reasonable inference from the attitudes and behavior of our more assimilated respondents that at the more extreme end of that scale, somewhere beyond our actual survivor pool—in terms of assimilation, religion, and integration in the larger Gentile society of their time—there were many whose reaction to the Holocaust was probably outright flight from Jewish identity. This was almost certainly true of most Jews who had voluntarily adopted the Christian religion before or during the war. These people wanted to forget about being Jewish. The Nazis insisted on reminding them of it on racial grounds. The end of the war probably brought a sense of relief to many such people. They could go back to being Christian and henceforth no one would, presumably, bother them again about their racial credentials. For such people, by and large, Jewishness was something to forget and abandon as quickly and as completely as possible. Analogous reactions probably occurred in some less extreme cases. People who did not become Christian but who had minimal Jewish affiliations before the war were probably also frequently disposed to attenuate these affiliations even further after the Holocaust.

This was the case historically with many Jewish radicals and Communists in Russia and Eastern Europe after 1945. They may have been born Jewish and may never have formally renounced their Jewish origins, but they were primarily interested in meeting the demands of Marxist orthodoxy out of ideological conviction and for career reasons, and even a modest manifestation of Jewish identity would have been a decided, perhaps even a fatal, handicap to them during this period. They simply could not "afford" it. The circumstances of Jewish Communists in the Soviet Bloc, beginning with the late 1940s and early 1950s, when Stalin launched his anti-Zionist and anticosmopolitan purges, made Jewish identity a virtual curse.

Although these may have been somewhat special cases, it is apparent that among strongly secularized Jews of Europe, both East and West, there have always been pressures to escape the handicaps of Jewish identity for reasons related to economic as well as social mobility and status.[15]

Our data demonstrate that the way in which the survivors reacted to the Holocaust was very strongly related to the legacy of assimilation—or nonassimilation. Obviously, all the respondents in our survey identified themselves as Jews, at least to some degree. But the assimilated identified less strongly, suggesting something about the fate of those Jews who shared some of the same characteristics and tendencies (e.g., being less religious or actually nonreligious and being indifferent to the reemergence of the Jewish state) but who possessed them presumably to an even greater degree than did our relatively less robust Jewish identifiers.

In fact, when we separated the elements of suffering and loss incurred by survivors during the Holocaust from their pre-1939 backgrounds, we found a very substantial difference in postwar Jewish identifications. Given analogous camp experiences and family losses, those whose prewar Jewish backgrounds were "strong" outscored those whose Jewish backgrounds were "weak" by a magnitude of some 20 percent.

However, what emerges from our analysis of the Jewish identifications of Holocaust survivors is a twofold insight. There are differences among them in which history and personal experience are uniquely important. There is also a certain impressive commonality here with respect to social cohesion and a very high level of community involvement and contribution.

NOTES

1. Most of our Jewish identity variables were not highly intercorrelated. However, using the Spearman rho correlation test, we found the following attitude-behavior chain moderately significant. Positive feelings about Israel show a .207 correlation, significant at the .01 level, with frequency of contributions to "Jewish causes." The latter is correlated at .256, also significant at the .01 level, with frequency of visits to Israel. People who at some time in the past considered making aliyah are more frequent visitors to Israel. A .198 correlation significant at the .01 level links dispositions and behavior in this area.

2. See Jacob Neusner, *Stranger At Home: 'The Holocaust,' Zionism, and American Judaism* (Chicago: University of Chicago, 1981) p. 1, who defined the role of the Holocaust in American Jewish consciousness as follows: "These events, far from America's shores and remote from American Jews' everyday experience,

constitute the generative myth by which the generality of American Jews make sense of themselves and decide what to do with that part of themselves set aside for 'being Jewish.' . . . [A] sizable sector of the American people sees the world in and along the lines of vision of reality beginning in death, 'the Holocaust,' and completed by resurrection or rebirth, 'Israel.'" The survivors are the living reminders of this concept.

See also Daniel J. Elazar, "The Political Tradition of the American Jew," in *Traditions of the American Jew*, ed. Stanley M. Wagner (New York: KTAV Publishing, 1977), pp. 105–30, who attributes a power of rediscovery of Jewish identity by American Jews "beginning with Zionism and the effort to restore the Jewish national home" (p. 105). He also observes, interestingly, that "the basic values, both positive and negative, of the American and Jewish civilizations are quite similar, encouraging a measure of convergence and identification not present in other civilizations that have been hosts to Jews" (p. 118).

3. See Chaim Waxman, "The Family and the American Jewish Community on the Threshold of the 1980s: An Inventory for Research and Planning," in *Understanding American Jewry*, ed. Marshall Sklare (New Brunswick, N. J.: Brandeis University, 1982), pp. 163–85. He makes the following observation: "Among Jews themselves . . . the divorce rate [has been] higher among those born in the United States than among those born elsewhere, and higher among Reform than among Conservative and Orthodox Jews . . . [with] divorce and separation . . . higher among those highly educated" (pp. 166–67). Even among the Orthodox, however, the rate of divorce was apparently increasing (p. 167). He also noted "sharp increases" in single-parent families among American Jews (p. 168) and a general decline in number of offspring (pp. 168–71).

See also James Yaffee, *The American Jews* (New York: Random House, 1968), who observes that "the most important attribute of traditional Judaism is that the family is the sacred foundation of all life, the heart not only of daily living but of religion itself. For this reason, in almost all Jewish religious holidays the home ceremonies are just as important as the synagogue ceremonies" (p. 279). Note also the discussion about Jewish attitudes toward divorce and toward children as the "real purpose" of marriage (p. 280–88).

4. "United States Population," *The World Almanac and Book of Facts, 2000* (Mahwah, N. J.: World Almanac Books, 1999), p. 381.

See also William Toll, *Women, Men and Ethnicity: Essays on the Structure and Thought of American Jewry* (Lanham, Md.: University Press of America, 1991). Writing about intermarriage, he says that "Jews in the West have not been stigmatized nor even challenged by politics of ethnic conflict" (p. 158). Integration and contact with the non-Jewish world have greatly increased over the years. Young people, with education and money, have tended to create new, multiethnic networks for themselves—in contrast to the patterns of their parents (pp. 158–59). He also points out that intermarriage may result, at least at times, in more conversions of people to Judaism, including the conversions of children of intermarried couples (p. 162).

Chaim Waxman, *America's Jews in Transition* (Philadelphia: Temple University, 1983), notes that in consequence of the Six-Day War of 1967, a spirit of "unity with Israel" was greatly strengthened in the American Jewish community. "The threat to Israel aroused the fear of another Holocaust in American Jewry and awakened a strong desire for survival" (p. 114). Note also his interesting chapter on "Religion without Religiosity: The Third Generation Community," pp. 81–103. Here Waxman describes the tendency among modern American Jews to see "religion" more as an ethnic, community-building set of activities and concerns than actually spiritual ones. "Jewishness" was more important to many people than "Judaism" (p. 84). Waxman's conclusion, "Diversification without Disintegration," pp. 225–36, seems to have considerable relevance for a significant "middle" stratum of Holocaust survivors. These are people who may be described as not really religious but nevertheless strongly Jewish in self-identification and significantly involved in Jewish community activities.

5. It is noteworthy that in his study of Jewish public opinion in the United States, *American Modernity and Jewish Identity* (New York: Tavistock Publications, 1984), Steven M. Cohen reports a 1981–82 national survey in which only 43 percent of American Jewish respondents described themselves as "very pro-Israel," only about half of the equivalent approval rate among our Holocaust survivors (p. 158). Only 12 percent of American Jews agreed with the statement that "each American Jew should give serious thought to settling in Israel" (p. 158). Among our survivor respondents, people who had considered such an option or had in fact lived in Israel as immigrants totaled 79 percent.

6. The activities of our respondents were consistent with the findings of some previous research. William B. Helmreich, *Against All Odds: Holocaust Survivors and the Successful Lives They Made in America* (New Brunswick, N. J.: Transaction Publishers, 1996), reports that "about 90 percent of all survivors queried in 1989 had visited Israel [at least] once, compared to 54 percent among American Jews. Moreover, survivors were much more likely to have visited Israel than American Jews even after Orthodox affiliation, income, occupation, and family size were taken into account. Depth of commitment to Israel can be better gauged by looking at the number of times people visit. Here the proportion among survivors was far higher. They were more than three times as likely to have gone to Israel twice or more than their American Jewish counterparts. Overall, 57.3 percent of the survivors had been to Israel two or more times compared to 15.5 percent of Americans" (pp. 184–85).

7. Gertrude Hirschler and Lester S. Echman, *Menachem Begin: From Freedom Fighter to Statesman* (New York: Shengold Publishers, 1979), note that Begin's first published book, translated into English as *Revolt* in 1950, addressed the theme of the Holocaust as a backdrop to his own political striving, "lest the Jew forget" the need to fight for national independence and self-respect (pp. 196–97).

See also Harry Zvi Harwitz, *Begin: A Portrait* (Jerusalem: B'nai Brith Books, 1994), p. 30: "Menachem Begin's great faith was derived from his parents, staunch

Zionists who believed implicitly in Shivat Zion, the return to Zion; it was derived from his school and his Jewish studies, which he devoured with the hunger of a starving man.

"His father, Zeev Dov Begin, had been the secretary of the Brest-Litovsk Jewish community, and . . . he went to his death at the hands of the Germans in the Holocaust, leading his fellow-Jews in defiant singing of Hatikvah (the Jewish song of Hope which later became the national anthem of the State of Israel)."

8. Frank Gervasi, *The Life and Times of Menachem Begin: Rebel to Statesman* (New York: G. P. Putnam's Sons, 1979), p. 308: "The memory of the Holocaust is ever-present in Begin's subconscious."

Among many sources on events in wartime Warsaw mentioned here, see especially Frank P. King, "British Policy and the Warsaw Uprising," *Journal of European Studies* 4, no. 1 (1974): 1–18. For an account of the Uganda raid, see Louis I. Rabinowitz, "Entebbe," in *Encyclopedia Judaica: Decennial Book, 1973–1982*, (Jerusalem: Keter Publishing, 1983), pp. 238–39.

9. Quoted in Eitan Haber, *Menahem Begin: The Legend and The Man* (New York: Delacorte Press, 1978), p. 52.

10. See Sarah Bershtel and Allen Graubard, *Saving Remnants: Feeling Jewish in America* (Berkeley and Los Angeles: University of California Press, 1993), who say: "If Israel were in no political or military danger, and did not need American Jewish financial contributions, the greatest source of Jewish community activity and concern would disappear. And if there were not enough antisemitism to talk about, even that gloomy incentive for Jewish assertion, awareness, and community action would be gone" (p. 160). Here are obviously two ways in which the survivors have contributed a powerful stimulant to the Jewish consciousness of the Diaspora: as promoters of Israel and as vigilant reminders of the tragic potential of anti-Semitism.

11. In his account of the Israeli War of Independence, Abram L. Sachar, *The Redemption of the Unwanted: From the Liberation of the Death Camps to the Founding of Israel* (New York: St. Martin's Press, 1983), notes that one of the most important elements in the Jewish victory over the powerful Arab coalition was the "no alternative" (*ain braira*) spirit with which the Israelis, and especially the immigrant [Holocaust survivor] reinforcements fought. The Arabs never understood how powerful a weapon desperation could be. . . . Jewish history had prepared [these Jews] not to expect to be welcomed anywhere" (pp. 272–73).

On the other hand, as David Biale, *Power and Powerlessness in Jewish History* (New York: Schocken Books, 1968), points out, in the 1940s many people in Israel viewed the victims of the Holocaust as part of a historically passive Jewry, acquiescent in its own destruction. They admired an allegedly alternative, militant approach to conflict represented by modern Zionism (p. 158). But the Eichmann trial and the Six-Day War changed perceptions: "The sense of encirclement preceding the war and the abandonment by Israel's Western allies caused many who had hitherto scorned Diaspora history to describe their situation in terms of the

Holocaust: they perceived themselves facing a 'second Auschwitz'" (p. 159). Ultimately, it was Menachem Begin, a Polish Jew who became prime minister in 1977, who transformed the prevalent Israeli view. "With Begin, the experience of the Holocaust survivors became the ethos of the state. . . . The Masada metaphor now converged with the Warsaw ghetto in a kind of telescoping of Jewish history" (pp. 160–61).

On October 12, 2000, amid violent clashes between Arabs and Jews in the West Bank and Gaza, the UN General Assembly voted—predictably—to condemn Israel by a margin of 92 to 6, with 46 nations abstaining. Excluding the vote of Israel itself, this meant that the margin of opposition to the Jewish state in the UN was 95 percent of those voting and 64 percent overall. The many abstentions were eerily reminiscent of an earlier crisis in Jewish history.

12. All this fits into the apparent progressive secularization of Jewish religious-cultural life in America, where the synagogue is a place that abounds with "cultural activities and learning programs . . . but the essential values of association as members [are increasingly] social, not religious" (Stuart E. Rosenberg, *The New Jewish Identity in America* [New York: Hippocrene Books, 1985], p. 153). Rosenberg also says, however, that "Jewishness—the ethnic-emotional awareness of a cultural, communal, and even political indivisibility—and Judaism—the religious matrix of Jewish personal and corporate life—crisscross, interlock and interpenetrate" (p. 63).

On the secular element in modern American Judaism, see Ernst Van den Haag, *The Jewish Mystique* (New York: Stein and Day, 1969). "As the waves of immigrants swelled to a flood, Jewish life was revitalized—albeit in secular form, in which synagogues became centers for women's clubs and humanitarian activities, and ceased to be centers of learning and of a life nearly coextensive with religion or, at least dominated by religious rituals and suffused by religious spirit" (p. 196). See also Jonathan S. Woocher, *Sacred Survival: The Civil Religion of American Jews* (Bloomington: Indiana University Press, 1986), who defines the American Jewish civil religion as an "activist religion emphasizing the pursuits of Jewish survival and social justice." He finds its first ingredient in the story of the Holocaust to the rebirth of Israel (p. 131).

13. Marshall Sklare and Joseph Greenbaum, *Jewish Identity on the Suburban Frontier: A Study of Group Survival in the Open Society* (Chicago: University of Chicago Press, 1979), pp. 323–24.

14. Ibid., p. 326.

15. See Louise A. Mayo, *The Ambivalent Image: Nineteenth Century America's Perception of the Jew* (London: Associated University Presses, 1988). She outlines both the way in which the American context has been different and more hospitable for Jews, but also the ingredients of "classical," European anti-Semitism, to a degree always present in many places, the United States included. Understandably, it would seem, for many Jews the adoption of secularism, a seamless blending with one's Gentile environment, is and has been a logical means of

minimizing the impact of rejection, opprobrium, and marginalization on account of being "Jewish" (p. 180).

See also Cary McWilliams, *A Mask for Privilege: Anti-Semitism in America* (Boston: Little, Brown, 1948), who says that the Jews are a "unique minority, the minority of minorities," and that "the very fact that the Jew has been traditionally used as a scapegoat leads to his being constantly recast in that role. . . . Anti-Semitism has long been a socially sanctioned and culturally conditioned mode of expressing aggressive impulses. Most of these factors have a general application in the United States as well as Europe" (pp. 82–83).

Chapter 5

THE RECKONING

Blame and Praise

This is our "balance sheet" chapter. Blame and praise are part of a critical literature of reckoning that goes back to the 1940s. In a tripartite perspective on the Holocaust, this literature has involved much describing and reporting but, above all, evaluating the roles of the direct participants—the oppressors and their victims—and the people who made up the surrounding world—the witnesses, the spectators, the auxiliaries, and the helpers. In the West, understandably, the literature of reckoning first focused upon the Nazi enemy, passing judgment upon the people who had initiated and implemented the Final Solution. Most of this literature began to pour out at the conclusion of the Second World War, but some came even earlier. It is ironic, in light of so many Western denials of knowledge about the fate of the Jews in Nazi-occupied Europe, that some of the earliest published, widely available, evaluative accounts go back to the war itself. In fact, some accurately foreshadowed in an earlier period of the war the terrible developments of later years.

One such source was *The Black Book of Poland*, issued by the Ministry of Information of the Polish government-in-exile in London in early 1942. This book contained an extensive section dealing with Nazi treatment of the Jews in Poland, with a great deal of specific information about the Warsaw ghetto, where over four hundred thousand Jews were herded into a relatively small urban area. Its focus was on the period from October 1939 to June 1941. The conditions described here with respect to food rations, shelter, and medical assistance, as well as actual mortality patterns, made it quite clear that Nazi policy involved genocide by attrition—by starvation, exposure, and disease.

In addition to documents, illustrations, statistics, and descriptions, the book included evaluative statements by the Polish Minister for Home Affairs (later Premier) Stanislaw Mikolajczyk, which explicitly identified the systematic extermination of the Jews of Warsaw as an objective of Nazi policy.[1] This was followed by a declaration speaking of the "wholesale extermination of the Jews" as a characteristic feature of Nazi conduct throughout Poland.[2] The book also contained a highly significant statement by Szmuel Zygielbojm, the Jewish Bund representative to the Polish National Council in London, a man who had spent some months in the Warsaw ghetto, and who within a year was to commit suicide over the passivity of the Allies regarding the murder of the Jews. In this statement he cited the Gestapo chief of Warsaw calling for the total extermination of Polish Jews as early as 1940. In fact, Zygielbojm declared that poison gas was already being used to kill Jews in 1941, and that "the monstrous plan to exterminate all Jews [was] being carried out in Poland"—well before the Wannsee Conference of January 1942.[3]

Of course, not too many people in the West—leaders included—paid much attention to all this published material. Jan Karski, the 1943 underground envoy to the West from occupied Poland, spoke to many incredulous or uncaring statesmen in Britain and America. He recorded the following conclusions about Nazi policy, citing his conversation with a Jewish underground leader whom he had secretly met in Warsaw sometime in the latter part of 1942: "We want you to tell Polish and Allied governments and the great leaders of the Allies that we are helpless in the face of the German criminals. . . . The Germans are not trying to enslave us as they have other people; we are being systematically murdered."[4]

And Karski himself concluded that "never in the history of mankind, never anywhere in the realm of human relations did anything occur to compare with what was inflicted on the Jewish population of Poland."[5] In addition to conveying this judgment to top allied leaders, Karski actually published them in early 1944 in the United States in his book *Story of the Secret State*.

In the immediate postwar period, the literature about the oppressors was supported and enriched by documents published in connection with the Nuremberg trials of 1945–46 as well as those of other major Nazi war criminals.[6] There were also works of individual eyewitnesses, like Eugen Kogon, whose book *The Theory and Practice of Hell: The German Con-*

centration Camps and the System behind Them, originally published in West Germany in 1946, presented not only facts but context as well. Kogon describes Nazi extermination practices in great and vivid detail, with special attention to the liquidations at Auschwitz, where, as he noted, the chief victims were "Jews from all the countries of Europe that had come under Hitler's rule."[7] Nor was this, of course, accidental, since apart from the complex bureaucrat-police apparatus he describes, there was a finding here of an underlying policy and dynamic—"organized liquidation campaigns . . . [and] after 1942 the systematic extermination of the Jews, especially in the east."[8] Kogon concluded his discussion of the fate of the Jews with this chilling assessment: "I hope that someday there will be an exhaustive documentation of the awful fate the Nazis prepared for the Jews of Eastern Europe. It is likely to be one of the ghastliest records in the history of the world."[9]

While telling us something about the crimes of the perpetrators, Kogon's account also foreshadowed more critical discussions of the behavior of the victims—in his coverage of life in Nazi camps under the murderous and willy-nilly corruptive conditions of SS rule. But what the Nuremberg disclosures and individual accounts like Kogon's had not yet touched upon was the very significant subject—using Raul Hilberg's terminology—of the bystanders. How did they figure in the story of the Holocaust? In the years immediately following the conclusion of the Second World War, this subject was largely taboo.

Certainly, the people who had organized the Nuremberg proceedings and other major trials of Nazi war criminals were not about to accuse themselves of complicity, passivity, or any other unfavorable guilty involvement in the tragedy of the Jews. And among the larger public, outside the sphere of governments and officialdom, people were still politically and psychologically disinclined to question the behavior of their heroic and victorious leaders. To have raised questions about people like Roosevelt or Churchill in 1945, 1946, or 1947 would have been, for most Westerners, an abomination, an act of ingratitude and downright disloyalty. Who could possibly question the conduct of these immensely popular and successful national chieftains? Politically, and psychologically, it was easiest to explore and to assail the record of the indisputable "bad guys"—and losers. It was much more difficult, perhaps downright embarrassing, painful, and even dangerous to criticize the winners, one's own leaders. Ultimately, it was much more difficult to speak unfavorably about "us" than it was to speak about the obvious "them."

It is noteworthy, parenthetically, that it was not until the "fall of Communism" and the disintegration of the Soviet Union in 1991 that the Nazi crimes against the Jews began to emerge from the shadows of the traditionally veiled Soviet interpretations. Under Stalin and his successors—at least until the time of Mikhail Gorbachev—the murder of the Jews was never recognized in its full magnitude and singularity. It was always part of a more amorphous story of Hitlerite, German-fascist atrocities committed against the peoples of the Soviet Union, a minor aspect of the sacrifices connected with the Great Patriotic War. The Final Solution was not part of the official understanding of what had happened in Europe and on Soviet territory between 1941 and 1945. In the Soviet Union of Stalin's time, and for some substantial period at least under his successors, for anyone to deviate from what was the official, cultural-ideological interpretation of the Party would have been downright perilous to the offender.

It was partly for such reasons, as well as the collateral aspect of the subsequent, increasing availability of documents, memoirs, and the like, that the literature that raised questions about "us" rather than only about "them" became a substantial and steady stream only in more recent years, in the late 1970s, '80s, and '90s. For reasons of policy and self-interest, even in Israel there was great reluctance to confront the passively complicit.

When Pope Pius XII died on October 9, 1958, Golda Meir, then Israel's Foreign Minister, issued the following statement on behalf of her government: "When fearful martyrdom came to our people in the decade of Nazi terror, the voice of the Pope was raised for the victims. The life of our times was enriched by a voice speaking out on the great moral truths above the tumult of daily conflict. We mourn a great servant of peace."[10] Some analogous constraints applied to critical treatment of various other by-standers and of the victims themselves. When Hannah Arendt published her book *Eichmann in Jerusalem* in 1963, it contained an unprecedented attack upon the conduct of the victims and the victims' leaders, causing a literary furor and, not without reason, earning Arendt great and intense disapproval from within the international Jewish community. But more discussion understandably followed.[11] The critical witnesses—Jewish victims of the Holocaust—found it difficult to discuss publicly the treatment meted out to them by the surrounding society, especially when that society was, and continued to be, hostile to them, and they, for whatever personal and existential reasons, continued to live within its confines.

Many Jews who had received assistance from non-Jews in their struggle for survival in countries such as Poland almost certainly were well aware of the prevailing, enormous hostility directed toward Jews by the general populace. The testimony of the Kielce Pogrom in Poland in 1946 was merely one reminder.[12] But for the few remaining Jews to publicly express their judgments would have seemed rank ingratitude to their Christian benefactors. It would also likely provoke considerable, potentially dangerous, local antagonism. For the small saved remnant of Polish Jewry still resident in Poland it was generally—personally, politically, and psychologically—easier to write accounts heaping praise upon the courage, altruism, and sacrifice of their Gentile benefactors than to deal factually with the more somber contours of the larger tragedy. One way of dealing with the subject, of course, was to say that in the outside world there were some people who helped and some who hurt. This might be somewhat analogous to reporting an American election by saying that some people voted Republican and some people voted Democratic. This way of dealing with the subject might have been quite astute for those seeking "not to give offense," even if it was not particularly revealing.

Among many accounts that focused on the "positive" side of the issue, that is, remarkable individual efforts to aid Jews by non-Jews during the Holocaust were, for example, two interesting works originally published in Poland in the late 1960s by Wladyslaw Bartoszewski and Zofia Levin, and translated in an American edition as *The Samaritans: Heroes of the Holocaust* (New York: Twayne Publishers, 1970) and Tatiana Berenstein and Adam Rutkowski, *Assistance to the Jews in Poland, 1939–1945* (Warsaw: Polonia Publishing House, 1963). So was the work of Philip Friedman, *Their Brother's Keepers*, published in the United States in 1978. In the preface to this volume, Father John A. O'Brien of the University of Notre Dame wrote that Friedman's work was "reassuring and inspiring" and that it showed that "nineteen centuries of Christian teaching were not without results."[13]

Among accounts that were personal and, necessarily, a blend of the good and the bad in terms of the attitudes of non-Jews to the Holocaust was the work of Michael Zylberberg, *A Warsaw Diary, 1939–1945*. On the one hand, the author recounted stories of Gentiles who had helped him survive the ordeal. On the other hand, he recounted his impressions of the many Poles whom he had encountered under his assumed Gentile identity in the following manner: "Jews were one of the main topics of conversation in the streets, markets, public houses and shops. They were discussed with callousness, often with hate; even as a scourge that had to be wiped out."[14]

Among impressionistic accounts, how could one ignore the observations made by Emanuel Ringelblum, the great Warsaw ghetto historian, known to us through a posthumously published book on Polish-Jewish relations, *To Live with Honor and Die with Honor: Selected Documents from the Warsaw Ghetto Underground Archives "O.S."* [Oneg Shabbath]:

> [D]iscussion of [Polish-Jewish relations] is accompanied by a sense of reluctance, since all the attempts to justify the Poles' attitude to Jews— even the most objective and characterized by goodwill, will be qualified by a wish to forgive the sins or "Let bygones be bygones."
>
> The Polish people, suffering perhaps more than any other nation from the yoke of misfortune together with the Jewish people, should have, above all, and at every opportunity, demonstrated sympathy, solidarity and brotherhood with the Jew.
>
> Alas, this is but a dream.
>
> [Whatever the positives] . . . the list of sins crying out to heaven for vengence is alas, heavier and much longer, far-reaching and unforgivable.
>
> This is, unfortunately, true in regard to the masses, commonly considered humble and unaware, as well as in regard to all the officials.
>
> It suffices to look at the faces of youngsters, rascals, peasant women and artisans, who cross the Jewish quarter by tramways: they are happily amused, they cheerfully crack shameless and crude jokes, betraying full satisfaction and malicious joy at the fact that Jews finally got what 'they deserved' and what everyone wished them.
>
> With what a contemptibly vile and thoughtless joy they often gaze at the bridge on Chlodna, at the passage ramps on Zelazna, at the body search of people returning from forced labor at the ghetto entrance!
>
> We know we must not generalize; there is often a compassionate silence, horror in the eyes, a mute expression of solidarity.
>
> But what the rabble, youngsters, peasant women, idlers, rascals, scoundrels and outcasts—warped and debased in German schools— express in words, sets the tone, wounds the heart, hurts the dignity of the Jews, who have not even been granted the satisfaction of having friends and comrades among the Poles.
>
> It makes things even sadder to realize that these expressions are not planned or directed. On the contrary: no political reason dictates this to the Poles, it is even against their best interests. These people are not voicing the sympathies or inclinations of any party or social group.
>
> It is just a genuine reaction of theirs, a reflex of elementary, spontaneous joy, that their wish has, at long last, been fulfilled.[15]

It is not at all clear, however, that one could draw any inferences about this issue from either this or any other individual case studies.[16] In an important way, clearly, the victim survivors must be allowed to testify about the matter of prevailing social attitudes in their time. Could the actions of a relatively few heroes, inspiring as they might be, make up for the attitudes of indifferent or hostile millions?

Increasingly, with the passage of years, a more critical literature has developed, principally focused on Western leaders and publics. Illustrative of these new developments was the work of Henry Feingold, who in 1970 managed to find fault with both the Roosevelt administration and the leadership of the Jewish community in America. Both failed in their responses to the Holocaust in Feingold's view. He concluded that "a passionate commitment to save [Jewish] lives did not exist in the Roosevelt Administration,"[17] and he blamed some of the problem, at least, on the divisions and vacillations within the Jewish community, which did not speak to FDR with one voice.[18] He also observed that the "Administration's reluctance to publicly acknowledge that a mass murder operation was taking place went far in keeping American public opinion ignorant and therefore unaroused while it helped convince men like Goebbels that the Allies approved or at least were indifferent to the fate of the Jews."[19]

In the mid-eighties, we saw an amply illustrated and documented conclusion of the rather substantial study by Seymour Maxwell Finger: "American Jews were not powerless during the Holocaust, they were weak. And they were weak because of divisiveness caused in part by ego conflicts, because of a lack of sophistication in recognizing the powers they actually did possess, and because of an irresoluteness derived from fear (real and imagined) and also because of a shortage of self-sacrificing leadership. They were a muscle, never fully flexed."[20]

Although some might argue that he was still pulling his punches, Bernard Wasserstein concluded in a 1979 study that "there is little to celebrate in [an] account of British policy towards the Jews of Europe between 1939 and 1945."[21] He found an "ocean of bureaucratic indifference and lack of concern." There was even "a tinge of antisemitism"[22] in all this, a "blunting of ordinary human feelings."[23] Indeed, "They came and looked, and passed by on the other side."[24]

Deborah Lipstadt's *Beyond Belief: The American People and The Coming of the Holocaust* constituted a powerful critique of the role of American media in effectively burying the story of the unfolding Final Solution in Europe. Lipstadt concluded: "There is no way of knowing whether the American people would have even been aroused enough to demand action to rescue Jews. But we can categorically state that most of the press refused to light its 'beacon,' making it virtually certain that there would be no public outcry and no 'common activity' to try to succor this suffering people."[25]

After some fifty years, when all the sounds of anguish and the clamor of conflict have faded away, how do survivor views fit into this evolving re-evaluation of the story of the Final Solution? Here we are interested not so much in what the survivors actually "saw out there," but rather in what evaluative meaning they assigned to what they saw.

On the subject of culpability, we have collected answers ranging from no or little wrong attributed to particular actors all the way to ascriptions of high condemnation. Using a coding system in which relatively positive judgments are scored at 1, relatively neutral judgments at 0, and clearly negative judgments at 2, we have constructed a scale based on responses to twenty-five questions assessing different actors in the drama of the Holocaust. The resultant scale is exhibited in Figure 5.1. It may be noted that our scale ranges from a low value of 3 points to a high value of 20 points, with at least some representation in each cell between 3 and 20, and with a tendency for values to cluster at the high end. The mean is 13.07 and the median is at 13.00, testifying to a fairly balanced distribution of values among our respondents. Having established the scale, we then linked it to the various personal attributes of the survivors in order to develop a better, fuller understanding of the forces driving these judgments, however critical they might be.

The blame scale is significantly and, it would appear, logically, correlated with two other scales in our study—cognition and learning. Essentially, people who attributed a great deal of blame to various Holocaust participants were also people who tended to view the initial circumstances of the Holocaust in the most negative or bleak terms; they were more likely, for example, to believe that the Nazis intended to exterminate all Jews even before or on September 1, 1939. They were also more likely to see their prewar societies as more hostile to Jews compared with "low-blame" respondents.

In addition, "high-blame" respondents tended to draw the most pessimistic and negative conclusions from their Holocaust experience to the present and the future. Illustratively, they were more likely to be pessimistic or uncertain about the future of the world and more likely to believe that anti-Semitism worldwide was on the rise as compared with the beliefs of low-blame respondents. There was a modestly direct correlation between Jewish identity and blame (.106)—the more of one, the more of

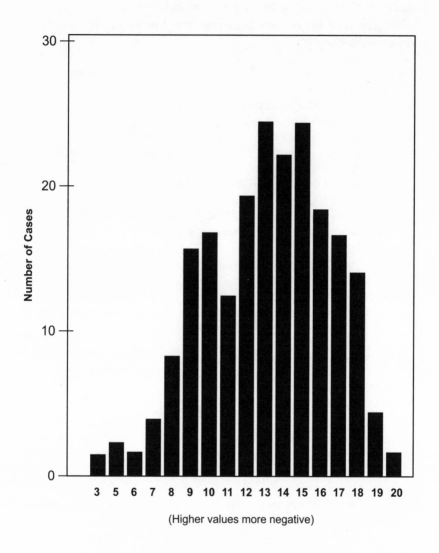

(Higher values more negative)

Fig. 5.1. Distribution of Values on the Blame Scale

the other. However, virtually no relationship existed between survivor empathy, as represented on the comparison scale, and the blame scale.

We reproduce below three questions used for the blame scale for the purpose of illustration:

What are your feelings about the role of the pope in the Jewish tragedy? Do you believe that:
a. He did all he could to save Jewish lives.
b. He deplored it but could not prevent it.
c. He was unaware of the true plight of the Jews.
d. He was a neutral observer throughout the war, trying to keep the church out of politics.
e. He held the power to save Jewish lives but did not use it out of fear of Nazi reprisals.
f. He was indifferent toward Jews.
g. He was anti-Semitic and was not opposed to Nazi policies.
h. Other: _____
i. Don't know; cannot say

What is your view about the claim that there was no reliable information about the fate of European Jewry in the free Western countries, even as late as 1943 and 1944? Do you believe that this claim is:
a. Genuine
b. Perhaps valid in some places, but not others
c. An excuse for passivity in the face of the Jewish catastrophe
d. No opinion
e. Other—explain:_____

Do you think the reason more assistance was not given to Jews [in the country of your residence] was
a. Lack of information about the fate of the Jews
b. Lack of resources
c. Fear of Nazi terror and reprisals
d. Ordinary human indifference
e. Lack of sympathy for Jews stemming from anti-Semitism
f. A combination of the above: specify _____
g. Other: _____

When one looks at the composite blame scales—divided by subjects (i.e., by victims, bystanders, and perpetrators and by blame "groups" low, medium, and high)—several important tendencies of survivor opinion are apparent (see Table 10). Given degrees of blame assignable in each of the subject categories, it is clear that the levels of blame assigned to perpetrators and bystanders are roughly similar in one important respect. The mean scores demonstrate that in each of these two categories, survivor respondents assigned analogously high levels of blame. Since the actions of perpetrators and bystanders were different, these scores are not equivalent in *substance*, but they are equivalent in the sense of eliciting the most negative interpretations available from the survivors.

Given a choice of placing responsibility for the Final Solution on many Germans or on all Germans, the former alternative prevailed by a margin of 51 to 43 percent. The remaining 6 percent of our respondents were willing to assign blame here only to the Nazis. Among those who thought that *all* Germans were responsible for the Final Solution, the overall blame scores were—as one might have perhaps expected—*higher* than among those who wanted to confine German responsibility to "many" but not to all. The mean score for the former was 13.59 versus 13.10 for the latter, a difference of about 4 percent. The differences in terms of exposure to suffering and current Jewish identifications were in line with our expectations. Among those who blamed all Germans, exposure-to-suffering scores were 12 percent higher than among those who only blamed "many." Jewish identity scores were 7 percent higher among those who blamed "all" as compared with those who only blamed "many."

With respect to the Germans' implementation of the Final Solution, as mentioned earlier, the survivor response was overwhelmingly along the lines of the Goldhagen thesis—most acted willingly, as if enjoying the job.[26] This was the judgment of 88 percent of all respondents; only 6 percent said that the implementors acted as if they feared their superiors, and

Table 10. Degree of Blame and Survivor Feelings about Victims, Bystanders, and Perpetrators

Blame Group	Means Scores on Questions*		
	Victims	**Bystanders**	**Perpetrators**
Low	0.416	1.06	1.31
Medium	0.744	1.38	1.31
High	0.976	1.67	1.49
All Respondents	0.718	1.36	1.35
* Average score of groups on all questions associated with feelings of blame.			

another 6 percent saw them as acting with indifference. Even in the West, where Nazi operatives are often perceived as having been more concerned with the sensibilities of local opinion than in Eastern Europe, 72 percent of our survivor respondents opted for the "enthusiastic" alternative, with only 22 percent choosing "indifference" and fewer than 6 percent saying that the perpetrators acted as if they feared their superiors.[27]

A related appraisal of the Germans in the Holocaust by our survivor respondents focused on the nature of the Nazis' public support at home as represented in answers to the following question:

How do you believe that the German people of the 1940s, by and large, supported Hitler's program of extermination of the Jews?
  a. Generally knew nothing about it
  b. Did not support it, but were forced into it by the Nazis
  c. With reluctance
  d. With indifference
  e. With enthusiasm
  f. Other—specify: _____
  g. Don't know; cannot say

Among all respondents, 66 percent saw the German people as enthusiastically supportive of the Final Solution, with a little under 25 percent attributing "indifference" to German public opinion. Less than 3 percent of the survivors saw the German people as merely reluctant supporters of Hitler's enterprise, and fewer than 5 percent saw the Germans as actually forced to accept this policy. Interestingly, however, among respondents from Western Europe, 50 percent described the Germans as indifferent and 44 percent as enthusiastic. Among Polish respondents, however, only 22 percent attributed indifference to the Germans and 68 percent saw them as enthusiastic. In Eastern Europe outside Poland, these figures were virtually identical: 23 versus 68 percent.

A remarkable commentary on the bitterness of memory among survivors, fifty years after the fact, was provided to us in response to two questions about Allied leaders and the people of Germany, respectively. We asked our respondents if in the post-Holocaust years their opinions of the roles of Franklin Roosevelt and Winston Churchill had *changed*, offering as principal choices three responses: "Yes, I feel more positive"; "No, unchanged"; and "Yes, I feel more negative." An equivalent question was asked with respect to survivor opinion of Germans, to wit, "Have your feelings [toward Germans] changed in more recent years?" Here the alternatives were "Yes, my feelings have softened"; "No, nothing has changed"; and "Yes, my feelings have hardened."

With respect to the FDR-Churchill question, the largest share of respondents—across all demographic categories—opted for change to a more negative attitude; in almost all cases, the smallest share of respondents was the one reporting a more positive opinion (see Table 11). With respect to the Germans, the direction of attitudinal change was exactly the same, but its magnitude was greater. Using seventeen demographic categories, including gender, age, level of education, current material welfare, life satisfaction, socioeconomic status (SES), region of residence during the Holocaust, and mode of survival based on the camp/noncamp distinction, we found an average of 68 percent of our respondents saying that they felt more negative toward Germans; the highest negative figure was 76.4 percent—oddly enough by those classified as having high socioeconomic status—and the lowest was 60.6 percent, among people classified as having low socioeconomic status (see Table 12).

The average of respondents reporting no change in attitude was 13.5 percent. The average reporting more positive feelings was only 18.4 percent. In overall terms, across all demographic categories, fifty years later, the ratio of more negative to more positive feelings was 3.7:1. People who were most likely to have become positive in attitudes toward Germans were survivors from Western Europe (26 percent) and people who were relatively young at the time of the Holocaust. Among those who were between one and thirteen years old in 1939, 23.3 percent expressed a change to more positive feelings.

Evaluating Roosevelt and Churchill, 53 percent across all categories reported having more negative views, and only 14 percent reported more positive views. This resulted in a ratio, 3.69:1, that is almost identical to the one presented above.

One of the more remarkable differences was among those who survived the war in concentration camps and those who lived outside them. Attitudes toward Allied leaders were much more positive among camp survivors. Only 48 percent reported more negative attitudes and 19 percent more positive ones, whereas among those having survived outside camps, 64 percent had become more negative and only 6 percent more positive toward Roosevelt and Churchill. Was a lingering factor of personal gratitude to their liberators perhaps involved in the outlook of many camp survivors? On the other hand, the differences in attitude toward Germans between these two categories of respondents were all but nil.

Table 11. Survivor Attitude Change toward Roosevelt and Churchill

Group	Feelings Softened		No Change		Feelings Hardened	
Gender	**Count**	**%**	**Count**	**%**	**Count**	**%**
Male	13	13.1	28	28.3	58	58.6
Female	15	16.1	32	34.4	46	49.5
Age in 1939						
1–13	8	10.7	27	36.0	40	53.3
14–31	20	17.2	32	27.6	64	55.2
Education						
High School/Below	26	17.7	36	24.5	85	57.8
College/Above	2	5.0	21	52.5	17	42.5
Current Welfare						
Well Off/Better	8	7.7	41	39.4	55	52.9
Ends Meet/Difficult	17	21.0	148	22.2	46	56.8
Life Satisfaction						
High/Mod. Satisfied	22	15.1	43	29.5	81	55.5
Disappointed	4	12.1	14	42.4	15	45.5
SES						
Low	9	28.1	9	28.1	14	43.8
High	3	5.9	21	41.2	27	52.9
Region						
Poland	14	12.8	37	33.9	58	53.2
Western Europe	4	20.0	6	30.0	10	50.0
Other	10	15.9	17	27.0	36	57.1
Camp Confinement						
Yes	24	19.4	40	32.3	60	48.4
No	4	6.0	20	29.9	43	64.2

Some of the negative assessments of Germans and Allied leaders actually ran counter to our hypothesized expectations. Those whom we classified as having high socioeconomic status were surprisingly *more* likely to express negative attitudes toward Allied leaders than the poorer respondents. With respect to Germans, the more prosperous demographic was more bitter than the poorer. In terms of life satisfaction, however, the results were in line with our initial expectations: those who had expressed

Table 12. Survivor Attitude Change toward the German People

Group	Feelings Softened		No Change		Feelings Hardened	
Gender	**Count**	**%**	**Count**	**%**	**Count**	**%**
Male	22	21.0	12	11.4	71	67.6
Female	13	14.3	15	16.5	63	69.2
Age in 1939						
1–13	17	23.3	6	8.2	50	68.5
14–31	17	13.9	21	17.2	84	68.9
Education						
High School/Below	26	17.3	22	14.7	102	68.0
College/Above	9	22.0	3	7.3	29	70.7
Current Welfare						
Well Off/Better	15	14.2	13	12.3	78	73.6
Ends Meet/Difficult	19	22.9	13	15.7	51	61.4
Life Satisfaction						
High/Mod. Satisfied	31	20.8	19	12.8	99	66.4
Disappointed	4	12.1	7	21.2	22	66.7
SES						
Low	7	21.2	6	18.2	20	60.6
High	7	12.7	6	10.9	42	76.4
Region						
Poland	19	16.7	17	14.9	78	68.4
Western Europe	5	26.3	2	10.5	12	63.2
Other	11	17.5	8	12.7	44	69.8
Camp Confinement						
Yes	23	17.8	19	14.7	87	67.4
No	12	18.2	7	10.6	47	71.2

greater satisfaction with their lives were also more likely to have softened their feelings toward Germans.

One of the more interesting divisions of opinion was based on gender. With respect to Roosevelt and Churchill, men were more negative in their attitudes than women. With respect to the Germans, however, the opposite was true. In all cases, however, the trend of survivor opinion was very strongly negative.

Contrary to the Hannah Arendt thesis, the Jewish collaborators were more often excused, and their conduct "rationalized away," rather than vigorously condemned by the surviving remnant. "They did it because they were forced to do it." "They did it because they desperately sought to save their lives." "They did it because they sought to make conditions as good as possible for as long as possible for their fellow Jews." These were the most frequently chosen alternatives by the survivors. Much more rare were attributions of malevolent self-interest or collaboration with the Nazis for seemingly ideological reasons.

On the other hand, an analysis of the "blame groups" involved indicates a certain paradox. The lowest blame group averaged only 0.416 points on "censure" directed toward Jewish officialdom in the Holocaust; the medium group averaged 0.744, and the highest blame group averaged a much more damning 0.976. Clearly, the severest judgment of Jewish collaborators was rendered by the relatively "most Jewish" of our survivors, and the greatest leniency was shown by those who might be described as "least Jewish." After all, people in the high-blame category, that is, those in the top 25 percent in terms of expressed resentment toward all categories of participants and bystanders in the Holocaust, ranked 8 percent higher in their average Jewish identity scores and 16 percent higher in their exposure-to-suffering scores than did the people in the low-blame category—the bottom 25 percent (see Table 13).

The difference in attitudes between high-blame and low-blame respondents was actually most dramatic with respect to their judgments about fellow Jews. The gap between blame attached to the perpetrators by the low and high groups was only 12 percent; it was 37 percent with respect to the bystanders. But it was almost $2^1/_2$ times as large with respect to the victims.

It is significant, nevertheless, that with respect to the roles of victims, i.e., European Jews in the Holocaust, the largest number of responses gen-

Table 13. Blame and Jewish Identity

Degree of Blame	Jewish Identity Score	
	Count	Mean*
Low	50	9.42
Medium	99	10.12
High	51	10.22

* Average score of groups on all questions associated with feelings of blame.

erally center on exculpatory variables. On the other hand, with respect to perpetrators and bystanders, including American Jews, responses all but invariably follow the rule of the most negative alternative. Thus, we find that, asked to evaluate the roles of Jewish community leaders during the Holocaust, 30 percent of our respondents say that what these leaders did was forced upon them by the Nazis. Some 18 percent of the respondents credit these leaders with actually improving conditions for their fellow Jews. Only 2 percent choose the pejorative alternative, that "they contributed to the killing"; about 6 percent said that the leaders "contributed little"; and some 17 percent said that these leaders simply looked out for themselves. Interestingly, the Jewish militia, organized under Nazi auspices in the various ghettos of occupied Europe, got even more positive evaluations. Some 39 percent of our respondents said that militia members did their best; about 19 percent saw them simply doing what the Nazis forced upon them; about 4 percent saw the militia as "often helpful" to other Jews. Only less than 18 percent of our respondents were willing to categorize militia behavior as "inexcusable."

These views of the survivors were reflected in the mix of comments volunteered to us on this subject:

> Nobody had experience or knowledge how to behave. Most Jewish militia helped where possible for at least some to survive.
>
> Without arms or support from the non-Jewish population no leaders could have changed the outcome.
>
> [They were] hoping to buy time, so a few could survive to be witnesses after the war.
>
> It depended on the individual persons.
>
> Some were very caring and some not.
>
> Some tried to improve conditions but not all.
>
> The Zionist leadership made heroic efforts.
>
> They did what they did mainly to save their own necks.
>
> They were misguided and lacking in character, in most cases intent on just improving their own situations.
>
> They could have helped organize resistance instead of cooperating with the Nazis.
>
> They saved their own.
>
> They were too passive.
>
> They had hope of liberation by the allies and tried to coexist.
>
> Each man or woman had different reasons. Some helped the resistance obtain weapons, etc.

One person simply wrote, "No comment." Another said, "I know of no Jewish collaboration with Nazis."

Approximately a quarter of our responses on questions relating to Jewish culpability scattered among various combinations of factors offered as explanations. We have attempted to gauge the direction of these multiple choices in the following manner. In cases where the respondent chose more than one alternative to answer a question, we classified the answer as either positive or negative if all the alternatives were either positive or negative. For example, if someone said that Jewish militia "often helped Jews to escape and mitigated Nazi orders" *and* also that "they were in a difficult situation and did the best they could," we interpreted this as a positive answer. We also classified as "positive" responses those that included relatively neutral as well as positive alternatives. For example, a response combining "they did what they were forced to do by the Nazis" with "they tried to improve conditions for Jews while they could," we classified as positive. We followed the same method with respect to "negative" responses. In cases where the respondents chose both some positive and some negative answers, we classified the responses as irreducibly mixed. Using this method, we classified 40 percent of the multiple responses as positive, 16 percent as negative, and 44 percent as mixed. Calculated as a fraction of all our respondents, these additional evaluations amounted to 10 percent positive, 4 percent negative, and 11 percent irreducibly mixed.

When considering the different survivor evaluations of victims, as opposed to bystanders and persecutors, the issue of motive is very important. Not only did the survivors see the activities of victims in a different light, they ascribed much more sympathetic motives to them as well. When respondents were asked to give reasons why Jews collaborated with Nazis, the most frequent answer was "desire to save oneself or to prolong one's own life" (69 percent).

When asked about the motives of non-Jewish collaborators, however, the most frequent survivor answers included anti-Semitism (28 percent) and material profit or gain (25 percent). In offering these different judgments, the survivors were not simply giving vent to ethnic prejudice on behalf of their own. In the perspective of years, they seemed to recognize the very different circumstances of Jewish and Gentile communities during the Holocaust. Physical-biological extermination in the case of Jews operated as a far more immediate and dire constraint upon would-be collaborators than in the case of the Gentiles. Nazi auxiliaries recruited from native populations in places like Holland, Hungary, or even Poland did not face the overwhelming negative incentive of their Jewish counterparts. For Gentiles, the alternative to helping the Nazis was very rarely death. It was more likely something that one might gain, or perhaps enjoy, as a consequence of collaboration. Though not entirely overlooking the Jewish collaborators' less worthy motives, the survivors seemed to recognize a difference in circumstances.

The discussion of motives reflected a significant estrangement of survivors from their surrounding Gentile communities. Asked to pass judgment on the motives of non-Jews who helped Jews, 48 percent of our respondents—quite understandably perhaps—replied with various combinations of motives. Among those willing to engage in single-cause explanations, 26 percent opted for humanitarian reasons. But an almost equal share—21 percent—chose financial or other personal gain, whereas personal friendships only drew 5 percent support.

In the second category of actors, persecutors and bystanders, we find only 8 percent of respondents willing to say that American Jews did all they could during the Holocaust. Only 16 percent saw them as not having been in a position to have helped much. But 72 percent said that they could have done much more. With respect to world opinion, 65 percent held the view that the reaction to the plight of Holocaust victims would have been definitely different and more helpful if the victims had not been Jewish. Only 5 percent were willing to say that it might not have been any different, and 4 percent that it might have been even less sympathetic.

When we asked our respondents if they thought that the outside world, "people outside the Nazi-occupied countries," could have done much more than they did to help the Jews of Europe, the answer was a virtually unanimous "yes." Out of 190 respondents, 98 percent (186 persons) agreed that it could have done much more. Only 2 percent (4 persons) disagreed. When we asked about specific measures that the "outside world" should have employed to help the Jews of Europe during the Holocaust, the single most frequently chosen response by the survivors was "allow Jews to enter their country(-ies)." The second-most frequent choice involved a combination of measures: ransom of Jews from the Nazi persecutors, threat of reprisals against the Nazis and Germans, bombing concentration/death camps, more effective publicizing of Nazi atrocities, raising money to help Jews, and allowing Jews places of escape.

When we looked at survivor choices of individual options of assistance, the second-most favored was the bombing of Nazi camps. This was a choice involving considerable irony, since the argument against bombing has often been predicated on the notion that it would have killed and maimed precisely those whom it was intending to aid.[28] The third-most frequent choice was the threat of reprisal against the Nazis; 12 percent of the respondents listed this option as their preference, compared with 18 percent who favored bombing the camps and the over 30 percent who favored emigration outlets. Some 11 percent chose the option of more significant publicity of Nazi crimes, which presumably would have included Allied, and possibly other (e.g., Vatican), exposure as well as denunciation of Nazi conduct and, implicitly or explicitly, appeals for help on behalf of the Jews.

The usefulness of emigration outlets to the Jews of wartime Europe is self-evident, even though not all Jews would have been able to reach the havens that might have been made available to them given Nazi presence and policies in Europe. But many would have, especially in and out of places such as Rumania, Hungary, and Italy. Bombing the camps could have temporarily disrupted the killing sites of the Final Solution; it would have also helped to publicize Hitler's crimes and rally popular opposition to them. Threats of reprisals against Germans and Nazis, in various possible forms, might have been significant deterrents against the murders, and the mere discussion of them would have had inhibiting effects similar to those involved in bombing the camps.

What the Allies might have done, with least cost and risk to themselves (but what they nevertheless did not do), was to make direct, top-level, public denunciations of the Nazi extermination of the Jews and to call upon the peoples of Europe to help the victims in all possible ways. Radio broadcasts by Franklin Roosevelt and Winston Churchill aimed at the occupied countries would have sent a powerful message: these leaders were seen as prestigious figures by the citizens of nations subjugated by Nazi Germany. There was a great and relatively inexpensive moral opportunity here. After, all if more people had been willing to hide Jews, and fewer people willing to denounce Jews, clearly more Jews would have been saved. Alas, the voices that should have been raised never were.

It is a matter of some interest that the least popular "might-have-been" measures of rescue selected by our Holocaust survivors involved infusions of money and the use of ransom to save the Jews of Europe. Only 4 percent saw the infusion of money, or more money, on behalf of Jews as being helpful, and fewer than 3 percent saw ransom as a good rescue option. Implicitly, the survivors seemed to recognize that money and ransom for the rescue of Jews could have had some undesirable side effect, such as strengthening the Nazi war machine and putting Allied governments into politically and morally untenable situations. This is not to say, of course, that more money to help Jews buy weapons and ammunition, or to ease their escapes in various ways, would not have been helpful, because it clearly would have been—just as it was in the case of the Yugoslavs and the Russians, to whom the Allies rendered all sorts of material assistance.

Asked to express an opinion on the claim that there was a lack of "reliable information" about the Holocaust in the Western world, the survivors emphatically rejected this idea. Some 79 percent described this opinion as an excuse for passivity, whereas only 13 percent were willing to recognize it as at least valid in some places, and 3 percent thought that it was factually genuine (see Fig. 5.2).

One of our key questions elicited survivor evaluations of culpability for the Holocaust in the following terms:

> Besides the Nazis, who would you say bears *major* responsibility for the Jewish tragedy in Europe?
> a. Western statesmen and public opinion
> b. Jews and Jewish organizations outside Europe
> c. Non-Jews in countries where the Final Solution was being carried out
> d. All of these equally
> e. None of these
> f. A combination of the above: specify _____
> g. Other
> h. Don't know; cannot say

By far the most frequent response to this question was *c*, "Non-Jews in countries where the Final Solution was being carried out" (43 percent). The next-most frequent choice was *a*, "Western statesmen and public opinion," which accounted for 34 percent of all responses. More than one-fifth, actually 22 percent, said, "All of these equally," thus including Jews and Jewish organizations outside Europe in the circle of blame. Three respondents—less than 2 percent—chose *h*, "Don't know; cannot say," as their answer to the question. Twelve respondents, slightly above 5 percent, actually checked off *b*, "Jews and Jewish organizations outside Europe." Eighteen persons offered their own comments, parts of each of which are cited below:

> Because the world didn't care—all of the above bear responsibility for the Jewish tragedy.

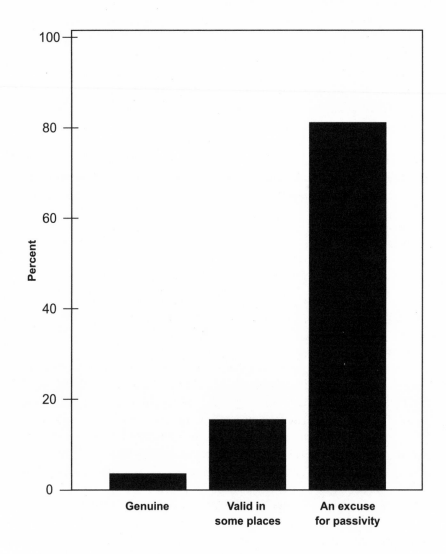

Fig. 5.2. Survivor Opinions of the Claim That Information about the Holocaust Was Lacking in the West

Western statesmen could have organized to permit Jewish immigration to save lives. Jewish organizations could have politically and financially helped the Jews in Poland, Ukraine, Hungary, etc. to escape. Local Gentiles could have prevented Jews from being removed from their communities.

Western countries and the world at large *did* want Jews exterminated and were glad Hitler did it for them.

Antisemitism in general was responsible for the tragedy. . . .

Allied governments were morally responsible for murder of 6 million Jews.

Western statesmen and Jewish organizations outside Europe. . . .

USA could do more. . . .

. . . Roosevelt did nothing to save European Jews. . . .

Roosevelt did not care, Churchill was more caring. . . .

President Roosevelt. . . .

U.S. President. . . .

Mr. Roosevelt. . . .

Winston Churchill, and his Foreign Secretary (A. Eden) and U.S. President Roosevelt. . . .

Western statesmen, in particular British. . . .

Poland, Ukraine. . . .

The Catholics should have stopped referring to the Jews as Christ Killers.

Christian instigation of 2,000 years. The Pope and prior Popes are to be blamed.

Jewish organizations and public opinion.

Interestingly, it would seem, not even one of our two hundred respondents volunteered the name of Stalin or the Soviet Union in response to the culpability question. To be sure, we did not include either option in our questionnaire. Was that a mistake? Probably not. Although no defense of a cruel and despotic leader is intended here, it should be pointed out that in the years 1939–41, when the Nazis and the Soviets divided up Poland, Stalin did something that no Western statesman had dared to do. He permitted essentially unrestricted immigration of Jews from Western, Nazi-occupied Poland to the Eastern, Soviet-occupied part.[29] (Of course, while the Warsaw ghetto rapidly starved to death under Nazi rule in 1940 and 1941, Stalin shipped valuable raw materials to his temporary ally—Nazi Germany.)

After the outbreak of the Nazi-Soviet conflict, Stalin showed no serious interest in the fate of the Jews, although the USSR was one of the parties to the December 17, 1942, declaration concerning the Holocaust, announced in London by British Foreign Secretary Anthony Eden. Soviet media, however, never responded to the relatively singular nature of the plight of European Jewry, either during the war or afterward. But it is also clear that there were some very important differences between the USSR and the Western Allies in the period 1941–45. The Russia of Stalin's time was a much poorer country than the United States, or Britain, or, for that matter, Canada, Australia, and New Zealand. And, whether measured in casualties, territories lost, total forces engaged, or any other reasonable indicator, it was involved in a far more desperate military struggle with Nazi Germany than were any of the Western nations, particularly in the years between 1941 and 1944.[30] Even if Stalin had "cared about" the Jews, he had much less to give them. Nor was this wholly a matter of tangible resources.

Stalin and his brand of Soviet Communism were widely loathed and feared in Europe of the 1940s, especially in Eastern Europe and in Poland, where the Final Solution was being carried out effectively. If, hypothetically speaking, Stalin had used his "moral authority" by directing a radio speech to Poland, appealing to the populace to help Jews, this might have stimulated a pogrom. It would probably have been seen by many Poles as confirmation of a classic stereotype of nationalist anti-Semitism—the alleged Jewish connection and foundation of Bolshevism. By contrast, Winston Churchill and Franklin Roosevelt were towering figures. They had much greater followings and prestige among the peoples of Europe. They had far more "moral capital" to employ for whatever purposes they might have chosen. Their silence was, by far, the greater practical wrong for the Jews of Europe.

Another factor discussed in this chapter was the perception by the survivors that Communist parties, armed forces, and guerrilla groups were much more favorably disposed toward Jews than most other, Western-oriented entities.[31] All this made it somewhat difficult to see Stalin as one of the *principal* villains of the Holocaust, especially with so many active and passive villains around.

Given an option of explaining Roosevelt's and Churchill's conduct toward the Jews of Europe as they and their historical defenders have most preferred—that they concentrated on the objective of winning the war against Hitler—only 17 percent of our respondents accepted this exculpatory alternative. But 39 percent said that these leaders simply did not care about the Jews of Europe. Still, only 5 percent of our respondents were willing to classify them as anti-Semites. (This was at least a much more favorable survivor attitude than that evidenced toward the pope.)

Assessing the roles of their Gentile fellow citizens during the Holocaust, 67 percent of the survivors opted for the most negative alternative—that they cooperated with and supported the Nazi Final Solution; only 27 percent opted for its passive acceptance by non-Jews, and a clearly amazing 2 percent chose the most favorable alternative, that is, that non-Jews were either opposed to or opposed to but powerless in the face of, the Final Solution (see Fig. 5.3). These were certainly remarkable numbers.

When asked if the response of world opinion during the Holocaust would have been different, and more favorable, if the victims not been Jewish, 65 percent of our respondents strongly agreed, and 26 percent offered the view that it *probably* would have been more favorable. Only 5 percent thought the identity of the victims did not really make any difference, and 4 percent thought that the world might have been even *less* concerned with the Holocaust if the victims involved were not Jewish. Those who were perceived as accomplices or accessories to the Holocaust tended to be judged very harshly by the survivors. There was little propensity here to indulge in "mitigating circumstances."

With respect to the role of the pope, the largest share of survivor respondents—34 percent—appeared to agree with the John Cornwell assessment—that Pius XII was personally anti-Semitic and not really opposed to Nazi policies toward Jews. Significantly, it would seem, not even 1 percent of our respondents agreed with the proposition that the pope had done all that he possibly could for the Jews of Europe. Less than 2 percent saw the pope as powerless to affect the course of events, and for that reason, conceivably at least, blameless. On the other hand, 22 percent sub-

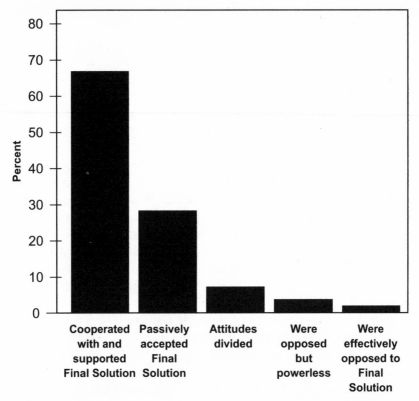

Fig. 5.3. Survivor Opinions of Non-Jews' Attitudes (in Their Own Society) toward the Holocaust

scribed to the proposition that he did have the power to help Jews, but that he did not use it out of fear of Nazi reprisals. About 10 percent saw him as trying to keep the Church out of politics in the Second World War and for that reason unwilling to take a stand on the treatment of Jews by Nazi Germany. There is, at best, an ambiguity in this opinion as to whether the pope's desire to keep the Church out of politics may be seen as an explanation of or an excuse for his conduct.

For a significant majority of our respondents, at least 56 percent, the choice of views about the pope was simply between an anti-Semite and a coward. The pope's reputation could not be saved, apparently, by the heroic deeds of at least some Catholic bishops, priests, monks, and nuns or by such rare personalities as Father Bernhard Lichtenberg, martyred by the Gestapo for his sympathy with the Jews of Germany. Nor did he benefit by the sympathetic hearts of some of his nuncios, notably Angelo Roncalli, the future Pope John XXIII. In the eyes of the Holocaust victims, Pius XII may well have dragged the Church down with him. It was noteworthy that when asked to specify religious denominations most hostile to Jews, 86 percent of those responding to the question named the Catholic Church. Only 2 percent opted for Protestantism, with a scattering of other responses as well as nonresponses. Among religious denominations most favorable to Jews, we found a plurality of our respondents choosing nonbelievers—some 31 percent. The next-largest choice was Jehovah's Witnesses at 23 percent. Protestants followed at 11 percent, and the Greek Orthodox Church and the Catholic Church were tied for last place with just under 8 percent each.

To be sure, there were some regional variations. Among our Western European respondents, the largest number, 39 percent, saw the pope as anti-Semitic, whereas 31 percent saw him as indifferent to Jewish survival. About 15 percent thought that he did not do more for Jews out of fear of Nazi reprisals, and an equal share believed that he tried to keep the Church out of politics. In Poland, 43 percent of respondents saw the pope as anti-Semitic and 26 percent as indifferent; 21 percent attributed his behavior during the Holocaust to fear of Nazi reprisals. The idea that he may have tried to keep the Church out of politics appealed to only 7 percent of our Polish respondents. In the rest of Eastern Europe, outside Poland, the dominant description of the pope's behavior was concession to fear at 35 percent, followed closely by anti-Semitic feelings at 33 percent; 15 percent of the respondents believed that the pope tried to maintain political neutrality for the Church; 12 percent thought that the pope was simply indifferent to the fate of the Jews.

On the question of which religious entities were most hostile to Jews, the greatest difference was apparent between West and East. In Poland, 91 percent of those responding identified Catholics as most hostile. In the rest of Eastern Europe, 81 percent did so. In Western Europe, 78 percent of those responding identified Catholics as most hostile, although a majority of survivors from this area simply did not respond to the question.

Alternatively, among our West European respondents, only 10 percent identified Catholics as the religious group most sympathetic to Jews, in a dead heat with Protestants. Some 15 percent chose nonbelievers. The rest actually did not respond to the question. In Poland, the top choice in terms of sympathy toward Jews was nonbelievers, at 27 percent. In the rest of Eastern Europe the same choice was made by 35 percent of our respondents. Jehovah's Witnesses were the choice of 24 percent of all Eastern Europeans. Only 3 percent of Polish survivors and 9 percent of other Eastern Europeans chose Catholics as the most sympathetic religious group.

Although the overall differences among these regions may not be overwhelming, the hostility to the Catholic Church and its supporters was clearly considerably greater among respondents from the East than from the West. There is an obvious connection, it would seem, between the behavior of Church officials as well as the Catholic rank and file in various Western countries, such as Holland, Belgium, and Italy, and the responses of the survivors. More churches and monasteries opened their doors to Jewish escapees of Nazi persecution here as compared with those in Eastern Europe, especially Poland. More voices among the episcopate were raised in defense of Jews than was the case in the East. These legacies probably played a role in lessening some of the sense of bitterness engendered by the silence of the pope during the Holocaust.

In another area of inquiry, we looked into respondent evaluations of anti-Semitism in different parts of Europe. Clearly, Holocaust survivors attached great importance to local anti-Semitism as an enabling factor in the success of the Nazi Final Solution. In view of this perception (see chapter 2), we attempted to get a sense of the survivors' own opinion about where it was that anti-Semitism was at its strongest and where it was at its weakest. In order to discover this, we asked our respondents to rank their five top choices of the most anti-Semitic environments in Europe as well as the five most sympathetic to Jews. Based on these answers, we were able to construct scales that awarded 5 points for a first-place choice and, in appropriate intervals, 1 point for fifth place. We subtracted opposite choices from each total. Illustratively, in the case of Poland, 59 respondents rated it most anti-Semitic, for a total of 295 points. But two respondents ranked Poland most sympathetic; we therefore subtracted 10 points. We then divided, in each case, the total number of points by the total pool of respondents in order to allow for the factor of prevalence in survivor opinions. (Obviously, if half of the respondents ranked ethnic entity X as "most anti-Semitic," this needed to be given much greater weight than if only two or three persons did so.)

On our 5-point scale of anti-Semitism, with first-place designation counting 5 points and fifth-place designation as 1 point, divided by the total number of respondents, the top ranking went to the Poles, with a score of 2.84; second place to the Germans at 2.55; and third place went to the Ukrainians, with a score of 2.36. No one else even came close to these scores. The top five are presented with their appropriate scores in Table 14 below, accompanied by the survivors' five most sympathetic ethnic groups. (At the bottom of each column, the survivors' sixth and seventh choices are also listed, based on analogous calculation.)

Among all survivors responding (184), 59 persons saw Poles as most anti-Semitic, and 58 identified Germans as such. Overall, Germans and Austrians jointly constituted 42 percent of first-place (most anti-Semitic) responses. But Poles and Ukrainians together accounted for 47 percent of first-place answers. Polish Jews were almost twice as likely to attribute anti-Semitic attitudes to Poles as to Germans.

What emerges from these data, among other things, is that the Jewish casualty rate, or, survivor rate in the Holocaust, is not unreasonably tied to survivor estimates of local anti-Semitism or its absence. Human losses were by far greater in the East, especially in Poland, than they were in the West.

Even in Bohemia and Moravia, the western Czech part of prewar Czechoslovakia, 11 percent of the Jewish population of some 117,000 in 1938 survived the war. Since about 26,000 Jews from this area succeeded in emigrating, legally and illegally, between 1939 and 1941, this made the share of survivors, 13,000 out of 90,900, more nearly 14 percent out of a total Jewish population "available" to the Nazis in this area at the time of the Wannsee Conference in early 1942.

On the other hand, in Poland, where the Jewish population was between 3.3 and 3.5 million in 1939, the number of surviving Jews, excluding the approximately 300,000 who had fled, or been deported, to the USSR, was much below 100,000, or less than 3 percent, of the population "available" to the Nazis at the same time period.[32] Jews surviving in the Ukraine, Belarus, and the Baltic states were, statistically speaking, all but nil.

Table 14. Perceived Anti-Semitism by Ethnic Groups

Most Anti-Semitic		Most Sympathetic	
Group	**Rank/Score**	**Group**	**Rank/Score**
Poles	1 (2.84)	**Danes**	1 (3.08)
Germans	2 (2.55)	**Dutch**	2 (1.98)
Ukrainians	3 (2.36)	**Czechs**	3 (1.34)
Austrians	4 (1.27)	**Norwegians**	4 (0.90)
Lithuanians	5 (0.98)	**Belgians**	5 (0.77)
Latvians	6 (0.73)	**Italians**	6 (0.57)
Croatians	7 (0.41)	**Bulgarians**	7 (0.53)

In Denmark, Holland, Norway, and Belgium, the comparisons were far more favorable. In Denmark, less than 2 percent of the Jewish population perished in the Holocaust. In Holland, 20 percent survived but 80 percent perished. In Norway, slightly less than half of the 1,700 Jews survived. In Belgium, between 90,000 and 110,000 Jews, from various countries, resided in the country at the time of German occupation in May 1940. A majority of these people fled Belgium between 1940 and 1941. Approximately 42,000 Jews were registered under Nazi racial laws in late 1940, and between 10,000 and 13,000 were estimated not to have registered at all. Based on a figure of 24,000 victims deported and not returning, the rate of Jewish population losses in Belgium was about 50 percent.

Parenthetically, in Italy and Bulgaria (the latter admittedly Eastern European but much less anti-Semitic), even larger shares of Jewish populations were saved. In Italy, about 78 percent out of a population of some 35,000 survived; in Bulgaria, where the number of Jews during the 1940s from all countries of origin was about 50,000, some 11,000 were deported to Nazi death camps in 1943. Virtually all of these Jews were of Macedonian and Thracian origin, absorbed into Bulgaria during the course of the war. In any case, more than three-quarters of Jews residing in Bulgaria during the Second World War survived the Holocaust.

How, concretely, was the anti-Semitism of the local populations an auxiliary to the Nazi Final Solution? One of our questions asked if more Jews might have been willing to risk escape from the ghettos and camps if non-Jews had been more sympathetic or less hostile to them. Eighty-eight percent of our respondents agreed that more would have fled. Slightly more than 11 percent thought that it was at least probable that more would have done so. Out of 193 respondents to this question, only one individual thought that attitudes toward escape would not have been affected by the climate of opinion outside the Jewish enclaves.

Would the Jews have been more likely to offer resistance to their Nazi executioners if the surrounding societies had been more supportive of them? Here, 90 percent of our respondents thought so, and 10 percent thought that it was at least possible though not certain. To be sure, there were some regional variations. Among Jews in Western Europe, 60 percent thought more would have escaped if the surrounding communities were more supportive. Some 40 percent thought that "maybe" they would have done so. In Poland, 97 percent of the respondents thought more would have escaped, and 3 percent opted for "maybe." In Eastern Europe outside Poland, 80 percent believed that more would have escaped. About 18 percent thought maybe more would have fled, and less than 2 percent thought that it would not have made any difference. About 95 percent of Western European respondents believed there would have been more Jewish resistance; in Poland, 94 percent of respondents agreed; in the rest of Eastern Europe, 81 percent agreed and 19 percent thought that there *might* have been more resistance. Although these questions addressed hypothetical issues, there is no doubt that for the victims who were there—"on the ground," as it were—these were not difficult questions at all. The responses were among the most consensual of our whole survey.

That anti-Semitism within the body of the surrounding populations might have a strong relationship to the general efficacy of the extermination of Jews would seem a fairly reasonable opinion. We have already alluded to the reasons, and the survivors confirm them. Presumably anti-Semitism could influence the rate at which non-Jews would help Jews, whether fleeing, hiding, or resisting. It could influence the rate at which non-Jews might cooperate with Nazi authorities by "turning in" Jews and by denouncing fellow Gentiles helping Jews. It could also influence the balance of passivity, that is, refusal to act or speak on behalf of Jews. But even serious scholarship, and even serious Jewish scholarship, has questioned the link between the success of the Final Solution and the strength of anti-Semitism in the surrounding communities.

The view of the eminent scholar Jacob Robinson is an example.[33] He points out that relatively more Jews survived the war in Rumania than in Holland, even though the apparent contrast in anti-Semitic attitudes of the respective populations—Rumanian and Dutch—might suggest just the opposite. But anti-Semitism among the local populace was not the only factor involved. An important consideration, among others, in the success of the extermination program was whether the Nazis exercised direct control over the areas inhabited by Jews, and also for how long they exercised such control. One of the reasons why relatively fewer Hungarian Jews than Polish Jews perished is that the Nazis did not achieve direct control of Hungary until relatively late in the Second World War. They did not have direct access to Hungarian Jews in 1940, 1941, 1942, and 1943. Of course, these were obviously very "productive" years for them in Poland! By 1944, there was less time and less opportunity for the Nazis in Hungary, and also more counterpressure from various sources—including the Western Allies and the Vatican. Analogous factors operated in Rumania. Rumanian governments did not always cooperate with the Nazis on the "Jewish question."[34]

Although in Holland, where the Nazis exercised direct control since

1940, a very large percentage of the Jewish population was exterminated, the percentage saved was nevertheless between five and six times greater than the share saved in Poland. In the latter case, only about 3 percent of the Jewish population *available* to the Nazis in 1941—at the beginning of Operation Barbarossa—survived the war. The difference was further compounded by the fact that a large percentage of the exterminated Jews of Holland consisted of people who had only recently fled there from Germany and other countries in the late 1930s—a less socially integrated population.

Without exhausting the issue of all the factors *other* than local anti-Semitism in the success of the Final Solution, some mention may be made of geography. A single glance at the map of Europe would demonstrate that the challenge of bringing Jews to a safe haven in the 1940s was much greater in what is now the Czech Republic than it was in Denmark. One area was surrounded by hostile and/or German-occupied territories, whereas the other was located only a few miles from the shores of neutral, democratic, and relatively friendly Sweden across an open sea.

Given the tendencies of Polish public opinion for several decades prior to the Second World War, and the policies of prewar Polish governments with respect to Jews, the results of our scale seem more confirmatory than surprising. The influential, highly anti-Semitic ideology of Polish National Democracy (Endecja), espoused most prominently by Roman Dmowski (1864–1939), had deep historical roots.

In books and articles published primarily between his 1903 *Thoughts of a Modern Pole* and his 1934 *Overthrow*, Dmowski elaborated on anti-Semitic ideology quite similar to Hitler's. Jews were seen as alien, hostile, and deeply corrosive, parasitic, and destructive ethnic elements. Dmowski's conclusion was that Poland needed to get rid of its Jews. How precisely that was to be done Dmowski did not specify. Hitler, whose anti-Semitism Dmowski had explicitly endorsed in 1934, similarly did not describe in *Mein Kampf* his own preferred solution of the "Jewish problem." What was analogous in both of these anti-Semitic doctrines, however, was the elaboration of such profound antagonism toward Jews that their elimination from the body politic by any means whatsoever could hardly be seen as an unreasonable inference.[35]

Every parliamentary election held in Poland during the 1919–1939 period reflected a majority following among ethnic Poles for parties espousing explicitly anti-Semitic ideals, including the Pilsudskiist BBWR (Bipartisan Bloc for Cooperation with the Government), which already in 1928 called for Jewish emigration as part of the solution to Poland's alleged

"Jewish problem." Anti-Semitism became part of the political weaponry of such movements as Christian Democracy, the National Workers' Party, part of the Peasant movement, and, above all, the successor to the BBWR, the OZN (Camp of National Unity).[36]

In each of the elections of 1919, 1922, 1928, 1930, and the nonparty elections of 1935, anti-Semitic orientations represented solid majorities of the ethnic Polish electorate. By way of comparison, under the German Weimar Republic, only in March of 1933—with Hitler already chancellor—did two anti-Semitic parties, the Nazis and the Nationalists, achieve a popular majority of 52 percent. This had not been the case in eight previous elections.

Under the governments of Poland's Pilsudskiist successors, in 1937, 1938, and 1939, the expulsion of the Jews (somewhat disguised as "encouraged emigration"), the substantial exclusion of Jews from secondary and higher education as well as from employment and contracts within the public sector, the regulatory persecution of Jews, and even a general boycott of Jewish businesses—publicly encouraged by the government of Premier (and General) Felicjan Slawoj-Skladkowski—had become official Polish policy toward Jews.

With this background, would it not be logical to assume that a Nazi program of "getting rid of the Jews" would have widespread local appeal? Would it not be only "natural" for a great many people—if not everyone, of course—to inform the Nazis as to who the Jews were and where they might be found? Would it not have been "natural" for many people to denounce Jews, and those helping Jews, to the Nazi authorities? Especially if one could expect to be materially rewarded for it by the Nazis, and especially if one could possibly seize the property of the Jews who were being denounced? Indeed, would not spontaneous violence against Jews, a widespread refusal to help them, and the willingness to assist Nazi roundups of Jews (such as those rendered by the Polish police, Policja Granatowa) be more likely to be the norms of popular conduct rather than the fringes?

That Hitler made Polish territory the graveyard of most of European Jewry is a fact. The origins of this decision are not known. But it is quite clear that Hitler was well aware of the prevalent public attitudes in Poland toward Jews quite consonant with his own. In fact, he had been told in 1938 by the Polish ambassador to Berlin, Joseph Lipski, that if he could facilitate Jewish emigration from Poland, the Poles would build him a monument in Warsaw.[37] Obviously, it was not only German or Nazi anti-Semitism that supported the actualization of the Final Solution.

(In his postwar memoirs, the 1943–44 commander of Poland's Home Army—the principal underground military organization—General Tadeusz Bór-Komorowski devotes eleven pages out of 370 to the fate of Polish Jews and to the Final Solution more generally. The general's only significant reference to assistance for Jews relates to the 1943 Warsaw ghetto uprising. He seems to concede that that assistance—in weapons and ammunition—was not very substantial but alleges that there was little to be shared at the time. He mentions over twenty-five thousand Polish attacks on the German railroad system and over five thousand assassinations of German officials but none apparently connected with the liquidation of the Jews.)[38]

It is not surprising that among our Jewish respondents from Poland, 72 percent characterized prevalent public opinion in that country as cooperative with and supportive of the Nazi Final Solution policy; 25 percent viewed prevalent Polish opinion as passively accepting of the Final Solution. We found only one respondent out of 120 who characterized prevalent Polish attitudes as "divided," and only one other who described them as sympathetic to Jews but powerless to help. Two persons declined to respond.

Looking in still another direction, we asked our respondents what social strata *within* ethnic groups were most hostile, or, alternately, most favorably disposed toward Jews. We asked them to identify the three most hostile strata as well as the three most sympathetic strata, and we attempted to create a scale here analogous to that we had devised for ethnic entities, the results of which are represented in Table 15. Without taking into account positive and negative designations, it appeared that the three most hostile strata in the minds of our respondents were the peasants (0.856), the clergy (0.716), and businesspeople (0.587). On the favorable side were workers (0.582), professionals (0.333), and, interestingly, very religious

Table 15. Anti-Semitism and Social Strata

Most Anti-Semitic		Most Sympathetic	
Stratum	**Rank/ Score**	**Stratum**	**Rank/ Score**
Peasants	1 (.617)	**Professionals**	1 (.249)
Clergy	2 (.466)	**Trade Unionists**	2 (.229)
Business People	3 (.438)	**Religious People**	3 (.109)
Workers	4 (.438)		

people (0.294). When, however, we discounted positive evaluations by negative ones, it was only possible to devise a very modest table of positive survivor perceptions of social strata within host countries.

Among political groupings most favorable toward Jews, 38 percent of our respondents identified Communists, followed by Socialists at 19 percent, with 14 percent opting for partisans of movements described as "liberal."

Looking to demographic data for explanations of attitudes (see Table 16), we see that the most negative judgments are rendered by people who, among other characteristics and experiences, survived the Final Solution in concentration camps, lived in Poland at the beginning of the war, were older, expressed disappointment with their lives, and—surprisingly, it would seem—were better off financially. Here, as if to bedevil logically coherent explanations, we find a significant disjunction. That disappointment in life translates into more bitterness displaced on public objects seems quite understandable in light of Harold Lasswell's pioneering political study of 1930, *Psychopathology and Politics*. That economic success translates into more public bitterness, and that lack of success is joined to more benign attitudes is clearly counterintuitive.

What seems to be happening here, however, is that money, or material welfare, is not the basis upon which survivors make their judgments. Their evaluations are driven much more strongly, it would appear, by memories of the Holocaust itself than by the experiences of a more recent past. When we compare the two groups of respondents with respect to other factors— factors relevant to the experience of trauma during the Holocaust—the anomalous results no longer seem anomalous. The more well-to-do respondents happen to be preponderantly derived from Poland, by a ratio of 2:1. Among the less well-to-do, there is an even split between survivors from Poland and from other countries, West and East. The well-to-do group is slightly older than its less affluent counterpart—another ingredient of our exposure-to-suffering scale. On the remaining elements of that scale, the less well-to-do actually exhibit a slightly higher rate of camp incarceration than the wealthier people, but that is easily offset by a significant difference with respect to the factor of assimilation.

It is instructive, we believe, to consider aggregate judgments by a variety of demographic categories. Looking across all the blame- or culpability-related questions, we discover that gender differences translated into no attitudinal differences whatsoever: men and women had identical blame scale scores of 13.07. Socioeconomic status contributed very little to differ-

Table 16. Degree of Blame Expressed in Selected Survivor Groups

Group	Low Blame		Medium Blame		High Blame	
Gender	**Count**	**%**	**Count**	**%**	**Count**	**%**
Male	28	26.7	49	46.7	28	26.7
Female	22	23.2	50	52.6	23	24.2
Age in 1939						
1–13	19	25.0	40	52.6	17	22.4
14–31	31	25.2	58	47.2	34	27.6
Education						
High School/Below	34	22.4	81	53.3	37	24.3
College/Above	15	35.7	16	38.1	11	26.2
Current Welfare						
Well Off/Better	24	22.0	53	48.6	32	29.4
Ends Meet/Difficult	24	28.6	43	51.2	17	20.2
Life Satisfaction						
High/Mod. Satisfied	40	26.5	75	49.7	36	23.8
Disappointed	5	14.7	19	55.9	10	29.4
SES						
Low	9	27.3	16	48.5	8	24.2
Medium	13	23.2	30	53.6	13	23.2
High	16	29.1	25	45.5	14	25.5
Region						
Poland	24	20.9	60	52.2	31	27.0
Western Europe	8	40.0	2	10.5	12	63.2
Other	18	27.7	31	47.7	16	24.6
Camp Confinement						
Yes	32	24.6	59	45.4	39	30.0
No	17	24.6	40	58.0	12	17.4

ences in attitude. Among people classified as professionals and managerial experts, the average blame score was 12.84. Among skilled workers and artisans, it was 12.89. Among students, it was 12.80, and among housewives 13.16. These were all but negligible differences.

Categories that produced moderate differences in attitudes, between 2 and 6 percent, included education, age, material welfare, belief in God, urban or small-town origins, assistance provided by Gentiles during the

Holocaust, religious background of pre-Holocaust household, incarceration in camps, and family losses during the Holocaust. Within this relatively modest range of differences, we find certain consistencies in attitudinal tendencies. People who were older, came from more religious homes and from small-town environments, were not assisted by Gentiles, survived in concentrations camps, and lost all or most of their relatives tended to have higher aggregate blame scores than people in contrasting categories.

Categories where attitudinal differences were at their greatest—between 7 and 12 percent—related to background of assimilation, country of origin at the beginning of the Second World War, and satisfaction with life. The single, most sharply discriminating factor was the legacy of assimilation. The difference in blame scores between those who came from nonassimilated homes and those whose prewar homes were assimilated was 12 percent (higher blame scores were recorded by those with nonassimilated backgrounds). Closely following was country of origin. The difference in blame scores between residents of Western Europe and of Poland was 11 percent, with the higher scores for those domiciled in Poland. The factor that introduced a contemporary dimension to these judgments, at least in part, was satisfaction with life. Those who described themselves as satisfied with their lives were 7 percent lower in their average blame scale scores than were the people who considered themselves somewhat or seriously disappointed with their lives.

A few specific illustrations based on more nuanced comparisons follow. Here, we divided our respondents into three blame categories: the lowest, 25 percent of all scores; the middle, with 50 percent; and the highest, with 25 percent. Socioeconomic status and formal education turned out to be fairly weak discriminators in survivor attitudes. There were virtually no differences in blame scores among people based on their low, middle, or high social status. Among respondents of low socioeconomic status, 24 percent were in the high-blame category; among the high-status persons, the figure was 26 percent—not much of a difference. The same was true at the low end of the blame scale, where 29 percent of the high-status people clustered, as compared with 27 percent in the low-status category.

There was a somewhat greater difference in terms of education. The college-educated were much more likely to be on the low-blame end of the scale, and the less-educated in the middle 50 percent. But there was not much difference at the high end of the scale. Among people with high school education or less, 24.3 percent were in the high-blame category, and among those with college education, 26.2 percent were—hardly much of a difference.

Once again, we discover the importance of cultural heritage in survivor attitudes. When we divided our respondents into those with nonassimilated versus assimilated backgrounds, we found twice as many in the high-blame category among the nonassimilated. At the low end of the blame scale, we found 36 percent of the assimilated but only 21 percent of the nonassimilated, also a very substantial difference—almost 70 percent more among the assimilated. These differences were reinforced by reference to places of origin. Among people whose family roots were in large cities, 23 percent were in the high-blame category and 27 percent in the low-blame category. But among people originating in the small towns and villages of the Jewish Diaspora, 29 percent were in the high-blame and only 21 percent in the low-blame categories.

Among the "better-integrated" Jews—those who received assistance from Gentiles during the Holocaust—21 percent were in the high-blame category and 29 percent in the low-blame end. But among the less integrated—those not receiving Gentile assistance—29 percent were at the high end of the scale, and less than 24 percent were at the low end. Among people who described themselves as "believers"—in the Deity—29 percent were at the high end of the blame scale and 29 at the low end. Among people who described themselves as nonbelievers, only 11 percent were at the high end of the blame scale versus 26 percent at the low end; 63 percent were in the middle blame stratum, whereas among the believers, only 42 percent fell into this middle category.

This, at last, brings us to the three compound models (besides SES), that is, models based on combinations of qualities or attributes among the survivors. The three models we used were personality, culture, and exposure to suffering. With respect to the first, differences between more "positive" respondents—that is, those simultaneously professing satisfaction with life and optimism about the world—amounted to 7.5 percent. The more positive tended to assign less blame, the more negative personalities more blame.

The distinction based on culture, separating those with nonassimilated and religious backgrounds who were also believers from assimilated nonbelievers, was the second largest in the survey. People whom we called Jewish traditionalists exhibited average blame scores 13 percent higher than the opposite, "modernist" respondents.

The largest single difference, however, emerged between those heavily exposed to the sufferings of the Holocaust (older respondents from Poland, incarcerated in camps, who come from nonassimilated family backgrounds) and those with less exposure: a robust 17 percent. Much greater degree of blame was attributed to various Holocaust actors by the "high-exposure" cases.

The powerful discriminating effects of culture and exposure to suffering testified to the domination of the past over the present in the judgments of survivors. What happened to them more than fifty years ago, both in terms of family life in adolescence and hardships endured at the hands of the Nazis during the Final Solution, mattered greatly. In fact, it seemed to be more critical to their current perspectives on the Holocaust than whatever they had achieved or learned in the years since the Second World War. Culture and history were apparently stronger shapers of survivor outlook fifty years after the Holocaust than material welfare, status, or formal education.

NOTES

1. *The Black Book of Poland* (New York: G. P. Putnam's Sons), p. 579.

2. Ibid., p. 582.

3. Ibid., pp. 584–85.

4. Jan Karski, *Story of the Secret State* (Boston: Houghton Mifflin, 1944), p. 323.

5. Ibid., p. 321.

6. The trial of Rudolf Höss, Nazi Commandant of Auschwitz, in Warsaw in 1946, with its implication of Himmler and Hitler in the Final Solution policy, was certainly very important. See Jadwiga Bezwinska and Danuta Czech, eds., *KL Auschwitz Seen By the SS: Höss, Broad, Kremer* (New York: Howard Fertig, 1984).

7. Kogon, *The Theory and Practice of Hell: The German Concentration Camps and the System behind Them* (New York: Farrar, Straus, 1950), p. 215.

8. Ibid., p. 162.

9. Ibid., p. 172.

10. John Cornwell, *Hitler's Pope: The Secret History of Pius XII* (New York: Viking, 1999), p. 357.

11. See, e.g., YIVO Colloquium (2–5 December 1967), *Imposed Jewish Governing Bodies Uunder Nazi Rule* (New York: YIVO Institute for Jewish Research, 1972).

12. See William Kornbluth, *Sentenced to Remember: My Legacy of Life in Pre-1939 Poland and Sixty-Eight Months of Nazi Occupation* (Bethlehem, Pa.: Lehigh University Press, 1994). Here we find substantial description of post-1945 events in Poland. See also Nechama Tec, *When Light Pierced the Darkness: Christian Rescue of Jews in Nazi-Occupied Poland* (New York: Oxford University Press,

1986). Note p. 140 on prevalent attitudes of Polish clergy toward Jews and other aspects of anti-Semitism. Tec maintains that some Polish anti-Semites actually helped rescue Jews—which raises the question of just how anti-Semitic those anti-Semites were, and also how widespread this sort of behavior was. See also Anthony Polonsky, *"My Brother's Keeper?" Recent Polish Debates on the Holocaust* (London: Routledge, 1990).

It is of great relevance, of course, that in their extensive and thoughtful study, Samuel P. Oliner and Pearl M. Oliner, *The Altruistic Personality: Rescuers of Jews in Nazi Europe* (New York: Free Press, 1988), found that when they compared the social contacts of people who were rescuers of Jews with those who were nonrescuers and bystanders, the social links between Jews and non-Jews turned out to be extremely important. For example, 59 percent of rescuers had Jewish friends before the war, but only 34 percent among nonrescuers; 34 percent of rescuers had had Jewish coworkers, whereas among the nonrescuers only 17 percent did. Among the former, 69 percent had Jewish neighbors before the war; among the latter, only 52 percent. Another interesting finding of this study, relevant to claims of authors like Nechama Tec, was that parents of nonrescuers and bystanders were much more likely to have expressed negative stereotypes of Jews to their children—by a factor of four to six times more often than the parents of rescuers (pp. 285, 288).

13. John A. O'Brien, preface to *Their Brother's Keepers*, by Philip Friedman (New York: Holocaust Library, 1978), p. 7.

14. Michael Zylberberg, *A Warsaw Diary, 1939–1945* (London: Vallentine, Mitchell, 1969), p. 121.

15. Emanuel Ringelblum, *To Live with Honor and Die With Honor: Selected Documents from the Warsaw Ghetto Underground and Archives "O.S.,"* ed. Joseph Kernish (Jerusalem: Yad Veshem, 1986), pp. 615–16.

16. A recent example of the case study approach is Nathan Stoltzfus, "Protest and Silence: Resistance Histories in Post-War Germany: The Missing Case of Intermarried Germans," in *Resisting the Holocaust*, ed. Ruby Rohrlich (New York: Oxford University Press, 1998), pp. 151–78. Among earlier works, see also Alexander Ramati, *The Assisi Underground: The Priests Who Rescued Jews* (New York: Stein and Day, 1978). This is, needless to say, a thoroughly positive account of some heroic people. There is even a suggestion here that one of the heroes of that rescue was a Wehrmacht colonel, Valentin Müller (p. 176).

17. Henry Feingold, *The Politics of Rescue: The Roosevelt Administration and the Holocaust, 1938–1945* (New Brunswick, N. J.: Rutgers University Press, 1970), p. 295. See also David S. Wyman, *The Abandonment of the Jews: America and the Holocaust, 1941–1945* (New York: Pantheon Books, 1984).

18. Feingold, *The Politics of Rescue*, p. 299.

19. Ibid., p. 305.

20. S. M. Finger, *American Jewry during the Holocaust* (New York: Holmes and Meier, 1984), p. 42.

21. Bernard Wasserstein, *Britain and the Jews of Europe, 1939–1945* (Oxford: Clarendon Press, 1979), p. 345.

22. Ibid., p. 351.

23. Ibid., p. 351.

24. Ibid., p. 357. See also Martin Gilbert, *Auschwitz and the Allies* (London: Michael Joseph, 1981); Michael J. Cohen, *Churchill and the Jews* (Totowa, N.J.: F. Cass, 1985); Arthur D. Morse, *While Six Million Died: A Chronicle of American Apathy* (New York: Random House, 1968); and V. W. Newton, ed., *FDR and the Holocaust* (New York: St. Martin's Press, 1996). A remarkable early work on Western responses and complicity in the Holocaust was Saul S. Friedman, *No Haven for the Oppressed: United States Policy toward Jewish Refugees, 1938–1945* (Detroit: Wayne State University Press, 1973). Friedman was not at all reluctant to focus upon "us" rather than "them." Note especially chapter 10, "The Yoke of Shame," pp. 225–35. "To untold numbers in the U.S.," he wrote, "the Nazis were merely the unwitting allies of God" (p. 230).

25 Deborah Lipstadt, *Beyond Belief: The American People and the Coming of the Holocaust*, (New York: Free Press, 1968), p. 278.

26. See Daniel Goldhagen, *Hitler's Willing Executioners: Ordinary Germans and the Holocaust* (New York: A. A. Knopf, 1996), p. 419, for the author's diagnosis that the German people generally shared Hitler's anti-Semitism.

27. See Michael R. Marrus and Robert Paxton, "The Nazis and the Jews in Occupied Western Europe, 1940–1944," in *Unanswered Questions: Nazi Germany and the Genocide of the Jews*, ed. Francois Furet (New York: Schocken Books, 1989), pp. 172–98. These authors speak of "caution" and of Nazi measures with respect to Jews that could be termed "slow and hesitant" in Western Europe, "anxious not to disturb local sensibilities." They also say that "considerable care and diplomacy were necessary" in carrying out the Final Solution, in large measure because "Jews tended to be well integrated in the societies in which they lived" (p. 184).

On the other hand, see also Ezra Mandelson, "Relations between Jews and Non-Jews in Eastern Europe between the Two World Wars," in Furet (ed.), *Unanswered Questions*, pp. 71–83. It makes the strong case that "during the interwar period . . . eastern Europe was a uniquely hostile environment for Jews as individuals, . . . [which constituted] a prelude to the Holocaust" (p. 82). Obviously, this state of public opinion in the region was a resource from the Nazi point of view in "solving" the so-called Jewish problem.

28. See James H. Kitchens III (U.S. Air Force archivist), "The Bombing of Auschwitz Reexamined," in Newton (ed.), *FDR and the Holocaust*, pp. 183–217. Kitchens severely challenges Wyman, *Abandonment of the Jews*, and others who believe that the Allies could have bombed Auschwitz in the latter part of 1944. Those included in the purview of his criticism are, among others, Morse, *While Six Million Died*, and Gilbert, *Auschwitz and the Allies*. Kitchens's critical conclusion is that "an objective look at targeting possibilities, available intelligence, opera-

tional constraints, and the realistic allocation of military resources . . . shows that the effective use of air power against Auschwitz is a chimera [!] having little to do with War Department policies, indifference, military ineptitude or negative ethnic attitudes" (p. 191). Says the author: "In the instance of Auschwitz, military policy was driven by availability of intelligence, operational possibilities, asset allocation, the rules of war, and conventional morality" (p. 204).

It is interesting to consider for a moment who or what decides "asset allocation" and even more interesting to know that the rules of war and conventional morality had no difficulties over Dresden and Hamburg, or Hiroshima and Nagasaki (or Mers el Kebir), though somehow insuperable moral military objections arose with respect to bombing Auschwitz.

29. See Don Levin, *The Lesser of Two Evils: East European Jewry under Soviet Rule, 1939–1941* (Philadelphia: Jewish Publication Society, 1995), p. 6; and Lucjan Dobroszycki, *Survivors of the Holocaust in Poland* (New York: M. E. Sharpe, 1994), pp. 18–19. About 500,000 Jews escaped from West to East in these years, but probably fewer than 350,000 managed to flee deep into Soviet territory before Operation Barbarossa, and of those at least 240,000 returned to the West after the war. Yehuda Bauer, *The Holocaust in Historical Perspective* (Seattle: University of Washington Press, 1978), p. 55, estimates that 264,000 Jews were actually deported to the USSR. See Shimon Redlick, ed., *War, Holocaust, and Stalinism: A Documented Study of the Jewish Anti-Fascist Committee in the USSR* (Luxembourg: Harwood Academic Publishers, 1995), who reports that 400,000 Jews from Soviet-annexed areas, "mainly refugees from German-occupied Poland," were deported to the interior of the USSR, and another 85,000 fled there voluntarily, for a total of about "half-a-million Jews who had not been Soviet citizens in 1939" (pp. 29–30). Keith Sword, *Deportation and Exile: Poles in the Soviet Union, 1939–1948* (London: St. Martin's Press, 1994), p. 26, gives a figure of 198,000 Jews in the so-called "refugee" category who were removed to the USSR between 1939 and 1941. He also estimates that 136,500 Jews returned to Poland from the USSR during the first half of 1946 (p. 195). Jeff Schatz, *The Generation: The Rise and Fall of the Jewish Communists of Poland* (Berkeley and Los Angeles: University of California Press, 1991), p. 203, reports 157,420 Jewish repatriates from the USSR who were registered with the Central Committee of Jews in Poland. It should be noted that many Polish Jews who left the USSR after the war went to countries other than Poland and also that many Polish Jews remained in Russia after 1945. Arkady Vaksberg, *Stalin Against the Jews* (New York: Alfred A. Knopf, 1944), provides an otherwise interesting catalogue of Stalin's anti-Semitic attitudes and actions; nevertheless, he engages in a curious misrepresentation of history when he provides the following account of the Jewish exodus to the East in 1939–41, to wit: "Taking advantage of the porous new border [between Germany and the USSR] . . . Jews from western and central regions of Poland tried to cross over as quickly as possible to the areas of Soviet military units. Knowing he would be sending them to Germany and not wishing to waste time or money on this

unwieldy operation, Stalin gave orders 'not to allow Jews onto Soviet territory.' They were shot at from both sides" (p. 105). On the whole, this is one of the more remarkable fantasies to be found in what professes to be serious literature.

30. See, e.g., Alexander J. Groth, *Democracies against Hitler: Myth, Reality and Prologue* (Brookfield, Vt.: Ashgate, 1999), pp. 211, 212–13.

31. See Louis Rapoport, *Stalin's War Against the Jews: The Doctors' Plot and the Soviet Solution* (New York: Free Press, 1990). Rapoport describes Stalin's anti-Semitism, the murders of various Jewish personages, and the conspicuous Soviet silence on the Holocaust. Although Rapoport mentions Stalin handing over six hundred German Communists to the Nazis, most of them Jews, he does not mention the hundreds of thousands of Jews allowed entry into the USSR between 1939 and 1941 from western Poland. His chapter titled "Rescue Denied: Stalin and Hitler Sacrifice the Jews" contains no acknowledgment of it. Curiously, his book does make reference to the many generals of the Red Army of Jewish extraction, including a relatively major figure, Colonel General Ivan Cherniakovsky, killed in East Prussia in early 1945. In fact, Stalin renamed the East Prussian city of Insterburg Cherniakovsk, after this Jewish general—the name it bears to this day.

32. Filip Friedman, "Zaglada Zydów Polskich w Latach 1939–1949" (The destruction of Polish Jews in the years 1939–1945), *Biuletyn Glownej Komisji Badania Zbrodni Niemieckich w Polse* (Bulletin of the Main Commission for the Study of German Crimes in Poland) (Poznan, Poland: Main Commission for the Study of German Crimes in Poland, 1946), p. 205, estimates that only between 1.3 and 1.8 percent of Jews who had inhabited Polish territories occupied by Nazi Germany survived the war in those territories; approximately 98 percent were exterminated.

33. See Robinson, "Holocaust," in *Encyclopedia Judaica*, vol. 8 (Jerusalem: Keter Publishing, 1972), p. 876: "With the exception of the Polish-Soviet area, the extent of indigenous antisemitism generally had no bearing on the number of victims. Outstanding examples are the Netherlands and Serbia, areas of no, or insignificant, anti-Jewish feelings but of high rate of losses, and Rumania, for decades antisemitic but with a relatively low rate of losses. However, friendly relations between Jews and non-Jews could prove a powerful rescue factor."

34. See, e.g., the article by Thedor Lavi in the *Encyclopedia Judaica*, vol. 14, p. 404, with references to 1942 and 1943: "Despite German efforts, the Rumanian government refused to deport its Jews to the 'east.' [In 1944,] Antonescu warned the Germans to avoid killing Jews while retreating."

35. See Alexander J. Groth, "Dmowski, Pilsudski, and Ethnic Conflict in Pre-1939 Poland," *Canadian Slavic Studies* 3, no. 1 (1969):69–91. The sum of Dmowski's views about Jews is best reflected in three quotations from his works:

> In the character of this race so many different values, strange to our moral constitution and harmful to our life, have accumulated that assimilation with a large number of [Jews] would destroy us [*zgubiloby nas*] replacing with decadent elements those young creative foundations upon which we

are building the future. (*Myśli nowoczesnego polaka* [Thoughts of a modern Pole] [Warsaw, 1903; 7th ed., London: n.p., 1953]), p. 91.

Even if Jews were morally angels, mentally geniuses, even if they were people of a higher kind than we are, the very fact of their existence among us and their close participation in our life is for our society *lethal* [*zabójczy*] and they have to be got rid of [*trzeba się ich pozbyc*]. (*Przewrót* [Overthrow] [Warsaw, 1934], p. 309.)

The incursion of a large wave of Jews into our life has resulted, in those social circles which have become connected with them, in such destruction of all preservative [*zachowawczych*] characteristics, such as rebellion against one's own national tradition, such decay in religious feelings and even elementary respect for religion, such repulsion toward every . . . hierarchy that it has in a sense threatened us with barbarization [*zdziczeniem*]. . . . If all society were to succumb to this influence, we would actually lose our capacity for societal life. (*Upadek myśli konserwatywnej* [The decline of conservative thought], in *Pisma* [Works] vol. 4 [Czestochowa, Poland, 1938], pp. 18–79.)

36. Among various sources, see Alexander J. Groth, "Proportional Representation in Prewar Poland," *Slavic Review* 23, no. 1 (1964):103–16; "Polish Elections, 1919–1928," *Slavic Review* 24, no. 4 (1965):653–65; and "Legacy of Three Crises: Parliament and Ethnic Issues in Prewar Poland," *Slavic Review* 27, no. 4 (1968):564–80.

37. The following passages from the papers and memoirs of Jozef Lipski, titled *Diplomat in Berlin, 1933–1939*, ed. Waclaw Jedrzejewicz (New York: Columbia University Press, 1968), pp. 408, 411, are amply illustrative:

DOCUMENT 99—Lipski to [Foreign Minister Jozef] Beck

September 20, 1938

Strictly Confidential

The Chancellor received me today in Obersalzberg in the presence of the Reich minister of foreign affairs, Ribbentrop, at 4 P.M. The conversation lasted for more than two hours. . . . From . . . long deliberations the following results were clear . . . that he has in mind an idea for settling the Jewish problem by way of emigration to the colonies in accordance with an understanding with Poland, Hungary, and possibly also Rumania (at which point I told him that if he finds such a solution we will erect him a beautiful monument in Warsaw).

See also William W. Hagen, "Before the 'Final Solution': Toward a Comparative Analysis of Political Anti-Semitism in Interwar Germany and Poland," *Journal of Modern History* 68, no. 2 (1996): 351–81.

38. Tadeusz Bór-Komorowski, *Armia Podziemna* (Underground army), 3d ed. (London: Veritas, 1951), pp. 95–106, 146–47. See also Israel Gutman, *The Jews of Warsaw, 1939–1942: Ghetto, Underground Revolt* (Bloomington: Indiana University Press, 1982). Note especially mortality rates in the ghetto, pp. 63–64. Among some sobering recent accounts, see Jan T. Gross, *Neighbors: The Destruction of the Jewish Community in Jedwabne, Poland* (Princeton, N. J.: Princeton University Press, 2001) and Jerzy Tomaszewski et al., *Najnowsze dzieje Żydów w Polsce w zarysie (do 1950 roku)* (Recent history of Jews in Poland in outline [till 1950]) (Warsaw: Wydawnictwo Naukowe PWN, 1993). Very revealing, and obviously useful, summaries on Polish-Jewish relations during the war may be found in the four-volume work of Israel Gutman (ed.), *Encyclopedia of the Holocaust* (New York: Macmillan 1990). See, for example, Gutman, "Poland: The Jews in Poland," 3:1171–74; Shumel Krakowski, "Polnische Polizei," 3:1178–79; Gutman, "Partisans," 3:1119–21; and 4:1607, 1622, 1624, 1628, 1630, also by Gutman, on the ghetto uprising of April–May 1943.

Chapter 6

COMPARING the HOLOCAUST

In this chapter, we focus primarily upon a single question, probing the survivors' view of the Holocaust in relation to three post–Second World War massacres. This question in our survey read as follows:

> Some people compare the tragic events in Bosnia, Rwanda, and Cambodia with the Holocaust. Do you see some or any equivalence to the Holocaust in these events?
> a. None
> b. Little
> c. Some
> d. Quite a lot
> e. Other—specify: _____

We were interested in the degree of empathy that survivors would demonstrate toward the sufferings and losses of people in the contemporary world under circumstances that, in some respects, might be seen as similar or analogous to their own earlier ordeal, and that might be seen, on the other hand, as somewhat different from their own. It should be noted that we did not actually offer our respondents the choice of full equivalence between the Holocaust and whatever had transpired in Bosnia, Cambodia, or Rwanda. (They were, of course, free to provide whatever alternative they wished in the "Other" rubric.)

Important questions are interrelated in the proposition about the comparability of the Holocaust. In one sense it may be plausibly maintained, as

Steven T. Katz has argued in his monumental *The Holocaust in Historical Context* that the Holocaust was a genuinely unique event in world history.[1] Hitler's Final Solution of the Jewish Question can be reasonably understood as unique in several interrelated respects (apart from the proposition that every occurrence and phenomenon in the cosmos may be seen as unique given the time, the place, and other particular configurations of it that cannot be precisely replicated).[2]

However the policy of the Nazi state toward the extermination of the Jewish people may have been generated—and there has been some disagreement on this between the aforementioned intentionalists and functionalists, for example—it clearly achieved a perceptibly comprehensive, total, and in this sense unique, character at least by sometime in 1942. All Jews—men, women, and children who resided within territories occupied by the Nazi Reich, or even in territories that could be subject to Nazi political-diplomatic pressure—became the quarry of the Nazi state. They were pursued by the authorities of the Hitlerian state for the purpose of an undifferentiated, relentless physical annihilation. Biology was destiny: no actions of Jews, such as religious conversion, profession of allegiance, or even the acceptance of slavery, to use extreme examples, could avert the fate that the Nazi state sought for them. The destruction of the Jews, unlike many previous acts of violence against civilian populations, in ancient and medieval as well as modern times, was not committed in connection with acts of conquest or warfare. It was carried out systematically and comprehensively in areas not involved in military operations and against people who could not be reasonably confused with or mingled with combatants offering resistance to the armed forces of the exterminator state. These were not crimes committed in the heat of battle—à la the My Lai atrocity in 1968 during the American conflict in Vietnam.

The destruction of the Jews had a prolonged, planned, and officially sanctioned character. This distinguished it from various massacres, however bloody, committed through sporadic, localized incidents, such as the Russian pogroms of the nineteenth century or in "collateral enterprises." Nazi extermination was not carried out under an umbrella of official indifference or inability of those formally in control of the state to curb the excesses of their nominal or actual subordinates. No letters of reprimand, even halfhearted ones, were ever sent by Hitler or Himmler to commandants of camps in Majdanek and Treblinka. No trains arriving in Auschwitz were ever greeted by officials telling the guards: "How could you possibly be doing what you are doing? Cease and desist."

In the great massacre of the Armenians by the Turks in 1915, when at least one million persons (perhaps even 1.5 million) were exterminated, the organizing motive was, ostensibly, at least, the removal of Armenians from areas near the war front. "It is probable that few deportees were anticipated to arrive at their destinations, which were the Syrian desert and the Mesopotamian Valley, and that those who did were expected to survive the inhospitable terrain and hostile tribesmen only briefly. Furthermore, the deportations were not actually confined to frontier regions. They developed into large-scale massacres. Some evidence, whose authenticity has been disputed, suggests that the central government had decided to exterminate the Armenians, and had issued orders accordingly."[3]

When the Romans destroyed Carthage, many Carthaginians survived the conquest through enslavement. Unlike the Nazis, Romans did not seek to kill persons of Carthaginian ancestry residing in, say, ancient Spain, or Turkey, or Judea.[4] When Tsarist officials participated in anti-Jewish pogroms in the Ukraine, this did not entail analogous consequences for Jews residing in St. Petersburg, Tomsk, or Vladivostok.[5] These are at least some of the more obvious differences between the treatment that Nazi Germany meted out to the Jews as opposed to sundry acts of violence committed against other people at different times and places throughout history.

None of the seemingly repeated events of history are duplicated exactly. For one thing, murder has taken place at different times with different weapons, in obvious response to changes in science and technology. Still, if Hitler had used laser guns instead of gas chambers to annihilate the Jews of Europe, would that have made the Holocaust an essentially different, and in any sense more humane, event? Each of the world's great massacres of the innocent differed from one another.

But the Holocaust does not stand outside of the more general human experience, past, present, or future. Simply put, it was mass murder of the innocent. In the case of the Jews, the murder was justified by Nazi racial theories that collectively demonized the Jews as vicious and implacable enemies of Germany and of all mankind. The Jews were Hitler's ultimate scapegoats. Every social wrong, in the Nazi view, was ultimately traceable to pestilential Jewish activity or influence. Characteristically, Nazism connected every living Jew to its aggregate lethal stereotype with no concern for the facts of any particular, actual cases. There was no individual appeal from the collective Nazi death sentence.

In this respect—the murder of the innocent under the cover of some hateful, collectively applied stereotype—the Holocaust clearly stands as part of a very prevalent human experience. It is part of the tragedy of humanity, extending into the all but immemorial recesses of history, that people—rulers, individuals, and groups—have repeatedly stigmatized other groups, various kinds of "out-groups." Under the cover of such stereotypes, whether ethnic, religious, tribal, cultural, racial, or political, they have murdered children, women, old people, young people, and everyone in sight, no questions asked.

In discussing the Armenian massacre of 1915, Richard Hovannisian refers to the United Nations convention on the prevention and punishment of genocide as consisting of five acts "intentionally perpetrated against a national, ethnic, racial or religious" entity: killing group members; causing serious bodily or mental harm to its members; inflicting conditions of life that are calculated to cause the physical annihilation of the group, in total or in part; prevention of the biological reproduction of the group; and forcibly taking away the group's children to give away to others. Says Hovannisian: "It is significant that in the Armenian Genocide and Holocaust all five categories apply, except possibly the final point to Jews because of Nazi racial ideology."[6]

Writing about Rwanda, Edward L. Nyankanzi offers this concept of genocide, supplementing the 1948 United Nations definition: "Genocide is . . . the promotion and execution of policies by a state or its agents that result in the deaths of a substantial portion of a group. . . . In a genocidal situation the targeted group is identified as the enemy or potential enemy. The group is accused of collective guilt. The targeted group is demonized, dehumanized, and denigrated." He also notes that "genocide recognizes neither geographic boundaries nor ethnic monopolies. It has become an incurable man-made disease."[7]

It is for this reason, above all else, that the story of the Holocaust communicates a meaning to all the rest of the world. It is for this reason that we have institutions such as the United States Holocaust Museum in Washington, D. C. Obviously, since the victims of the Holocaust were Jews, it is of particular and understandably greater interest to Jews than to anyone else. But it is also of great interest to other people precisely because the underlying formula—the murder of innocents through the agency of stereotyped hatred—has many precedents and analogues around the globe. Bosnia, Cambodia, and Rwanda are merely three modern examples of the formula.

Beginning chronologically with the Cambodian mass killings in the 1970s and moving on to those in Bosnia and Rwanda in the 1990s, atrocities involving in the aggregate millions of people have been widely publicized in the Western world in all sorts of print media, on radio and on television. With all certainty, these tragic developments have received considerably more media attention in the last three decades in the Western world than did the murder of the Jews during the 1940s.[8] One could hardly escape this more recent coverage. The substance of the events was unquestionably grave: "In the Cambodian revolution a greater proportion of the population perished than in any other revolution during the twentieth century. The exact number of deaths due to K[hmer] R[ouge] execution or mistreatment between 1975 and 1979 will never be known. Estimates run from the low figures of 400,000 or 740,000 . . . to the State Department high of 1.5 to 3 million. Although around one million became the most widely accepted number, later research indicated a much higher figure . . . In any case, the K[hmer] R[ouge] genocide certainly ranks with the crimes of Stalin, Hitler, and Mao Zedong."[9]

Another author observes: "For Cambodia's ethnic Chinese, Democratic Kampuchea was the worst disaster ever to befall any ethnic Chinese community in Southeast Asia. Of a 1975 population of 430,000, only about 214,000 Chinese survived the next four years. . . . The 50 percent of them who perished is a higher proportion than that estimated for city dwellers in general (about one-third). . . . The Chinese language, like all foreign and minority languages, was banned, and so was any tolerance of a culturally and ethnically distinguishable Chinese community. The Chinese community was to be destroyed 'as such.' This [Communist Party] policy . . . could be construed as genocide."[10]

It seems a fair inference that much of the interest in the subject of the Holocaust, especially by non-Jews, is premised on the notion that this horrendous experience can teach people something of universal validity about man's inhumanity to man, about ethnic and racial persecution, and perhaps about unacceptable extremes of political tyranny, among a variety of possible subjects. The killing of innocent human beings on a mass scale, over extended periods of time, for ideological, racial, religious, and political reasons has been, sadly, one of the more important, salient features of world history down to the present time.

Our anticipation was that Holocaust survivors, having personally experienced, deeply and profoundly, the horrors of extermination and persecution by the Nazis, would demonstrate a great deal of empathy with respect to Bosnians, Cambodians, and Rwandans. A breakdown of individual responses to our survey question, however, provided unexpected results (see Table 17). A plurality of our respondents, 40 percent, saw no equiva-

Table 17. Survivor Views on Comparability of the Holocaust and Three Postwar Mass Killings

Comparability	Number of Respondents	Percent
None	78	39.8%
Little	28	14.3%
Some	66	33.7%
Quite a lot	24	12.2%
TOTAL	196	100.0%

lence in these situations, answering "none," 14 percent answered "little," 34 percent answered "some," and only 12 percent of the 196 respondents to this particular question said "quite a lot."

In overall terms, 60 percent of our respondents, those ranging from "little" to "quite a lot," saw *some* degree of relatedness among these events or situations. On the other hand, those who had said "none" or "little" accounted for 54 percent; those who composed the "some" and "quite a lot" categories constituted 46 percent.

The responses to our survey question can also be treated as a four-point ordinal scale that measures the degree of empathy among our survivors, with a score of four representing the most empathetic feelings. The mean score on our four-point empathy scale was 2.18, and the scores were not distributed in a normal bell-shaped manner but rather had a distinctly bimodal shape, with the largest number of cases falling at the lowest end of the scale. Clearly, the level of empathy among our survivor group was relatively low.

Comments volunteered by our respondents preponderantly emphasized the differences between the Holocaust and the post–Second World War massacres:

Can not compare.

There are no gas chambers in the above countries neither are the people worked to death.

Tragic as Bosnia, Rwand [*sic*] and Cambodia are—they can *never* be compared or equated to the Holocaust.

This was not done systematically as in Germany.

The Civil Wars have little in common with Final Solution.

No comparison.

Nothing is equivalent to the Holocaust. It is unique in its brutality and scope.

There were armed forces on each side. At least in the case of Bosnia both or all three sides did their own killing and cruelty during the last few centuries.

Addressing both similarities and differences, another respondent noted:

These are civil wars with combatants armed and living in their own country, only the brutality is comparable.

Still another, however, observed:

Ethnic Cleansing—Judenrein. Similar Ideology—Same Hate.

Looking at different demographic groups of respondents, we found little variation in responses. For example, there was virtually no difference in responses by gender. The average score for men on the empathy scale was 2.17, versus 2.19 for women: little evidence here of greater female sympathy for the misfortunes of other people.

There was virtually no difference in empathy between the more affluent and the less affluent respondents based on a self-assessment of their current material welfare. Those who had declared themselves as "very well-off or moderately well-off" posted an average score of 2.18, and those who were making ends meet or who had experienced financial difficulties recorded a 2.20 empathy score—not much of a difference.

On the other hand, using a multidimensional measure of class, or socioeconomic status, that takes into account levels of education attained, occupation, *and* self-assessment of current material welfare, much larger differences emerge. People with low SES reporteed an average empathy score of 1.91, whereas the high-SES group scored 2.29, or nearly 20 percent higher. This result amply met our hypothetical expectations.

More surprising perhaps was the outcome in relation to the respondent's education alone. Here we had expected that higher education might be related to more information, and perhaps to a more acute and detailed understanding of, the events in Bosnia, Cambodia, and Rwanda. Perhaps the more educated would exhibit more sensitive judgments given more information about the atrocities committed in these areas; we expected more exposure to television and print media as a backdrop to any discussion of this question. But the results confounded these expectations. If the educated were more logical or better thinkers, and if they possessed more information, it did not really matter. Those with high school education or less scored 2.17 on the empathy scale, and those with some college or more just 2.24. Although the difference was at least in the direction we had expected, it was only a difference of about 3 percent between the two groups, hardly significant in any sense. If the educated knew more about the situations in Cambodia, Bosnia, and Rwanda than the rest, it made virtually no difference in terms of the attitudes expressed by the two groups.

Although money per se and education did not seem to make much difference on the empathy question, a somewhat wider gap existed between those who expressed a relatively high degree of satisfaction with life and those who expressed less. Unfortunately, from the standpoint of our initial assumptions, the differences ran in the wrong direction. The more satisfied individuals showed *less* empathy—a 2.07 average score, compared with 2.22 from the moderately and substantially disappointed; this was a difference of about 7 percent. Obviously, contrary to our assumption, those less happy with their lives could relate more sympathetically to the persecuted in other countries than the more fulfilled. The differences were quite modest, but there was at least a slight suggestion in this comparison of some association between empathy and disappointment or misfortune in life.

This also seemed to be the case with our personality model, based on the following two criteria of respondent views: anticipation of the future and life satisfaction. The more negative personalities—i.e., those who were more pessimistic about the future and also less satisfied with their own lives—actually recorded a higher average empathy score at 2.29, compared with only 2.19 for the more positive types—a difference of nearly 5 percent. These tendencies were quite clearly evident in the separate components of our personality model. Among those professing optimism about the future of the world, 42 percent expressed the more empathetic "some" and "quite a lot" responses, whereas among the pessimists, 58 percent did. Among the optimists, the most empathetic response accounted for about 12 percent of all answers; among the pessimists, it accounted for 23 percent.

Two subgroups of respondents reveal somewhat counterintuitive attitudes on the empathy issue. One of our surprises emerges from the division of respondents into those who profess belief in God and those who describe themselves either as nonbelievers or as doubters. Among believers, 44 percent see no equivalence between the Holocaust and post–Second World War massacres, 14 percent see little equivalence, 32 percent see some, and 10 percent "quite a lot."

In contrast, among the nonbelievers and doubters, only 34 percent see no equivalence; 15 percent see little equivalence; a plurality, 35 percent, see some; and 16 percent recognize "quite a lot" of common elements. These findings, albeit modestly, suggest that the effect of belief in God, or religiosity, may be somewhat insulative, making it harder rather than easier to identify with the plight of people in an "out group."

Generally speaking, however, the *greater* the respondents' *past* suffering, the *less* sympathetic their reactions to the Bosnians, the Cambodians, and the Rwandans. First, let us consider some of the components of our exposure-to-suffering model before we discuss a more comprehensive summary. Among people who had lived in Poland during the war, the mean empathy score was 2.12, whereas among those outside Poland it was 2.29, a difference of about 8 percent. More strikingly, among those who had survived the war in concentration camps, the empathy score was 2.07, as compared with 2.42 for all others, a difference of 15 percent. Among those who had received no assistance from Gentiles in their personal struggle for survival, the average empathy score was 2.09, but among those who had received such assistance, it was 2.40—a difference of 13 percent. Among those who had reported losing all or most members of their family, the average empathy score was 2.12, but among those who had reported losing only some or none, the score was 2.80, a rather large difference of 24 percent. Among the older respondents, those between ages fourteen and thirty-one in 1939, the empathy index was only 2.04, but among the younger group—ages one to thirteen in 1939—it was 2.43. This was a difference of nearly 16 percent—with much less empathy among the older group.

The cultural factors that we had associated with isolation from the non-Jewish world, and therefore with more acute suffering in the process, all operated in the same direction. People who had described themselves as coming from nonassimilated families reported an empathy score of 2.11, whereas among the assimilated the figure was 2.44, a difference of about 14 percent. Predictably, analogous differences prevailed among people who had described themselves as coming from very religious families, as compared with those coming from the less religious or even nonreligious backgrounds. Thus, we found that among those from very religious families, 43 percent saw *no* equivalence between the plight of the Jews and the situations of the Bosnians, Cambodians, and Rwandans. Only about 10 percent in this group opted for the most empathetic response. On the other hand, among the "somewhat religious," only 32 percent opted for the "none" response, and 15 percent chose "quite a lot." Among people who had described their backgrounds as "not at all religious," a majority chose the "some" and "quite a lot" responses, with 19 percent in the latter category.

The differences carried over to the reported cultural factors with respect to the present, post-Holocaust period. As indicated earlier, among those who were reporting current belief in God, the empathy score was 2.08, whereas among nonbelievers it was 2.34, a difference of over 11 percent in the same direction. It may be noted also, parenthetically, that among those of our respondents who had classified themselves as regular or frequent contributors to Jewish causes, the mean empathy score on our scale was only 2.11, whereas among those declaring themselves in the "rare to never" category of contributors, the mean score was 2.36, or about 11 percent higher.

When the cultural differences were considered in the more complex model, with those identified as traditionalists versus those characterized as modernists, the difference in degree of empathy was indicated by average scores of 2.12 for the former and 2.86 for the latter—a gap of almost 35 percent.

Looking at the exposure-to-suffering model in all its four aspects, the gap is at its widest. People who may be classified as low-exposure respondents showed an average empathy score of 2.82, whereas the "high-exposure" respondents revealed a score of only 1.75. This represented a difference of 61 percent—by far the most substantial difference in our survey.

It should be noted that people who represented the upper tier of the exposure to suffering model tended to identify themselves with Jewish causes and activities in the post-Holocaust period. Put in another way, the index of Jewish identity in the time since the Second World War was 27 percent smaller for the low-exposure group (7.27 versus 9.86) than for the high-exposure group. The correlation between current Jewish identity and empathy on the compare scale was a predictably negative $-.070$; the correlation between our exposure-to-suffering model and empathy on the compare scale was $-.46$.

In essence, those survivors who had had the most negative assessments of conditions facing them during the Holocaust, whose assessments of the roles of various participants in the Holocaust were the harshest, and who had drawn the most somber and pessimistic inferences from that experience were also least likely to express empathy with people victimized in post–Second World War genocides.

Given our results, it appears that the experience of suffering in the Holocaust, at least in the sense in which we have defined it, is, in effect, inversely related to empathy. It was those who had seemingly suffered more, or even the most, who exhibited the lowest sense of identification with the persecutions of the Bosnians, Cambodians, and Rwandans. And, by contrast, it was the people who had suffered much less who actually identified more strongly with the depredations inflicted in the postwar period on non-Jewish victims in the three instances we employed in our comparison question.

What is also of considerable interest is that given the intermingling, or actually the reinforcement of "culture" with "suffering," as shown in our earlier analyses, it would appear that a stronger sense of ethnic identification is inversely related to empathy directed toward out-groups. There appears to be some significant trade-off here in social attitudes toward the collective "self." More cohesion within may mean somewhat less sympathy without. Perhaps such trade-offs may be related to a more general phenomenon, not merely or only Jewish, relating to the psychological, cultural, and political consequences of what some authors have termed "tribalism."[11]

To be sure, certain significant reservations attach to our conclusion, and those should not be minimized by any means. Our finding is, like the findings of all analogous surveys, a "snapshot in time." In order to be able to establish it as an enduring, dominant feature of survivor opinion, one would need substantial replication—more respondents, more questions on the analogous theme, more occasions on which those questions would be asked and answered.

This question, with all its unavoidable moral overtones, is fraught with some obviously disturbing implications. The survivors, overwhelmingly, favor teaching schoolchildren about the Holocaust (see Fig. 6.1). They do so in the expectation, or at least the hope, that education might help prevent the repetition of what happened to them. But if so many survivors—people who have had the most direct, intense, and prolonged experience of the Holocaust themselves—do not, fifty years after the fact, manifest great empathy for the (arguably *somewhat* different) sufferings of so many innocent others, what hope is there for this classroom education? And does not

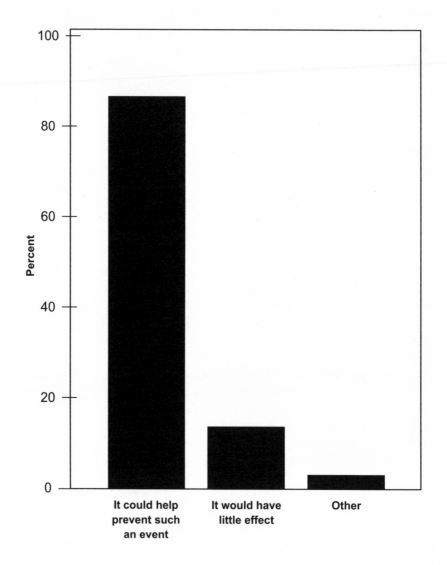

Fig. 6.1. Survivor Views of the Value of Teaching Children about the Holocaust

this particular phenomenon of one's own response cast an eerie light upon the undeniable, tragically indifferent response to the fate of the Jews rendered by the world community of nations in the 1940s?

There is an interesting issue of meaning that may or may not be accurately communicated by the sort of written (or for that matter, possibly even verbal) responses we elicited. This applies to all surveys, not only ours. It is never certain that two or more persons who employ the same expression in response to a question actually mean equivalent things. It is difficult to evaluate the sincerity, the depth of conviction, the thoughtfulness, and certainly various possible nuances involved in people's verbal or written responses to survey questions. Perhaps when X says that something is "somewhat important" to him, but Y says that it is "very important" to her, the actual, behaviorally related difference may not be what it seems. Our subject X may actually be more concerned about the issue than Y perhaps because of the sort of person he is—thoughtful, reflective, absorbed, engaged. Y may be rather superficial and may therefore give answers that she thinks would simply make her "look good" in the eyes of people who administer the survey.

This is related to another problem. Verbal expressions of attitude are not the only possible attitudinal measures. Under some circumstances, they may be much less important than simply behavioral indications. The practical point here is that people who may not express great sympathy for Rwandans in a mail survey may nevertheless be the same people who join with others through civic and charitable Jewish organizations to donate money and bring help and relief to the Rwandan victims of ethnically motivated massacres, whereas some people who express great apparent sympathy in a mail questionnaire may, conceivably, never act in any meaningful sense on the beliefs that they express.

Still, caveats aside, our findings bear upon the question of the transmissibility or convertibility of personal experience and knowledge. Does "information," whether acquired through one's own experience, exposure, and suffering or through learning really enable people to be empathetic toward the analogous, or perhaps only somewhat analogous, experiences of others?

The overwhelming majority of our respondents agreed with the view that teaching children about the Holocaust would serve the purpose of actually preventing its repetition in the future. But, as is evident from the opinions discussed earlier, the survivors have not been putting quite as much faith in educational efforts as Figure 6.1 would indicate. Clearly, a great deal of information about the Holocaust had been disseminated before the time of our survey in 1996–98. Yet, very few survivors agreed with the proposition that "a great deal" had been learned thus far about the Holocaust. A substantial majority of our respondents believed either that very little or nothing had been learned, and, perhaps even more importantly, that whatever may have been learned, it would not make much difference anyway.

As indicated earlier, only a minority of our respondents was willing to commit itself to the proposition that it was unlikely that the Holocaust would ever be repeated. Even fewer thought it a certainty that it would not recur. Many more expressed pessimistic views. Survivors who saw anti-Semitism weakening since 1945 constituted a distinct minority of those answering the question about world trends in attitudes toward Jews.

These responses taken together seem to suggest that while most survivors of the Holocaust tend to see their experience under Nazi rule as basically unique, there is no consensus among them as to how the Holocaust relates to other genocidal events of the century. Moreover, the paradox of Figure 6.1 notwithstanding, the survivors display considerable pessimism with respect to the learning potential implicit in the Holocaust.

NOTES

1. Steven T. Katz, *The Holocaust in Historical Context* (New York: Oxford University Press, 1994), pp. 15, 27. See also the discussion, by various authors, in *Is the Holocaust Unique? Perspectives on Comparative Genocide*, ed. Alan S. Rosenbaum (Boulder, Colo.: Westview Press, 1996).

2. Katz, *The Holocaust in Historical Context*, p. 54.

3. A. E. Redgate, *The Armenians* (Oxford: Blackwell, 1998), p. 272.

4. See, for example, Michael Bloch, *Ribbentrop* (New York: Bantam Press, 1992), esp. pp. 353–57, 372–74, on the activities of Nazi Foreign Minister Joachim von Ribbentrop, who sought to persuade Germany's allies throughout Europe to kill their Jews, or at least to hand them over for precisely this purpose to Nazi Germany.

When, on completion of their conquest, the Romans leveled the city of Carthage, they also "buried it deep in sand and scattered salt upon the site so that nothing should ever grow again where it had stood" (John Peddie, *Hannibal's War* [Thrupp Stroud, U.K.: Sutton Publishing, 1997], p. 204). There is, however, no record of an extermination campaign against persons of Carthaginian extraction throughout the Roman empire and among its neighbors after 146 B.C.E. See T. A. Dorey and D. R. Dudley, *Rome against Carthage* (London: Secker and Warburg,

1971). Some fifty thousand Carthaginians were allowed to surrender by the Romans, their lives spared, upon the fall of the city in 146 B.C.E. These fifty thousand were all sold into slavery.

5. Yehuda Slutsky, in his article on pogroms in the *Encyclopedia Judaica*, vol. 13 (1972), pp. 696–98, notes that in the 1880s in Russia, a three-day pogrom in Kiev "was perpetrated . . . before the eyes of the governor-general and his staff of officials and police force while no attempt was made to restrain the rioters." On the other hand, in Odessa, where 300 died, and in some other cities during the early 1900s, pogroms "were inspired by government circles. The local authorities received instructions to give the pogromists a free hand and to protect them from the Jewish self-defense." But at least one pogrom in 1906 in Siedlce was "directly perpetrated by the police and military forces."

6. Richard G. Hovannisian, ed., *The Armenian Genocide: History, Politics, Ethics* (New York: St. Martin's Press, 1992), p. xv. See also Christopher J. Walker, "World War I and the Armenian Genocide," in *The Armenian People from Ancient to Modern Times*, ed. R. G. Hovannisian, vol. 2 (New York: St. Martin's Press, 1997) pp. 239–73. Also on earlier massacres, see E. B. Bliss, *Turkey and the Armenian Atrocities* (New York: Edgewood Publishing, 1986).

7. Edward L. Nyankanzi, *Genocide, Rwanda and Burundi* (Rochester, Vt.: Schenkman Books, 1998), pp. 1, 94. For dramatic accounts of killings in Rwanda, see especially Peter Gourevitch, *We Wish to Inform You That Tomorrow We Will Be Killed with Our Families: Stories from Rwanda* (New York: Farrar, Straus, and Giroux, 1998). As the author notes, although the killing was "low tech—performed largely by machete—it was carried out at dazzling speed; of an original population of about seven and a half million, at least eight hundred thousand people were killed in just a hundred days" (p. 1).

See also the work of Carole Rogel, The Breakup of Yugoslavia and the War in Bosnia (Westport, Conn.: Greenwood Press, 1998), who defines ethnic cleansing in the following manner: "A Serbian war aim implemented first in Eastern Croatia in the summer of 1991 and then rigorously applied in Bosnia-Herzegovina after fighting began there in April 1992. In Bosnia the victims were primarily Bosnian Muslims who were harassed, terrorized, raped, and murdered. Some were forced into detention camps; others were driven from their homes and became refugees. The policy of genocide was probably initiated by Belgrade, and evoked comparisons to the Holocaust against European Jews in World War II" (p. 158). See also Jim Seroka and Vukasin Pavlovic, eds., *The Tragedy of Yugoslavia: The Failure of Democratic Transformation* (New York: M. E. Sharpe, 1992). Among many other sources, see for example House Commission on Security and Cooperation in Europe, *Mass Graves and Other Atrocities in Bosnia: Hearing before the Commission on Security and Cooperation in Europe*, 104th Cong., 1st sess., 6 December 1995, and House Committee on International Relations, *Human Rights, Refugees, and War Crimes: The Prospects for Peace in Bosnia: Hearing before the Committee on International Relations*, 104th Cong. 1st sess., 15 November 1995.

8. Deborah Lipstadt, *Beyond Belief: The American People and the Coming of the Holocaust* (New York: The Free Press, 1986), p. 278, observes that during the Holocaust the American press "refused to light its 'beacon' making it virtually certain that there would be no public outcry," and that, in general, it reacted to the story of the persecution and destruction of the Jewish people with "equanimity" and "dispassion."

9. Wilfred D. Deac, *Road to the Killing Fields: The Cambodian War of 1970–1975*, (College Station, Tex.: Texas A & M University Press, 1997) pp. 234–35.

10. Ben Kiernan, *The Pol Pot Regime: Race, Power, and Genocide in Cambodia under the Khmer Rouge, 1975–79* (New Haven, Conn.: Yale University Press, 1996), pp. 295–96.

11. Jack David Eller, *From Culture to Ethnicity to Conflict: An Anthropological Perspective on International Ethnic Conflict* (Ann Arbor: University of Michigan Press, 1999), defines "ethnicity" as "consciousness of difference and the subjective salience of that difference. It is also mobilization around difference—a camaraderie with or preference for socially similar others. It is in this sense a 'familial' kind of relationship, with emotional characteristics—a bond, a tie, a sentiment, an attachment. . . . Ethnicity is . . . subjective, even while it is based on, refers to, or invokes 'objective' or shared cultural or historical markers" (p. 9). "Ethnicity does not always or necessarily make for conflict" (p. 11), but Eller notes its unique potential for making absolute, unique claims out of primordial grounds from the fabric of ethnicity and hence the potential for being "extremely corrosive" to various forms of political integration (p. 16). Contemporary nationalism, as a political vehicle of ethnicity, he notes, "connotes particularism, not homogenization; separation, not inclusion" (p. 24).

See also Kenneth Christie, ed., *Ethnic Conflict, Tribal Politics: A Global Perspective* (London: Curzon, 1998), p. 6, who says in his introduction, discussing extant literature, that "tribes [may be seen as] . . . operating at a high level of internal conformity, coupled with external conflict, with little tolerance for others (others being those who have set themselves outside the collectivity or have been excluded from it by characteristics or conscious decisions [of] those who are in [power]). . . . Hence, the notion that retribalization carries with it the idea that society is regressing from a higher form (e.g., civil society) to the older more primitive form of the tribe." He also writes of an inherent "inclusiveness and exclusiveness of the tribe."

Anthony D. Smith, *Ethnic Revival* (Cambridge: Cambridge University Press, 1981), p. 195, notes that ethnic nationalism represents and defends "unique, incommeasurable, symbolically personalized" communities. This implies an aspiration to high internal cohesion opposed to the "mechanical, impersonal culture of the state" and presumably other, more amorphous, communities.

On this subject, see likewise Feliks Gross, *The Civic and the Tribal State: The State, Ethnicity and the Multiethnic State* (Westport, Conn.: Greenwood Press,

1998); and Stephan Van Evera, Jack Snyder, and Karen Ballentine, "Hypotheses on Nationalism and War," *Nationalism and Ethnic Conflict*, ed. Michael Brown et al. (Cambridge: MIT Press, 1997), pp. 26–60. "Nations can co-exist most easily . . . when they share a common image of their mutual history and one another's current conduct and character. . . . Relations are worst if images diverge in self-justifying directions" (p. 47). For the relationship between "tribe" and "nation," see Anthony D. Smith, *Theories of Nationalism* (London: Duckworth, 1971), p. 180: "[The tribe] is a relatively small group of people who share a common culture and who are descended from a common ancestor. The tribe is the largest social group defined in terms of kinship and is normally an aggregate of clans, intermediate to nationality."

Chapter 7

THE PART-TERM SURVIVORS

In this chapter we look at those victims of the Holocaust who, for a variety of reasons, did not spend the duration of the war in territories under Nazi control or influence. Most of this group consists of persons who had escaped from western Poland to Soviet-occupied eastern Poland, and who were subsequently transported—voluntarily or involuntarily—into the deeper recesses of the Soviet Union. They thus escaped the advancing German troops once Operation Barbarossa had begun. In a few cases, these survivors were people who fled westward, from Poland (and in one case, Austria) after the war began. One person managed to get to Switzerland; another fled to Lithuania, and through a circuitous route through the Far East, reached the United States before the end of the war.

What distinguished this group from the rest of our survivors is that they did not directly experience the effects of Nazi policy toward Jews after the Wannsee Conference of January 1942, considered the key threshold of the Final Solution: with its plan for mass gas chamber liquidations of the Jewish population of Europe.

Nevertheless, these people did share a number of important characteristics with the rest of the survivors. They were generationally and culturally similar to the other survivors. Their roots were found in the same European societies. In most cases, they shared the human and material losses suffered by the full-term, 1939–45, survivors. Whereas 90 percent of the latter reported losing either all or most family members in the Holocaust, equivalent family losses were reported by 86 percent of respondents among the former group. Those who reported losing only some or none of their family members made up 10 percent of the full-term survivors but 14 percent of the part-term survivors. This was a difference, but hardly an overwhelming one.

There were also roughly equivalent losses between the two groups in terms of property. Generally speaking, Jews who had escaped to the Soviet Union in 1939 or 1940, or even early 1941, took no more than a few meager personal belongings with them—a suitcase or two at best. Homes, houses, all sorts of businesses and real property, were left behind and lost as certainly and as inevitably as was the case with the so-called full-term survivors. The Polish government, Communist or post-Communist, paid no reparations to private Jewish individuals for any material losses they may have suffered as a consequence of the Holocaust—even if the appropriators of the stolen property were Poles.

Although the part-term survivors did not experience the post-Wannsee treatment of European Jewry, they did generally experience the initial occupation and to some degree the early harassment of Jews by Nazis. They therefore had some firsthand knowledge of the conditions of Jews—and others—under Nazi occupation. Moreover, they shared in the suffering caused by Hitler's war against the Jews, even if much of this suffering occurred not at the hands of the Germans but rather at the hands of their temporary hosts—the Russians. Many of the Jews who had fled to the East spent the war years in Soviet prisons and hard-labor camps, where maltreatment and malnutrition represented standard treatment of inmates. These were very bitter years in their lives: there were few freedoms and few amenities, as well as hunger, cold, and various degrees of mistreatment. Even for those Jews in the Soviet Union who were not incarcerated, life was generally harsh and bleak. Indirectly, however, it was the Nazi invasion of Poland and the persecution of the Jews that drove these people into the hands of their less than genial hosts.

There was still another sense in which the two groups of survivors were linked. For the most part, they have been socially connected in their postwar lives in the United States, Canada, or Israel. Common origins, analogous backgrounds, linguistic and cultural commonalties, and common Jewish social interests brought and kept these two survivor groups together, usually for many years. In a sense, therefore, they constituted one reference group, with significant social and cultural bonds over many years. Based on their affinities, one might expect the two groups of survivors to have shared much of their world outlook.

In this particular case, however, there were also some important differences between our larger, full-term survivor group and the smaller, part-term survivor group. For one thing, the part-term group was, on average, much older. While among the full-term survivors 38.5 percent were people who were less than thirteen years old in 1939, the equivalent age group constituted only 8.8 percent of the part-term survivors—more than a fourfold difference. Among the full-term survivors, 57 percent came from Poland, but among the part-term survivors, that figure exceeded 77 percent. Among the former there was a virtually even distribution between men and women. But among the latter, over 71 percent were men, and only about 29 percent were women (see Table 18).

The part-term survivors were more substantially drawn from larger cities and were more likely to come from nonreligious families. The two groups, however, were virtually equal in current material affluence and in life satisfaction scores. Their backgrounds in terms of assimilation (or nonassimilation, preponderantly), were virtually identical, and the share of believers in the Deity among the smaller group was 49 percent, with only 6 percent clearly identifying themselves as nonbelievers and the rest as doubters. Believers constituted over 56 percent of the full-term survivors, but, apart from the doubters, there were 15 percent in this group who identified themselves as nonbelievers.

Although the part-term survivor group included about 7 percent more respondents with college and even postcollege training, the differences were less favorable to it at the lower rung of educational attainment. The proportion of people with a completed primary education or less was 37 percent in the smaller group, whereas it was only about 24 percent for the larger, full-term aggregate. Some 25 percent of the latter group had completed high school, but among the part-term people, the figure was only 20 percent. Whereas within the larger group there were 26 percent who had completed school at some level between primary and high school, only 11 percent of the part-term group achieved comparable levels of formal training. Taken as a whole, the part-term survivor group averaged slightly lower levels of formal education than did the larger, full-term group.

What implications might all this have on attitudinal responses among the smaller, part-term survivor group? To be sure, there was the presumably unknown effect of direct contact with the Nazi killers during the critical years 1941–45. By and large, the people in this group did not experience long-term incarceration in the ghettos, let alone Nazi concentration camps. They did not need to hide or assume false identities in order to save their

Table 18. Demographic Comparison of Full-Term and Part-Term Survivors

	Full-Term %	Part-Term %
Age in 1939		
Young (1–13)	38.5	8.8
Older (14–31)	61.5	91.2
Gender		
Female	47.3	28.6
Male	52.7	71.4
Nation		
Poland	57.2	77.1
Other	42.8	22.9
Residence		
Large city	57.8	68.6
Town or countryside	42.2	31.4
Employment at Time of Holocaust		
Working	21.8	45.7
Student	69.5	51.4
Other	8.7	2.9
Family Assimilation		
Strong/somewhat	29.1	29.4
Not assimilated	70.9	70.6
Family Wealth		
Very/moderate	73.2	62.9
Making ends meet/poor	26.8	37.1
Family Religious		
Very/somewhat	91.9	80.0
Not at all	8.1	20.0
Family Lost		
All/most	89.9	85.7
Some/none	10.1	14.3

lives as did those Jews of occupied Europe who had escaped the ghettos and the camps. They did not personally witness as much violence and brutality by the Nazis as did the larger group. Perhaps the sufferings of the part-term group were more indirect and vicarious. It was not they but rather their families and their personal friends who were being killed. It was their property that was being destroyed and looted. And it was the Nazis who had forced upon them their bitter exile, and thus were the cause of their grief far from the site of the Holocaust itself.

It is clear that this group of respondents shared to a high degree three of the four elements of our definition of high exposure to suffering during the Holocaust. One of these, of course, was nonassimilated family backgrounds. In this respect, the part-term survivors were virtually identical with the full-term survivors. There were also many older people here with contemporaneous residence in Poland. The last, absent element was incarceration in Nazi concentration camps. Even so, we also know that the partial survivors did not nearly get a complete "free pass" on this score, either physically or psychologically. For many—more than a third—there was a substitution of Soviet camps for Nazi camps, quite different to be sure, but hardly a picnic.

Samuel Honig, a Polish Jew exiled in the Soviet Union, records the following vignette—a recollection of his life in a Russian labor camp, actually not nearly the worst option for Jewish survivors in the USSR:

> It was now late October. In the evening, a cold wind blew from the north. When we woke up in the morning the whole world was white. The wind subsided and the snowflakes were falling majestically to the ground. The snow was dry. It wasn't like at home, rain mixed with snow, and then wet snow. Here the first snow that fell stayed on the ground until spring.
>
> We were issued some old quilted jackets and pants and old fur hats, but no shoes. They claimed the bark shoes we wore were warmer and better than anything in the cold weather. They gave us a few pieces of cloth to better cover our feet.
>
> At the beginning of November, winter was in full swing, a winter we only heard of in books at home. The temperatures started to drop from the beginning to $-20°C$ and later to $-40°C$ and lower. We were obliged to work up to $-40°C$. We were getting up in the dark and returning in the dark. The worst part was the march to our job site. The snow was deep and the wind was bitter in the open spaces. We tried to cover our faces to avoid frostbite.
>
> When you urinated outside, it turned almost immediately to ice. When you had to move your bowels and take off your pants it was a dis-

aster. We tried to hold on. The only consolation was the mosquitoes were gone. The rest of our lot in winter was much harder, physically and mentally. The woods were a relief. It was still and peaceful, and we were able to warm ourselves and cook our meals once we lit the fires. We also had to quit much earlier to be able to return to camp before darkness and had to fill our quota in a shorter time.

Our barracks were always cold, despite the ovens going all the time. The windows were frozen and the outside walls were covered by frost. We slept in all the clothes we had, and were still freezing. We were only able to keep clean with a great amount of determination. I was lucky Mrs. Schwartz, who stayed in the barracks all day, helped me keep my things dry and clean.

Once in a while we were allowed to go to the steam bath. It was only a small one, and for about 400 people it took a long time to get your turn. It felt wonderful to get undressed and wash your whole body.

By December the winter started in all its fury. The snow fell day and night. Our barracks were covered by snow, half way up our doors. Sometimes the wind would blow away the snow from one side and pile it up metres high on the other. It was so fine and dry, just like powder. It was almost impossible to get to work. The roads were impassable.[1]

If the presumably lesser sufferings of the part-term survivors were not in themselves an offsetting factor, the smaller survivor group would probably outdo the larger group in certain respects with reference to all of our attitudinal categories. This is a fairly reasonable inference from the data presented in our earlier analyses.

Advanced age and residence in Poland were factors strongly associated with more negative perceptions of the world, as shown in both in our cognition and learning chapters. They were also linked to a greater propensity not only to assign blame to actors involved in the Holocaust but also to exhibit lower levels of empathy in comparing the Holocaust with other violent, genocidal events of the century and to evidence higher levels of Jewish identification.

Although the smaller group contained relatively fewer women, differences in attitude attributable to gender on all these issues were not sufficiently strong to decisively separate the two groups. A significant demographic difference—about 10 percent—in urban versus rural backgrounds in the two groups was, however, an important attitudinal factor. So was religious family background. The part-term survivors were, in their backgrounds, a more secular group than their full-term Holocaust counterparts, with 20 percent of respondents coming from nonreligious households, as compared with only 8 percent for the latter. Both of these factors would have predisposed the part-term survivor group in the opposite direction—toward less Jewish identification, more empathy on the comparison scale, more positive (or less negative) perceptions in the cognition and learning areas, and lower levels of blame assigned to the several types of participants involved in the Holocaust experience—perpetrators, victims, and bystanders. But secular backgrounds and big-city origins were seemingly offset by two very substantial attitudinal discriminants—age and country of residence.

In the upshot, the part-term survivors recorded lower—less negative—scores on three of our principal scales: cognition, blame, and learning. They were virtually even with the full-term survivors on the Jewish identity scale; and, somewhat surprisingly perhaps, they exceeded the negativity of the larger group in scores on the comparison scale (see Table 19). The mean score for the part-term respondents was 2.09, whereas the full-term group recorded a 2.18 average. On a scale of "none," "little," "some," and "quite a lot," both groups scored slightly above "little." However, the Russian survivors were less empathetic than the full-term group by almost 4 percent.

Indeed, we found that among the part-term survivor group, a near majority of respondents, 49 percent, opted for the "none" response, professing to see no equivalence between the Holocaust and the other genocidal events of the century listed in the question. About 11 percent of this group saw "quite a lot" of equivalence, 6 percent of the smaller group saw a "little" equivalence, and only about a third (34 percent), was willing to say that there was "some" comparability in all these events.

The nonempathetic attitudes were reflected in only one comment volun-

Table 19. Two Survivor Groups' Views on Comparability of the Holocaust with Three Postwar Mass Killings

Comparability	Full-Term		Part-Term	
	Count	Percent	Count	Percent
None	78	39.8	17	48.6
Little	28	14.3	2	5.7
Some	66	33.7	12	34.3
Quite a lot	24	12.1	4	11.1
TOTAL	196	100.0	35	100.0

teered from among our thirty-five respondents in this group: "I believe that no war or any government misbehavior is comparable to the Holocaust."

By contrast, one empathetic respondent noted: "The reaction of the free world is the same as it was to the Holocaust."

On the cognition scale, the difference between the two groups was 8 percent. The part-term group averaged 11.14 and the full-term 12.12, indicating somewhat more pessimistic and negative perceptions of circumstances surrounding the Holocaust on the part of the people who witnessed it all. On the blame scale, the scores were 12.63 and 13.07, respectively, a difference of about 4 percent, with greater culpability attributed to various actors by the full-term survivors, as perhaps one might have expected. The difference was greater still with respect to the learning scale, where the part-term survivors averaged 5.94 and the full-term 6.49. This was a difference of almost 9 percent. It demonstrated considerably greater overall optimism on the part of the people who had survived the war largely in Russia as compared with those who had survived it under Nazi control and occupation.

Given our earlier findings on the relationship between religious family background, gender, and urban residence on the one hand, and Jewish identification on the other, it was surprising that this group of part-term survivors—predominantly male, with strong urban and nonreligious backgrounds—exhibited such a firm sense of Jewish identity.

Scales, of course, aggregate and homogenize responses. They may be useful for the purpose of illustrating tendencies and trends. We think they are. But every scale is open to the charge of lumping some more important responses with some less important responses, and issues that are substantially discrete, in order to create an amorphous whole. For this reason, it may be useful to illustrate some of the major differences between our two survivor entities by focusing on several particular, seemingly crucial questions.

Looking at cognitive aspects, what anticipations of disaster did the part-term survivors have in 1939? Actually, somewhat more alarming than those of the full-term survivors, these anticipations were consistent with their actions: flight, especially flight to the USSR. It turns out that 37 percent of these survivors anticipated total extermination; 40 percent thought the Nazis would undertake severe measures against Jews although not mass killings; 20 percent said they did not know what to expect. Among the larger, full-term group, only 30 percent said they anticipated Nazi annihilation; 32 percent anticipated severe measures, while 6 percent actually thought the Nazis would be no worse than anyone else.

It was not surprising probably, given the Polish origins of most of the survivors from the USSR, that the perception of anti-Semitism as very strong in their native land on the eve of the Holocaust was expressed by 89 percent of the respondents; 11 percent opted for the term "moderately strong." On the other hand, among the full-term survivors, with less than 60 percent originating in Poland, the view that anti-Semitism was very strong in the country of origin was expressed by 79 percent of the respondents; about 17 percent viewed it as "moderately strong," and almost 4 percent opted for the categories of "fairly weak" or even virtually nonexistent.

What were the expectations of *other* Jews, in the judgment of our respondents, at the beginning of the war? According to the part-term survivors, 48 percent saw severe measures but not total extermination as the objective of Nazi policy. Only 24 percent saw total destruction as the Nazi goal in the perception of other Jews. These figures, too, were very similar to those of the full-term survivors: 41 percent of them believed that severe measures—but not total extermination—were the likely Nazi policy; total extermination was the choice of only 26 percent; 25 percent saw Nazi intentions as unclear; and 7 percent allowed themselves the hope that Nazi policies would not be really worse than anyone else's.

An interesting cognitive consensus existed between the two groups of survivors with respect to the diagnosis of Nazi designs in 1942. Among the people who had spent most of the war years in Russia, the summer of 1942 was an obviously difficult time to sort out Nazi intentions. After all, they were far from the scene of the action. Nevertheless, 36 percent said they were certain that the Nazis intended to exterminate all Jews; 27 percent reported that they suspected this; 18 percent said they did not know what to expect; 9 percent did not believe that the Nazis could have such totally destructive intentions; and 6 percent actually thought that the Nazis would try to kill some, but not all, Jews. Among the survivors from Nazi-occupied Europe, the figures were oddly similar. Here, 38 percent reported their certainty in 1942 about the Final Solution; 28 percent suspected it; 16 percent did not know what to expect; 14 percent could not believe the Nazis could really intend this; and 4 percent thought only some Jews might be killed.

Looking at specific questions related to blame and praise, we can see that the part-term respondents tended to blame both fellow Jews and Germans appreciably *less* than did their full-term counterparts. On the other hand, their attitude toward the so-called bystanders tended to be more mixed. In some cases, such as that of the pope, it was actually even more negative.

With respect to the critical query about Nazi destruction of the Jews and German responsibility for it, 63 percent of our part-term group opted for the alternative placing responsibility on "many Germans, Nazi and non-Nazi, but not upon all Germans"; 34 percent placed it upon the whole German people; and 3 percent on the Nazis alone. However, among survivors who had spent all of the war under Nazi control or influence, the division of opinion was much closer, with 42 percent blaming all Germans and 51 percent blaming many Germans; 6 percent blamed only Nazis (see Table 20). Asked whether in recent years they had changed their views about the Germans, 79 percent of our part-term respondents said that they had not. Among those who did change, four individuals (11 percent) said that their views had actually hardened, but three individuals (9 percent) said that their views had softened.

This was a striking difference between the two survivor groups. Among those who had spent the whole war under direct or even indirect control of the Nazis, only 14 percent reported no change of views since the war. Whereas 68 percent indicated that their attitudes toward Germans had become more negative over time, only 18 percent reported a positive change of views. Clearly, there was much less closure in survivor reflections on Holocaust among people who had experienced the trauma of Nazi persecution directly and for a more extended period.

Only 11 percent of the part-term respondents expressed the view that Jews should have nothing to do with Germans in the aftermath of the Holocaust; 20 percent thought that relations between Jews and Germans should be the same as with anyone else; 23 percent advocated "being on guard" against the Germans; and 43 percent believed that German acknowledgment of responsibility was a prerequisite to Jewish-German relations. In sharp contrast, among full-term survivors, a much larger share of respon-

Table 20. Full-Term and Part-Term Survivor Views on Germans Who Are to Blame in the Holocaust

Blame	Full-Term		Part-Term	
	Count	Percent	Count	Percent
All Germans	83	42.8	11	31.4
Many Germans	99	51.0	23	65.7
Only Nazis	12	6.2	1	2.9
TOTAL	194	100.0	35	100.0

dents (25 percent) offered the view that Jews should have nothing to do with Germans; 16 percent believed that relations should be as with anyone else in the world; 15 percent opted for the "on guard" choice; and 39 percent demanded acknowledgment of their guilt as a precondition for dealings with Germans.

This pattern of relatively less antagonism toward Germans on the part of the part-term survivors was demonstrated also, marginally but consistently, with respect to the following question: "Looking back over the years, do you think that what the Nazis did to the Jews of Europe is strictly or especially *German*, or do you feel that other people might have possibly done it, too, given certain 'appropriate circumstances'?" Among our part-term respondents, 83 percent said that what was done to the Jews could have been possibly done by others. In fact, 8.5 percent agreed with the proposition that it could have been done by virtually anyone; an equal number thought that only Germans could have done it. In contrast, however, among our full-term respondents, 13 percent thought that only Germans could have done what they did to the Jews, and only 4 percent said that anyone could have done it.

On the other hand, asked about the roles of Franklin Roosevelt and Winston Churchill, 54 percent of our part-term respondents said that their views of these leaders were mixed, only 9 percent said that they were largely positive, whereas 29 percent said they were largely negative. Among the full-term group, 43 percent of respondent views were mixed, 38 percent were largely negative, and 19 percent were largely positive. The full-term survivors were actually more divided in their views with respect to these Allied leaders.

Among the larger group of full-term survivors, the notion that FDR and Churchill did not do much for the Jews because they concentrated on winning the war was believed by only 17 percent of respondents; 39 percent thought that these leaders simply did not care about Jews. The constraints of their own domestic anti-Semites as an explanation of the Allied leaders' conduct was in effect rejected, with only 1 percent agreeing to this proposition. On the other hand, only 5 percent of the full-term survivors saw these leaders as anti-Semitic themselves.

Among the smaller group or part-term respondents, 43 percent believed that if FDR and Churchill "did not do all that they could" to help Jews during the Holocaust, this was because "they did not really care about Jews," but 30 percent believed that this was because "they concentrated on fighting the war against the Nazis"; 15 percent thought these leaders were constrained in their actions by fear of anti-Semites in their own countries; no one attributed anti-Semitism to either Roosevelt or Churchill.

The smaller group seemed to have a somewhat more idealistic view of why it was that some Gentiles had helped Jews during the Holocaust. A clear majority of 51 percent opted for "humanitarian motives" as the reason for assistance by Gentiles to Jews; 31 percent opted for financial gain; and 13 percent chose friendship as motives of Gentiles. Among the full-term survivors, however, humanitarian motives had the support of only 21 percent of the respondents, and 5 percent opted for friendship as a motive. Financial gain was the choice of 26 percent of the respondents, whereas 48 percent chose a variety of explanatory combinations with a mix of motives, good and bad.

Among full-term survivors, only 49 percent subscribed to the view that efforts by Gentiles to rescue Jews were "somewhat effective." Forty percent saw Gentile efforts as "not effective," while among the part-term survivors, this was the opinion of only 26 percent; 60 percent saw them as somewhat effective. However, asked about the likely world response if the Holocaust had been inflicted on non-Jews, these respondents were divided between those who thought it would have been *definitely* more helpful to non-Jews—67 percent—and those who thought that it *probably* would have been more helpful—29 percent. This was a more negative response than among full-term survivors. Among these, about 8 percent actually believed that the world would have been no different, or even less helpful, if the victims were non-Jewish.

In another variant of this question, only one of the thirty-five part-term respondents (3 percent) agreed with the proposition that Jewish leaders generally "contributed their share to killing fellow Jews," and 21 percent believed that they were selfish and "looked out only for themselves." This left a balance of 74 percent of respondents who either chose exculpatory characterizations or, in a few cases, simply refused to pass judgment on these leaders.

Among the full-term survivors who were willing to settle on a single alternative in order to describe the role of Jewish leaders during the Holocaust, the judgments were more sharply divided. More than 40 percent—a plurality—described Jewish leaders as doing what they could to improve conditions for all Jews. Only 21 percent described them as timid and ineffectual, and 12 percent saw them as acting differently in different places. But 27 percent of these respondents chose the most negative alternative— that they appeased the Nazis at every turn. These divisions of opinion were augmented by respondents who had chosen combinations of alternatives to describe the leaders' roles. Based on our earlier classification of "mixed" (good and bad), "positive" (either two or more favorable alternatives, or a mix of favorable and neutral), and "negative" (two or more unfavorable alternatives, or a mix of unfavorable and neutral alternatives) the remaining forty-odd cases divided roughly 2:2:1 among mixed, positive, and negative evaluations.

When asked about the roles of Jewish community leaders during the Holocaust, our part-term respondents rarely attributed the most negative characterizations to such persons. A plurality of them—42 percent—said that the best description of the Jewish leaders' role was that they were "generally weak, timid, and ineffectual." The most negative alternative, "They tried to appease the Nazis at every turn," was chosen by only two out of thirty-five respondents—all of 6.5 percent; 29 percent thought that the leaders did what they could under the circumstances; 16 percent thought that they acted differently in different places.

There was a very large difference between the two groups of survivors on the culpability attributed to American Jews during the Holocaust. Among the full-term group, 72 percent expressed the view that American Jews could have done much more to help. Only 16 percent said that American Jews were not in a position to make much of a difference in the fate of European Jewry. On the other hand, among the part-term respondents, only 55 percent agreed that American Jews could have done much more, while 31 percent believed that they could not have made much difference in any case. Interestingly, however, only a single part-term respondent agreed with the proposition that American Jews did all they could to help European Jews given what they knew.

On the issue of anti-Semitism on the one hand and sympathy for Jews on the other, among different ethnic groups the responses of the two types of survivors were in part analogous (see Table 21). Although the choices of the most anti-Semitic ethnicities were identical for both types with respect to the top three nationalities, the "distances" between Poles, Germans, and Ukrainians were not. The smaller group, made up largely of Polish Jews, rated Poles more anti-Semitic than Germans by a wider margin. It analogously ranked Germans more anti-Semitic than Ukrainians by 24 points. But among full-term survivors, the spread among these three nationalities was much more narrow. Among the five most sympathetic nationalities chosen by the part-term group, all but one represented Western Europe. Here we note the opposite tendency—the spread between the Danes and the

Table 21. Part-Term Survivor Evaluations of Ethnic Attitudes toward Jews

Most Anti-Semitic		Most Sympathetic	
Group	**Rank/Score**	**Group**	**Rank/Score**
Poles	1 (3.94)	**Danes**	1 (3.70)
Germans	2 (3.26)	**Dutch**	2 (3.09)
Ukrainians	3 (2.47)	**Czechs**	3 (1.47)
Lithuanians	4 (1.41)	**Bulgarians**	4 (1.00)
Latvians	5 (0.91)	**Belgians**	5 (0.88)

Dutch is only 16.5 percent; among the full-term group, the spread is almost 36 percent. In comparing the two survivor groups, these choices seem to indicate that the more exposed, full-term survivors view the differences among the most anti-Semitic entities confronting them as more roughly comparable, whereas the credit which they bestow upon the solidarity and assistance rendered to Jews by the Danes is much more exclusive.

On the issue of religious entities least and most sympathetic to Jews during the Holocaust, there were similarities but also differences. Catholics were identified as least sympathetic by 86 percent among the full-term survivors but only 77 percent of the part-term group. Among the larger group of full-term survivors, nonbelievers accounted for the largest favorable category, with 31 percent, followed by a scattering of religious denominations. Among the most sympathetic within the part-term group, it was, significantly, "don't know." This choice accounted for 54 percent of all responses in this group. It was followed by a scattering of preferences, with 17 percent opting for nonbelievers, 11 percent for Protestants, and the same percentage for Jehovah's Witnesses.

Turning to social strata, we discovered that the three most hostile designations by the part-term survivors went to the clergy, the peasantry, and shopkeepers. The three most favorable or empathetic designations went to trade unionists, workers, and professionals, including doctors and lawyers. However, the most popular response among these survivors, by a wide margin, was "don't know," which was chosen by eighteen of thirty-five respondents—a very telling 51 percent. Apart from the prevalence of the "don't knows," the main difference in the selection of most and least favorable social strata by the two survivor groups related to workers and the very religious. The part-term survivors were more given to positive evaluations of workers, and they were also more dismissive of the sympathies of the very religious.

Among the full-term survivors, only 39 percent viewed the pope as anti-Semitic, 22 percent saw him as indifferent to the fate of the Jews; 25 percent thought he was constrained by fear of Nazi reprisals; 12 percent believed he tried to maintain political neutrality by his silence on the murder of the Jews; and nearly 3 percent believed that he either could do no more or that, in fact, he had done all he could do for the Jews. Among the part-term survivors, the verdict on Pope Pius XII split three ways: 54 percent of the respondents viewed the pope as anti-Semitic, 29 percent said he was indifferent to the fate of the Jews, and 17 percent indicated that he was constrained in helping Jews by fear of Nazi reprisals.

Looking to issues of Jewish identity, it is clear that a key component, focusing on behavior rather than mere opinion, concerned contributions. Within the larger, full-term group, the regular, frequent contributors made up 70 percent of the total, while 29 percent had described themselves as doing so "from time to time"; just 1 percent said they contributed only rarely. The part-term survivors showed themselves to be slightly more frequent and regular contributors to Jewish causes than were the full-term survivors. Among the thirty-five in this smaller group, twenty-seven persons, or 77 percent, described themselves in this most active category; seven individuals, or 20 percent, said they made contributions "from time to time"; and only one person, representing less than 3 percent of the total, responded with "rarely."

An analogous question concerned travel to Israel by our respondents. In the case of the part-term survivors, *every* member of the group—thirty-five respondents—had visited Israel at least once. The average number of trips was 6.86. In both respects, the part-term survivors exceeded the analogous commitment of the full-term survivors. Within the latter group, about 4 percent had never visited Israel. The average number of trips was 5.61, or 18 percent less than within the smaller group.

Among the full-term survivors, only 37 percent said that they discussed the Holocaust with their children "frequently"; 50 percent said that they discussed it "occasionally"; and 11 percent said that they discussed it only "rarely." In fact, 2 percent reported that they never discussed the subject with their families (see Table 22). The part-term survivors were actually *more* willing to discuss the Holocaust with their children than were the people who had experienced Nazi persecution directly and for a much longer period of time. Among part-term survivors, 50 percent declared that they had talked with their children about the Holocaust "frequently," and 44 percent said they did so "occasionally"; just 6 percent said that they had discussed it only "rarely."

Table 22. Full-Term and Part-Term Survivors Discussing the Holocaust with Their Children

Frequency	Full-Term		Part-Term	
	Count	Percent	Count	Percent
Frequently	71	36.8	15	46.9
Occasionally	97	50.3	16	50.0
Rarely	21	10.9	1	3.1
Never	4	2.1	0	0.0
TOTAL	193	100.0	32	100.0

What inferences for the future did the survivors draw from their experiences? Among the full-term survivors, 44 percent declared themselves optimistic about the future of the world; 41 percent said they were uncertain; and 15 percent expressed pessimism. The part-term group seemed, at least outwardly, more guarded in outlook than their full-term Holocaust counterparts. Among the former, 59 percent declared themselves unsure about world prospects for peace, prosperity, and progress for all peoples. About 15 percent were openly pessimistic, and 24 percent openly optimistic.

On the subject of human nature, the full-term group was—somewhat surprisingly—more positive than the part-term respondents. Twenty-one percent expressed the view that human nature was generally good. Only 3 percent thought it was generally bad; 17 percent refused to categorize it; and 55 percent took the position that it was unpredictably good one minute and bad the next. The part-term group split predominantly between two categories: 60 percent thought it was good one minute and bad the next, and 27 percent thought it was too hard to categorize. Only 6 percent thought human nature was good, and even fewer, 3 percent, that it was bad.

But on specific questions, the differences narrowed. How likely was a revival of Nazism in Germany from the perspective of the part-term survivor group? About as likely as it was in the eyes of the full-term survivors. Actually, 51 percent of the part-term group said that a revival of Nazism was unlikely, while 34 percent thought that it was probable; only 14 percent thought that it was happening already. Among Jews who had spent all of the war under Nazi control or domination, 53 percent viewed such revival as unlikely, 25 percent as probable, and 22 percent as already happening.

Did Germany still pose a danger to the world in the last decade of the twentieth century? Among the full-term survivors, 31 percent thought it did, 37 percent said they were unsure, and another 31 percent thought that it did not pose a danger. On the other hand, among the part-term group, 44 percent were unsure, 35 percent believed Germany was still a danger, and 21 percent did not think that it was.

Was anti-Semitism on the rise in the postwar world? Within the part-term group, 26 percent saw anti-Semitism weakening, whereas 37 percent saw it increasing; 17 percent saw it at about the same level as at the time of the Second World War, and 20 percent said it was too hard to tell. Within the other, larger group, the proportion saying that anti-Semitism was on the decline constituted 24 percent of respondents. But those saying that it was on the increase constituted 43 percent, with 32 percent saying it was unchanged. Obviously, this was a substantially more negative judgment than that of the part-term survivors.

Our last analytic category involved summary comments by the survivors. What spontaneous reflections did the victims have about the Holocaust? Approximately 30 percent of our part-term respondents availed themselves of the opportunity to volunteer opinions. Among them were four characteristic themes, all given roughly equal emphasis by our respondents. One of these was the issue of justice—the failure to adequately punish thus far those who had helped prepare and implement the Final Solution. A second theme was intellectual and historical. What events and, broadly speaking, causes were involved in the tragedy of the Holocaust? How could something so terrible happen? A third theme was concern with education as a means of immunizing present-day society against the virus of racism and ethnic hatred. And, finally, there was the matter of security— political, diplomatic, and military—to prevent such a tragedy from recurring.

One of our respondents noted that it was tragic in this day and age to see war criminals "running around the world," evading justice. Something clearly needed to be done.[2] Another survivor noted that the Eichmann trial had the effect of breaking the widespread silence surrounding Nazi crimes against the Jews. Another asked how the whole world could have allowed all this to happen.

Still another, rather atypical individual, suggested that a better investigation into Jewish history was needed to deal with the "role of Jews in killing Jesus"—the main reason, as he put it, for the hatred of Jews in Europe. Another said that it was necessary to educate youth, Jewish and non-Jewish, about the dangers of racial hatred and its effect upon people's minds. Still another wrote that the great Allied powers of the Second World War knew what was being done to the Jews by the Nazis but chose to ignore it and kept silent for selfish, political reasons. This matter, he implied, clearly deserved rigorous inquiry.[3] One respondent advocated the need to fight extreme manifestations of both nationalism and religion, which have recently brought so much grief in Yugoslavia and in Africa. Another respondent said that the world would soon come to regret the fact that Germany has again been allowed to become an industrial giant.

Finally, one of the survivors urged that a film of then General Dwight D. Eisenhower visiting the death camps and gas chambers left behind by the defeated Nazis should be shown to all those people around the world who still continue to deny the reality of the Holocaust.

With both survivor groups, the comments offered spontaneously by our respondents were similar in their frequency—about 30 percent in each group chose to write such comments; and they were also similar in most of the topics mentioned. But there was an important difference, quantitative and qualitative. There was seemingly a greater sense of anguish among the full-term survivors, strong evidence of the continuing pain and unspeakable nightmare born of the experiences of what they had faced during the Holocaust.[4] It was clearly not accidental that the full-term survivors were significantly less likely to talk about the Holocaust with their families than were the people who had spent much of the war in Russia.

Arguably, suffering may be seen as subjective. What brings great trauma to one person does not necessarily bring it to another—or at least not with an equivalent effect. But, with all the possible caveats, seeing one's family members or closest friends killed, or being taken to be killed, and living in the perpetual fear for one's own life, that one effectively has forfeited one's life in the eyes of the state, is a more dreadful experience than feeling cold and hungry, or living in cramped and uncomfortable quarters, or being forced into menial and exhausting work, or having one's freedoms severely restricted—or even all of these things together.

Although we defer a full-scale discussion of the responses of the full-term survivors to the concluding chapter, two differences between them and those of the survivors who mostly spent the war years in the Soviet Union may be pointed out. Quantitatively, there was much greater concentration among the former on just two basic issues: the seemingly unanswerable query as to why it happened and how it could possibly have happened, and the question of justice, still substantially thwarted and denied: how could it be that having inflicted such prolonged and unbelievable horror upon so many people, so relatively few murderers and tormentors suffered punishment, and so many got away, to all appearances without any serious consequence to themselves? The qualitative aspect of the difference was in the sense of anguish evident in so many comments: a language of sadness and pain, and profound disappointment with the sensibilities of civilized humanity. It was also a language of deep anxiety. If something so awful had happened under such unlikely circumstances—by civilized Germany against civilized Europeans—might it not happen again, even "here," wherever that "here" might be?

NOTES

1. Samuel Honig, *From Poland to Russia and Back, 1939–1946* (Windsor, Ont.: Black Moss Press, 1996), pp. 118–19. For other accounts, Bernhard Roeder, *Katorga: The Aspect of Modern Slavery* (London: Heinemann, 1958); L. Zorin, *Soviet Prisons and Concentration Camps, 1917–1980* (Newtonville, Mass.: Oriental Research Partners, 1980); and Aleksander Solzhenitsyn, *The Gulag Archipelago, 1918–1956* (New York: Harper and Row, 1985). See also Robert Conquest, ed., *The Soviet Police System* (New York: Praeger, 1968); Peter S. Deriabin and Frank Gibney, *The Secret World* (Garden City, N.Y.: Doubleday, 1959); and Borys Lewytzkyj, *The Uses of Terror* (London: Sidgerick and Jackson, 1971).

2. With respect to war crimes trials and denazification, the record of the Western powers and the revived, postwar Germany has been generally disappointing. Between 1945 and 1949, the Western Allies managed to convict only 5,025 persons of war crimes. Among these, 486 were actually executed. From 1949 to 1962, the German Federal Republic convicted another 5,426 persons, and of those, only 3 were executed. Considering the magnitude and the scope of the Final Solution, as well as all the other Nazi crimes committed over most of the European continent in a period of 5½ years, these were clearly very paltry numbers. (It should be noted that the SS alone, declared a criminal organization by the International Tribunal at Nuremberg in 1946, had 240,000 members as early as 1939 and was greatly expanded during the war.)

3. Despite the official British (and Allied) declaration in London about the Nazi extermination of the Jewish people of Europe made on December 17, 1942, Prime Minister Winston Churchill never publicly referred to the killing of the Jews or even specifically to their persecution between 1940 and 1945. Franklin Roosevelt made one reluctant statement in December 1942 and another rather oblique and very brief reference in March 1944. See Richard Breitman, "Roosevelt and the Holocaust," *FDR and the Holocaust*, ed. Verne W. Newton (New York: St. Martin's

Press, 1996), pp. 116–17. Neither Churchill nor Roosevelt ever directly protested to or warned the Nazis about their policies concerning the Jews of Europe.

4. The *American Heritage Dictionary* of 1975 defines *anguish* as "an agonizing physical or mental pain; torment; torture"; i.e., to feel anguish is to suffer. The tenth edition of *Webster's Collegiate Dictionary* (1997) defines *anguish* as "extreme pain, distress, or anxiety."

Chapter 8

CONCLUSION

When one contemplates the survivors' perspective on the Holocaust, a single tragic event inevitably comes to mind. It is an event connected to the heroic uprising of the Jews of the Warsaw ghetto, commenced on April 19, 1943, and extinguished by Nazi power in early May.

On May 12, 1943, the Jewish (Bundist) deputy to the Polish National Council in London, Szmuel Zygielbojm, committed suicide in protest of world passivity toward the murder of the Jews. He left a letter, memorable in history, but hardly noticed by Western public opinion at the time:

> The responsibility for this crime—the assassination of the Jewish population in Poland—rests above all on the murderers themselves, but falls indirectly upon the whole human race, on the Allies and their governments, who so far have taken no firm steps to put a stop to these crimes. . . . My companions of the Warsaw ghetto fell in a last heroic battle with their weapons in their hands. I did not have the honour to die with them, but I belong to them and to their common grave. Let my death be an energetic cry of protest against the indifference of the world which witnesses the extermination of the Jewish people without taking any steps to prevent it.[1]

Alas, Zygielbojm's cry went unheeded. What remained, however, was a survivor memory calling the indifferent and the passive to harsh account.

The "conventional" view of the Holocaust—the view most often found in the relevant literature—identifies the mass murder of the Jewish people

---

as beginning with Hitler's campaign against Russia. It is often seen as started by the so-called *Einsatzgruppen* and then transmuted into the still more massive gas chamber liquidations that followed the Wannsee Conference of January 1942. But what is frequently overlooked is the fact that Nazi mass murder of the Jews really began with the ghettoization process of 1940 and 1941. Here was both the true beginning of the mass extermination of the Jews and also the most flagrant abandonment of them by what nowadays is referred to as the "world community."

In the so-called general government part of occupied Poland, under the auspices of Hans Frank and other German authorities, the Nazis forced millions of Jews into small urban spaces, where a combination of starvation, exposure, crowding, denial of adequate medical facilities, and especially the severing of normal economic activity doomed the lives of the persecuted. Warsaw's 184 calories per day's ration of food was a symbol of the Nazi policy of starvation. Even though it was countered to some extent, at least, by the black market supported by the smuggling of food into the ghetto, how long would the Jews be able to keep alive without recurrent, reasonable income generating opportunities? The ghetto was a doomsday scenario.

In Warsaw, where at times between four hundred and five hundred thousand Jews lived in the ghetto, 60 percent had no source of income at all. Those who did work at various trades and professions generally did so at wages that the Nazis set at absurdly low levels. Among the effects of all this was, as Danuta Dombrowska notes in her article in the *Encyclopedia Judaica*, the discovery in the winter of 1941–42 that 718 out of 780 Warsaw ghetto apartments surveyed for the purpose had no heat and "by the summer of 1942 over 100,000 Jews [had] died in the . . . ghetto."[2] The only reason that this gradual and differentiated Nazi extermination of the Jews (the poor die first, those with some accumulated money die later . . .) did not become wholly transparent was because it had been overtaken by the still more "activist" Nazi extermination program of 1942.

And, of course, what is critically important about the 1940–41 Nazi measures was that the ghettos were much more openly acknowledged, administratively described, accessible, and exhibited by the Nazis than the extermination camps such as Majdanek, Treblinka, or Auschwitz. The chief of the Polish underground army (Armia Krajowa), General Tadeusz Bór-Komorowski, reported in his 1951 memoirs that he had taken rides on a Warsaw streetcar that took him through the ghetto and gave him memorable glimpses into its existence, with its emaciated corpses left all about in the streets.[3] Yet none of these things evoked any public response from Allied leaders, from the leaders of the International Red Cross (who might have understood, one might think, the meaning of 184 calories per day), from the Vatican, from the so-called neutral countries in Europe and elsewhere (including the United States until December 1941). It is only against this somber background of the Final Solution that the reflections and judgments of our survivor respondents may be properly appreciated.

In our introductory chapter we discussed some of the more obvious issues involved in interviewing survivors about events occurring half a century earlier. One might have worried perhaps about memories that were blurred by time and by physical decline, and also, of course, by the overlay of more recent experiences and impressions imprinted in the minds of surviving victims. Judging by the nature of the answers, however, it seemed that the memories were still very strong, even among the very old, people in their late seventies and even late eighties in many cases. There was a remarkable consistency in the responses of virtually all of those who participated in our survey testifying to, among other things, logically coherent views.

When all is said and done, it seems that there was actually a great advantage in conducting this survey many years after the catastrophe itself, at least in certain respects. The world of 1945 and 1946 was probably not quite ready to listen to the testimonies of the survivors on the central issues of the Holocaust. Some of those most remarkably guilty of the crimes of indifference and complicity were still in power or close to it. It was still a world of Winston Churchill, Joseph Stalin, and Pope Pius XII, even if it was no longer the world of Franklin D. Roosevelt.

On the other hand, the survivors of the Holocaust were preponderantly young people who had found themselves with a miraculous gift of life at the conclusion of the war. Their collective and inexorable death sentence had been lifted. For the most part, they were people who were interested in making something of their lives, building or rebuilding careers and families, enjoying their personal freedoms, and focusing on achievements, not on painful memories and recriminations. The survivors were generally not the sort of people who picketed and demonstrated in front of public buildings.

The experiences of many of them suggested that—notwithstanding the interests of our own day—even relatives and friends in places like the United States and Canada in the 1940s and 1950s were not really eager to immerse themselves in the miseries of the Holocaust. They were often made to feel that it was the sort of memory better left behind. More importantly still, to have raised basic issues of culpability involving the by-standers of the Holocaust, in Europe and throughout the world, would have exposed these survivors, in their vulnerable years, at the beginning of their new lives and careers, to public censure, hostility, and to the incurrence of all sorts of social costs as presumed malcontents, ingrates, and trouble-makers. In the late 1990s, most of these problems were largely resolved.

There were generational changes, including leadership changes in the societies from which victims, perpetrators, and bystanders were drawn. More importantly still, the survivors who remained alive in the late 1990s were people whose careers and productive years were now largely behind them. The battles had been fought and won, lost, or drawn. Children had been raised. Retirement incomes, such as they might be, were now secured. It was clearly an opportunity for greater candor than might have been pos-sible forty years earlier.

Looking at the whole study, there is something to be said for the value of reflection, balancing, as it were, the accuracy of memories against the wisdom of experience. One of the important functions of time is to provide perspective on events. There is worth in the judgments of older, more mature people who have lived through the full spectrum, the full com-plexity, of the human journey in this world. It is precisely these people who are our respondents, and although the Holocaust may never have "closure," victims' voices should be weighed seriously in any judgment of what hap-pened, how it happened, and why it happened.

In the view of these older survivors, the Holocaust was a horror inflicted by the Nazis upon the Jews with very substantial assistance, pas-sive and active, of a world external to both. That assistance was rendered, in part, by the silence of people occupying positions of influence and power who knew what was being done to the Jews of Europe but would not pub-licly speak of it. And merely speaking of it would have alerted the victims, forced the perpetrators to face up to their actions, and mobilized public sup-port for the rescue and assistance to the persecuted. Apart from silence was the failure to provide refuge to those escaping, or trying to escape, from Hitler's inferno, as well as the failure to render material assistance, including the provision of arms to those resisting the murderers. This was especially and tragically the case of the Jews of Warsaw in 1943. Obvi-ously, if some had been helped, others would have been encouraged. Yet none were helped, and none were encouraged. The diplomatic interventions of the Allies and of the Holy See in Hungary in 1944 were much too late to have any effect on the bulk of Hitler's extermination of the Jews of Europe.

Among ordinary people, the rank and file of the societies in which the Jews were being deported and murdered, there were some exceptionally compassionate and heroic individuals who helped and sheltered the Jewish victims. But, in much larger numbers, there was passivity and indifference toward the fate of the Jews, and even massive hostility and collaboration with the killers. Local police forces were frequently used to round up Jews for deportation to their deaths, and local citizenry, with alarming frequency, turned in Jews seeking to escape, often in the hope of seizing their property. In Poland, those who helped Jews were at as much risk of being apprehended by Nazi executioners as the Jews themselves, precisely because there were so many people eager and willing to inform the Germans of their whereabouts. In addition there were many, ostensibly anti-Nazi, partisan detachments in Eastern Europe that not only refused to accept Jews in their ranks but actually killed Jews when they had the opportunity.

How frequent were such occurrences? What was the balance between the heroism of the self-sacrificing helpers and the callous brutality of the collaborators? Part of the answer, at least, emerges from this study in the evaluation by the victims of the circumstances that were best known to them. The balance was overwhelmingly negative. It is certainly nothing short of remarkable that in the aftermath of Hitler's Final Solution, the anti-Semitism of the Poles is judged by the survivors to have been even greater than that of the Germans, and that of the Ukrainians nearly equal to that of the Germans.

What role did the Jewish victims play in the process of their own destruction? There were—in aggregate numbers—many people within the Jewish communities of Europe who cooperated and collaborated with the Nazis in a variety of ways during the Holocaust. Some of these people were members of the ghetto militias, some were leaders and members of local Jewish councils, some were inmates of camps. All were subject to Nazi orders and supervision. All acted, in lesser or greater degree, depending on circumstances, as conveyors of Nazi will and regulations to the masses of Jews incarcerated in the ghettos and camps of Europe. Given some degree of authority and discretion to act, how did they use their powers? Did they try to ameliorate the conditions for their fellow Jews and minimize, if possible, the effect of the unspeakable wrong to which they were joined? Or were they perhaps ruthless self-seekers interested only in advancing their own personal interests and in saving their own necks? More than that, were they themselves perhaps sadistic killers eager to do to their fellow Jews precisely what the Nazis were doing? Were they perhaps a mix of many different things?

In all likelihood, given the scope and the chronology of the Holocaust, every conceivable type of person was to be found, at least at some time and some place during those years. Once again, however, the issue is one of ultimate balance. What roles were, or seemed, predominant to the people who actually lived under the dispensations of these Jewish collaborators? There is considerable condemnation among our respondents of the Jewish participants in the Holocaust, with many negative characterizations by many people. The overall balance, however, is not nearly supportive of Hannah Arendt's scenario of the Holocaust.

Many more survivors see the Jews who acted under some sort of official authority during the Nazi regime as doing what they could to help and to ameliorate conditions for fellow Jews rather than the opposite. There is a predominant tendency among survivors to see the collaborator-Jews as victims themselves, forced by the Nazis into horrendous, unwelcome roles at the peril of their own lives. To be sure, some also identify ruthlessly self-serving Jewish collaborators. Many more still see the behavior and the motives of the Jews in authority as mixed, good in some ways, bad in others. But, in the balance, the judgment of the survivors does not make fellow Jews the principal villains of the Holocaust. That distinction is reserved to the Nazi-German perpetrators. And, in the order of blame, Jewish collaborators rank far behind not only Nazis but the collectivity of bystanders made up of the European societies of the time and international actors outside the Nazi sphere of occupation and influence.

Daniel Goldhagen's view of the Final Solution, like Arendt's, is much too dismissive of the role of so-called bystanders in the destruction of European Jewry. The survivors' identification of Poles, rather than Germans, as the most anti-Semitic ethnic entity of Europe during the Second World War is one aspect of it. This identification supports the view that Nazi placement, and development, of major Jewish destruction sites in Poland was not a mere accident. Indeed, if simple logistical considerations had governed Nazi choices, then at least one or more camps such as Treblinka, Majdanek, Sobibor, Chełmno, Bełżec, or Auschwitz would have been located in Germany proper, or perhaps in Austria. By way of illustration, it may be noted that some five hundred thousand Jews from Germany, Austria, France, Holland, Belgium, Luxembourg, and Italy were shipped to their deaths in Poland. Hundreds of thousands were also shipped there from Hungary, Greece, Yugoslavia, and even Bulgaria. This was hardly the simplest, the most direct, or most economical use of the Nazi transportation system. Certainly, by late 1941, and clearly by the time of the Wannsee Conference of

January 1942, Nazi aspirations to the murder of all European Jews were reasonably well crystallized. Did Hitler think that it was politically more palatable to do what he had in mind in Poland rather than in Germany itself, no matter the logistical-economic considerations? No documentary evidence known at this time explains the Nazi choice. But the question certainly strongly suggests itself.

Analogously, looking at the Final Solution still more broadly, if one blames "ordinary Germans" for their passivity, as Goldhagen does, is there not even greater culpability on the part of, say, powerful American and British political leaders, who knowingly refused even so much as to *speak* on behalf of the murdered Jews? What did these leaders say, let alone do, when the Warsaw ghetto burned in April and May of 1943? The survivors, unlike Goldhagen, are keenly aware of this important reality of the Holocaust. In order for the murderers to succeed, many people, neither Nazis nor Germans, had to passively stand aside and let the murders take their course.

Among the perpetrators, our survivor respondents draw certain important distinctions. By a clear majority, they say that the responsibilities for Nazi destruction of the Jews should be placed upon many Germans, Nazi and non-Nazi, but not upon all Germans. On the other hand, by rather decisive majorities, the survivors attribute "enthusiasm" to the actual implementers of the Final Solution; they see enthusiastic support for it on the part of most of the German people; and they believe that the German people back home knew what was being done to the Jews of Europe at least by 1943 or 1944. Understandably, in light of such opinions, there is a great deal of aversion and reluctance on the part of the survivors with respect to any postwar contacts with Germany and Germans.

What is, however, remarkable about the inferences drawn by the victims from their experiences is that, by a significant majority, they believe that what the Nazis did to the Jews of Europe was *not* something that could only have been done by Germans. They believe that, under "appropriate circumstances," other national entities might have been—or might yet be—involved in analogous acts of mass extermination. This is surely a very grim assessment of human potential by people who have experienced its underside as few ever have.

The survivors' recollections of what they knew and understood of the conditions of their lives in 1939 and the years immediately following seem retrospectively tragic. Most Jews did not know what fate awaited them under Nazi rule when the Second World War began. Great uncertainty prevailed. In countless cases, this uncertainty spelled doom for Jewish lives.

Even as late as the summer of 1942—when the trains repeatedly rolled toward the gas chambers of Auschwitz, Majdanek, and Treblinka—there was still no majority victim awareness of the basic Nazi policy toward the Jews of Europe. It is with respect to this very ignorance among Hitler's victims that one can more fully appreciate the consequences of official silence from the non-Nazi and anti-Nazi power brokers of wartime Europe.

In effect, whatever may be said of their moral failure, they assisted Hitler's extermination of the Jews by treating it as a nonevent. The Final Solution was never publicly declared by the Nazis. (No wonder it could be denied by some to this day and in perpetuity!) And to the extent that Hitler wanted to keep it a secret, he was very ably and effectively assisted by his wartime enemies in both East and West, and also by all the prestigious neutrals. No public word from the International Red Cross, the Vatican, Sweden, Switzerland, Portugal, Spain, or Turkey ever really interfered with the Nazi design. The perpetrators and the bystanders could thus feign ignorance even if they had reasons for profound suspicion about events that they witnessed or in which they may have taken part. The victims could continue to believe, or delude themselves, that perhaps these train journeys that the Nazis were forcing upon them would turn out to be less than lethal, after all. On the other hand, from the very outset, victim perceptions of anti-Semitic attitudes within the surrounding, non-Jewish communities were very strong. There was virtually no doubt among the survivors that these attitudes strongly contributed to the success of the Nazi extermination program—with great effect on the possibilities of Jewish flight and resistance.

In examining the "lessons of the Holocaust"—the more general inferences and conclusions about the world that the survivors seem to draw from their tragic experience—we have encountered a paradox. On the one hand, many of our respondents—in fact, a plurality—are attracted to the label of optimism. This is how they choose to designate themselves—optimistic about the future of the world and of humanity. But with respect to many specific questions closely related to the Holocaust, such as the contemporary prevalence of anti-Semitism, the possible repetition of a Final Solution, the prospects of a Nazi revival in Germany, and what if anything the world at large has learned from the Holocaust, survivor opinions are strongly tinged with pessimism and anxiety.

The ray of sunshine in the survivors' outlook is Israel. The support and enthusiasm for the state of Israel is overwhelming. The record of our respondents' trips to Israel greatly exceeds the comparable effort of "ordinary" American (and presumably all other) Jews. Israel is the source of hope and pride for a huge majority of the survivors. It is, to all appearances, a miraculous rebirth following the dominion of death. There is a strong general sense of Jewish identification among the survivors of the Holocaust, a tendency to participate and to contribute to Jewish causes. It is strongest, however, among those survivors whose cultural roots are in the nonassimilated, more traditional and religious families of prewar Europe. It appears that among the survivors, the rule is: the more Jewish before the Holocaust, the more Jewish after the Holocaust. Conversely, however, there is some implication in our data that among people whose Jewish roots before the Holocaust were generally weak, the opposite effect was likely to have asserted itself.

There are some indications here that Jewish identification and belief in God have been sources of comfort and satisfaction in the lives of our respondents. Belief in God even seems to have provided a certain psychological offset to material deprivation: the religious are happier in their lives even when poorer. Although faith in God is more common among those who came from religious, nonassimilated families before the war, our data support considerable general success for God in the Holocaust experience. Over 56 percent of our respondents describe themselves as believers, and even among those who came from assimilated, nonreligious backgrounds, the share of believers is still quite impressive. Although philosophers and theologians may have great difficulty with the role of God in the Holocaust, the survivor respondents, for the most part, appear capable of reconciling their experiences with the continuing presence and influence of the Divine. Especially among people who have had high exposure to the Holocaust according to our definition, there is a tendency toward a higher degree of Jewish identification after the Holocaust.

In our analysis of the empathy question—how the survivors compare the Holocaust with other genocidal events of the twentieth century—we discovered a paradox. Within the full-term group, it seems that empathy is at its lowest among those survivors who have had the most exposure to the brutalities of the Holocaust. It appears to be highest among those who seemingly have suffered, and who remember suffering, much less than their high-exposure counterparts. It also appears, since exposure and Jewish identity are interrelated phenomena, that empathy is inversely related to both Jewish identity and the belief in God. These findings clearly raise questions about the link between the nature of personal experience and the capacity for empathy. The relationship appears to be counterintuitive—to seemingly understand more is to sympathize less? Is it possible that severe personal suffering actually diminishes the human potential for empathy?

Subject to all the caveats discussed in chapter 6, one implication here is an intriguing trade-off between the cultivation of a particular ethnic and religious identification on the one hand and a sense of universalist empathy on the other. The tendency suggested by our findings is that there is a moderately inverse relationship between these propensities. The greater the interest in and emphasis upon the particularism of one's own identity, in this case "Jewishness," the less substantial, it would seem, is empathy projected toward persons and objects in what may be termed out-groups. More attention focused on the in-group may imply a diminution of moral and intellectual energies turned in other directions. This seems to be a matter of great interest and importance. Given the limited empirical base of this tendency in our study, and all manner of complexity in its ramifications, more substantial research is clearly warranted.

In looking at the factors that seem to drive the victims' reactions to their experience, we find that the influences of the past strongly dominate over the influences of the present. When one looks at any of the specific topics—such as drawing inferences from the Holocaust to the present and the future, or assigning blame to particular actors, or simply diagnosing the general circumstances of the Holocaust—the exposure to suffering and the cultural legacy are predominant. What matters most is what happened to the victims during the period 1939–45 and what was the character of the Jewish identifications of their families in the pre-1939 era.

In common-sense terms, if we ask how much difference is there in the survivor outlook depending on any particular characteristic—for example, whether survivors are male or female, or whether they are rich or poor, older or younger—all these are secondary to cultural background and events experienced long ago. The third most important factor seems to be timeless—something that has probably characterized each respondent most or all of his or her life—personality.

It will be recalled, of course, that our definition of exposure was based on four factors: residence in Poland in 1939, age (taking into account greater maturity at the beginning of the war), incarceration in a concentration/destruction camp, and nonassimilated family background. Nonassimilation was associated with greater social isolation of the individual from the surrounding Gentile world. Culture was defined in terms of prewar families' relationship to assimilation and religion and the respondent's belief in God. People who came from nonassimilated and religious families and who professed belief in God we considered to be "traditionalists." Those who came from nonreligious, assimilated homes and who professed themselves either atheists or agnostics (doubters) we classified as "modernists." Personality was defined in terms of professed optimism about world future and satisfaction with life, with optimists and pessimists at opposite ends of this classification.

Taking into account all the questions we asked, and with respect to all of our topics here—cognition, learning, Jewish identity, blame, and comparison—only exposure to suffering and culture were associated with double-digit percentage point differences in outlook. For example, in questions dealing with cognition, difference in opinion based on exposure to suffering averaged 23.8 percent; learning, 22.0 percent; identity, 25.9 percent; blame, 13.2 percent; comparison, 32.4 percent. Differences based on culture averaged 16.2 percent with respect to cognition and 15.5 percent with respect to learning; they averaged 20.0 percent on Jewish identity, 13.0 percent on blame, and 26 percent on comparison questions. Personality was associated with double-digit differences in four out of five of these scales. In each case, that is, with respect to each of the topics of our study, the factors that appeared to be least important in differentiating respondent attitudes were gender, education, and socioeconomic status.

If we were to aggregate all of our Holocaust-related questions in this study, the greatest attitudinal variations would be attributable to differences in exposure to suffering. The average difference on all questions between those highly exposed to the Holocaust and those with less exposure was 23.46 percent. Differences based on culture, between those with more traditionally Jewish backgrounds and those with less, averaged 18.12 percent. Personality differences between people who could be broadly described as optimists as against the pessimists averaged 13.32 percent.

With respect to gender, average scores for women were about 98 percent of those of men on four of our scales—cognition, identity, blame, and comparison. The one substantial, statistically significant difference occurred with respect to the learning scale, with women about 12 percent more negative in their assessments than men.

The correlations of the seventeen independent continuous variables are listed here in the order of magnitude:

1. Exposure to suffering   .208
2. Degree of assimilation of family in 1939   .160
3. Wartime residence by country   .153
4. Culture   .136
5. Religious background of family   .128

6. Mode of Holocaust survival (camp versus hiding, etc.)	.122
7. Belief in God	.111*
8. Family losses in Holocaust	.110
9. Residence before Holocaust (urban versus rural)	.105
10. Life satisfaction	.086*
11. Age in 1939	.072
12. Socioeconomic status	.056*
13. Education	.055*
14. Current material welfare	.054*
15. Outlook on future	.047*
16. Family prewar wealth	.047
17. Personality (optimistic versus pessimistic)	.047*

(Note: Variables with an asterisk refer to opinions or conditions characterizing respondents primarily in the contemporary period when the survey was completed, 1996–98.)

It is remarkable that the correlation between exposure to suffering and all our attitudinal variables is nearly four times greater than that of socioeconomic status. It is also nearly four times as strong as that of education and of current material welfare. Present-day satisfaction with life, outlook on the future, and personality traits related to optimism are not nearly as "important"—as closely linked to attitudes—as, say, religious background of one's family in 1939, or whether one happened to live in Poland or in Western Europe in 1939.

The average correlations of the top nine independent variables, largely based on Holocaust and pre-Holocaust factors, are .137, while the correlations of the bottom eight based largely on respondents' post-Holocaust existence are only .058, a very sizeable difference at a ratio of 2.36:1. Ten of our correlations are significant at the .001 level. Of these, eight derive from the pre-Holocaust and Holocaust periods. There are also twelve correlations significant at the .005 level, and of these, ten are based on the Holocaust and on the pre-Holocaust periods.

Given the obvious uncertainty with respect to the underlying *causes* of attitudinal differences within and between various categories of respondents, we turn to multiple regression for further clues. Here, too, we are handicapped by the fact that in only 90 out of 203 cases do we have information on *all* the relevant variables. This amounts to slightly less than 45 percent of our cases. Limitations notwithstanding, what do the multiple regression results suggest?

The results support, inter alia, the notion of the primacy of the past over the present. Looking at standardized beta coefficients, we find that the first eight largest betas in the blame regression represent pre-Holocaust and Holocaust factors.[4] With respect to cognition, comparison, and learning equations, the first six are also in that category. Only with respect to Jewish identity do we find somewhat greater importance for contemporary variables. Here current material welfare follows in fourth place behind wartime residence, culture, and gender as most important explanatory variable. In four of our five equations, the single most powerful variable is exposure to suffering. Among the thirteen variables reaching T values of 2.0 or better in our five equations, only one represents post-Holocaust experience: that one variable—socioeconomic status—ranks thirteenth in magnitude.

In addition to this more inclusive analysis, we devised a simplified, "bare-bones" test of the factors at work. Considering that past and present events, as well as (quite likely) more timeless factors such as personality characteristics influence survivor attitudes, we chose a few major variables as proxies for a whole variety of the presumed forces at work. Avoiding redundancies, we selected the following independent variables: socioeconomic status as a measure of present-day well-being, religion of respondent's prewar family as a proxy for cultural background, the suffering scale as a measure of the hardships endured by respondents during the Holocaust, and respondent view of the future as a proxy for personality, at least with respect to optimism (or pessimism) on the part of the respondents.

Looking at the effect of these "minimalist" variables on the cognition, learning, blame, identity, and comparison issues, we understandably find the total explanatory power of our regression equations decline. Our R^2 values range from a mere .033 for the learning index to the somewhat more sizeable .181 for the cognition index.

What is of real interest here, however, is that the size and signs of the standardized betas generally point in the direction of our earlier findings. Exposure to suffering is the single most powerful predictor, followed by religion (as a proxy for culture), socioeconomic status, and personality. Note the following summaries:

Order of standardized betas for the cognition scale:
1. Suffering scale   .364
2. Religious background   −.167
3. Socioeconomic status   .053
4. Outlook on future   −.003

Order of standardized betas for the blame scale:
1. Suffering scale   .185
2. Socioeconomic status   .099
3. Religious background   .082
4. Outlook on future   −.040

Order of standardized betas for the learning scale:
1. Religious background   −.122
2. Suffering scale   .110
3. Socioeconomic status   .096
4. Outlook on future   −.043

Order of standardized betas for the identity scale:
1. Suffering scale   .178
2. Socioeconomic status   .136
3. Outlook on future   .130
4. Religious background   .127

Order of standardized betas for the comparison question:
1. Outlook on future   .111
2. Socioeconomic status   .094
3. Suffering scale   −.068
4. Religious background   −.062

Order of averaged standardized betas for all five independent variables:
1. Suffering scale   .181
2. Religious background   .112
3. Socioeconomic status   .096
4. Outlook on future   .065

Among our group of survivor respondents, men and women are closely matched in terms of educational attainments and religious family backgrounds; they are virtually identical in both respects. But women are significantly poorer than men; they rank lower in socioeconomic status, and they express significantly more disappointment with their lives. They are also more pessimistic about the future. However, women declare themselves believers in God more frequently—by a margin of ten percent. As noted earlier, they also exhibit higher scores of Jewish identification. Because the general patterns of Holocaust experience between men and women are virtually the same (i.e., equal proportions incarcerated in camps, as well as comparable family losses, frequency of assistance by Gentiles, and overall levels of exposure to suffering), how could these gender differences be explained? Certainly in part by the post-Holocaust gap between men and women in achievements and gratifications. But some of the attitudinal differences suggest either idiosyncratic aspects of gender or perhaps factors not identified in our study—or, conceivably, both.

Even though our women respondents tended to be more religious than the men, they are actually drawn more frequently from assimilated pre-1939 families and from more urban areas associated with greater secularism. This suggests a somewhat stronger "crossover" attraction for the Deity on the part of female Holocaust survivors. On the other hand, the meaning of "belief" for men and women also seems to be somewhat different. Among men, religious belief is associated with higher levels of optimism about the future and with greater life satisfaction than it is among women (refer back to chapter 3, Tables 4–7). It is also apparent from the inspection of the standardized betas in our regression equations that the attitudes of women are more strongly influenced by contemporary factors, and the attitudes of men more strongly by the legacy of the past.

Among the twenty largest betas—four for each of our five dependent variables—we find that only three pertain to current circumstances among men. One of these, with respect to blame, is the personality scale, representing respondent outlook on the future and satisfaction with one's own life. The others are socioeconomic status with respect to Jewish identity and age. But among women there are five such current factors, including belief in God, current material welfare, outlook on the future, age, and the combined personality scale. On the other hand, it is a matter of more than passing interest that with respect to the learning scale—the broadest measure of world outlook—both men and women survivors respond most strongly to factors outside of current experience. The largest beta in each case is exposure to suffering in the Holocaust, followed by region of residence during the Holocaust.

If the trauma of the Holocaust, and the legacy of pre-Holocaust circumstances, seem to be so strongly reflected in survivor attitudes fifty years later, is there still a way for us to measure, in some manner at least, the mediating impact of all the intervening years? Obviously one way of dealing with this question is to ask whether, or to what degree, respondents with equivalent Holocaust legacies differ in their attitudes depending on how they have fared in their post-Holocaust lives. We have already addressed the more fundamental question of whether—for example, money today, or suffering then—are more important factors in shaping current survivor attitudes with respect to cognition, Jewish identity, blame, learning, and comparison of genocidal events. But to what degree has money influenced, perhaps softened, the impact of suffering on survivor attitudes? To what degree have memories of lives productively and happily lived in the United States and in Canada over the last several decades modified the images and memories of the 1940s?

In order to explore this aspect of the problem, we tested the effect of the association between suffering—our seemingly most powerful variable—and two proxies, as it were, of the survivors' intervening lives: current material welfare and satisfaction with life. Given the substantial attitudinal differences between those who ranked in the upper half of the suffering scale and those in the lower half, how would success or failure in the post-Holocaust period affect the results?

Taking the lower half of the suffering scale at 9 or less and the upper half at 10 and higher, we discover a difference of about 11 percent on average in the five dependent variables. Those in the upper half have higher Jewish identity scores, higher blame scores, less empathetic comparison scores, more negative learning scores, and, above all, their perceptions of the circumstances leading up to the Holocaust (cognition) are much more negative—by about 20 percent.

The difference between those more exposed to suffering who succeeded in achieving *high* levels of material welfare after the Holocaust and those sufferers who only achieved *low* levels of material welfare was only 6 percent across all of our dependent variables. High levels of material welfare usually appear to be mitigating circumstances; low levels appear to be aggravating circumstances. Identity was somewhat lower among the poorer strata.

When we compared the same high-end sufferers on the basis of life satisfaction, the difference between the more satisfied and the less satisfied was on average only 5.5 percent. In fact, it was virtually nil with respect to Jewish identity and blame attributed to various actors; it was, however, about 6 percent with respect to empathy—higher among the more satisfied individuals; it was a robust 16 percent with respect to what people learned about the world from their Holocaust experience—with the less satisfied also more negative in their assessments; finally, we found a 4 percent difference in cognition of pre-Holocaust circumstances, with the less satisfied respondents also more negative in their perceptions.

Those whose sufferings in the Holocaust were followed by travail in the succeeding years tend to have relatively more negative, more bitter views of the past but sometimes more positive inferences about the present and the future. Those who suffered less, and those whose Holocaust experiences were followed by more personally rewarding lives, tend to be significantly less negative in their retrospective assessments. Sometimes, if they are more secular in background and outlook, as shown in chapters 3 and 5, they are actually more pessimistic about future prospects. Such people, however, also tend to be more empathetic, as shown in chapter 6.

Our comparison of the so-called part-term survivors, a group of 35 mainly Polish Jewish respondents who spent several years of the war in the Soviet Union, with the larger aggregate of 203 full-term survivors proved expectedly instructive. Both groups suffered human and property losses under the Nazis. Both suffered through very trying personal circumstances during the war, with many of the part-term survivors in Soviet gulags. But there was an important difference.

The full-term survivors lived most of the war years under a collective death sentence. If confined in camps, they expected execution at any moment. If outside camps, discovery and apprehension by the Nazis meant the prompt end of their lives, often also by summary execution. There were no exemptions, exceptions, or appeals. It was not just a question of hardships; the Jews' right to life had been forfeited to the Nazi state in perpetuity. This difference had an attitudinal impact. The full-term survivors evidenced a significantly greater sense of bitterness, especially with respect to Germans and Germany, than did their part-term counterparts, and to all appearances, also a greater sense of anguish about the memories of the Holocaust. This sense of anguish was reflected in numerous comments volunteered by respondents. Characteristically, these focused upon two themes. One was the uncanny failure of seemingly advanced civilization manifested in the Holocaust. How was that possible? How could so many people stand aside and let it happen? The second theme was the apparent failure of justice in the aftermath of so great a crime. How could so many colossal wrongdoers go unpunished in the postwar world?

Below are some unedited responses to our questions about unexplored topics concerning the Holocaust as well as some reflections on our survey:

> What has happened to all the murderers who were involved in killing and torturing us in the labor and concentration camps?

> Why the educated and highly organized German people did not stop the murder of their own handicapped children and adults . . .

Why so many people willingly participated . . .

How and why can something so terrible happen in a civilized world . . .

How come that the camp at Auschwitz was never bombed by the Allied forces from the beginning?

How seemingly well educated and cultured people could be made to change their behavior willingly and to do things so inhuman, then deny it . . .

Why did not anybody convince Roosevelt to let the ship come to the USA? Instead they sank the ship so Hitler saw this, that nobody cared about the Jews . . .

Justice has not been done. . . . too slow to prosecute the killers . . .

Very little has been done to punish those guilty in our family destruction. . . .

The German people never faced the truth about their crime, never acknowledged the wrong doing. They themselves should write books, make movies, and plays about the Nazi era. It must come from them. . . .
    If God is everywhere how do we explain evil? If God is good how do we explain suffering? How could God let this happen to the Jews? I will never forget or forgive the Nazis. . . .

How come so few Nazis were punished for their crimes after the war?

A thorough study on how people can sink so low to be able to do what they had done. . . .

How a normal, every day person and a very educated person can be turned into a monstrous Nazi killer without remorse . . .

The lack of punishment of Germans involved in Nazis' sponsored crimes, the farce of denazification of Germans in 1945, no retribution demanded . . .

The real factors behind the Nazi party like I. G. Farben, Krupp and other industrialists—the real war criminals who never were brought to face justice. . . .

The role the International Red Cross played, or should we say *not* played, in Europe, during the Second World War . . .

A sense of bitterness, disappointment with Canada for its lack of commitment for bringing justice to the many murderers among us. . . . Acute pain that revisionists spread their lies while we, the witnesses, are still alive . . .

A deepening sense of alienation and loneliness (often hidden) many of us feel as we are aging . . .

Why was the world silent and did not come to their rescue?

The silence of the U.S.A.!

Justice after the Holocaust . . .

We must never forget the past if we want that history should not repeat itself. . . .

We must remember because it could even happen here in the USA. . . .

The distortion that Jews were passive. What had to happen for the world to learn from history?

The brutality, cruelty, ruthlessness of the Nazis—when death was a luxury to many, many Jews. Many more Jews could have survived if they would be able or willing to abandon elderly parents and or young children. The family that stayed together died together. . . .The heroism of the Jewish mothers . . .

Please make sure to mention in your book that there were decent people who helped Jews in Hungary, Slovakia, Poland. . . .

When survivors returned to their respective homelands, they were frequently met with violent antisemitism. Why is it, that this is never mentioned?

Why were we survivors so silent about what happened to us for so long?

As long as humanity maintains faculties of memory and conscience, these voices with their immeasurable sorrow, pain, bewilderment, and anguish, will echo through all conceivable time, a reminder of hell created by men on earth.

The "Holocaust" represents a multitude of events; it stands for millions of individual agonies lived out on a whole continent over several years' time. It is obviously a complex tragedy with all sorts of mutually interactive aspects. There is a technological side to it with its gas chambers and railroads and index cards. There is a bureaucratic side to it with huge Nazi—and also non-Nazi—officialdoms routinely involved in the killings. It occurred within a context of time, culture, and social relations generally identified with "modernity," in an age of mass communications, mass ideologies, highly differentiated social structures, more complex social roles, more powerful economies, and more rapid human interactions than ever before. It has also been identified with some distinctive political forms, especially the totalitarian dictatorship of the Nazi state under the supreme leader and warlord, Adolf Hitler. None of this need obscure the fundamental moral meaning of this catastrophe, the commission of well-nigh unbelievable evil upon millions of innocent human beings by huge numbers of other human beings.

No finding here seems more important than the victims' "three-party" perspective of the Holocaust. The Nazis were the principal executioners, and the Jews their victims, but it could only have happened as it did because many other people either helped the killers or passively stood aside. Certainly not all people everywhere—not "everybody." But most people in most places, most of the time. The heroes were in the hundreds and thousands. The indifferent and the hostile were in the millions. That is the preponderant, overwhelming view of the survivors. Why that was the case is a haunting question with which the remaining victims have struggled all the years of their lives. It is a question ultimately as puzzling as the problem of good and evil in human nature. It will never cease to haunt the survivors, and it will forever haunt future generations.

Reflecting on it with the aid of survivor testimonies points to some fundamental issues of human potential and propensity—even beyond the events of the 1940s. One cannot help but notice that a plurality of our Holocaust survivors professed to see no connection whatsoever between their own earlier ordeal and some of the most dramatic postwar massacres of civilian, noncombatant, and legally innocent populations. Together with those who saw merely "little" connection, there was a survivor majority for a relatively unsympathetic view of three of the largest extermination experiences in the postwar world. This response raises a troubling question. Obviously, the survivors were horribly victimized in Nazi occupied Europe. There can be no "revising" of that fundamental truth. Assigning blame to the victims would be tantamount to a grotesque lie.

But, given the findings of chapter six with respect to the survivor views about Cambodia, Rwanda, and Bosnia, it is not unreasonable to speculate on just how these particular victims might have behaved had they traded places with all those "indifferents" of the 1940s. Is it possible that they, too, would have adopted a position of substantially passive indifference? Certainly, survivors themselves agree, and extant literature supports this view, that Jewish organizations, and by implication many Jews, in the United States during the Second World War fell far short of vigorously challenging American and Allied policies concerning Nazi extermination of European Jewry.[5] (This, of course, is but an illustration of attitudes that were not confined solely to the United States.)

Those who contributed to the Holocaust by commission as well as omission were, for the most part, underneath all sorts of labels and roles, ordinary human beings, even if all kinds of human beings. By the clearly exceptional nature of rectitude, heroism, sympathy, and solidarity among them, the Holocaust experience suggests—to those willing to admit it— that the pathology of Nazism was compounded by a more general human pathology, both active and passive.

In narrowly historical terms, Nazism was a particular, transitory phenomenon. It was a twelve-year criminal mass rampage through Germany and Europe, led by a singularly depraved homicidal maniac. But the Holocaust was not only about Hitler, the Nazis, the Germans, and the Jews, all within a relatively short span of time. It was also about millions of "ordinary people." It was more than an episode in history. As Szmuel Zygielbojm had accurately intimated in May of 1943, the Final Solution was really a test for the whole human race, a test that, on balance, it failed. That failure, insofar as it reflects recurring, endemic human propensities to commit evil, deny evil, countenance evil, is likely to have enduring consequences. The Holocaust is, and indeed already has been, a portent of future cataclysmic human implosions whose precise times and places are generally no more predictable than those of cyclones and earthquakes. But in terms of human potential, such occurrences have been, are, and probably always will be part of the human legacy, its characteristic pathology.

On a vastly greater and more horrifying scale, the Holocaust was an analogue and an amalgam of "ordinary," everyday crimes committed in all societies known to history, such as murder, assault, arson, mayhem, robbery, theft, rape, and fraud—all morally damnable and all justly punishable crimes with the addition of such significantly recurring episodes as war and terror as well.

Optimistic descendants of the Age of Reason might perhaps believe that such acts are, or were, the mere consequence of material deprivation or want of proper learning, or, somehow, of extraordinary circumstances. Is it not likely, however, that evil acts have repeatedly sprung from motives that were well understood by Jeremiah, Sophocles, Shakespeare, Cervantes, and Freud? That they derive from profoundly irrational and self-destructive impulses of the human personality? From that darker side of human nature, usually avoided in optimistic discourse, where hate, greed, fear, delusion, envy, mindless mayhem, bloodlust, and rampant sadism hold sway—just as far as vision and memory can reach?

Evil deeds have historically flourished not only in consequence of greed, hate, or want, but also in consequence of human indifference: a frightening propensity to see other human beings—at various times and places—in purely impersonal or instrumental terms, as if they were inanimate objects wholly outside our own individual sensibilities. Empathy may be a very strong human characteristic, but so is the complete lack of empathy. Evil instigators find dispassionate followers, "ice-cold" accomplices, and passively accepting observers, usually through the time-honored medium of commonly shared self-interests.

The continuing significance of the Holocaust for the future derives precisely from the fact that it was *not* an aberration in the stream of human experience. Aberrations can be safely left to the attention of antiquarians. The Holocaust was a sinister and foreboding magnification of humanity's most pathological tendencies, tendencies not easily separated from our fundamental nature—tendencies that are evident in the perpetual, though ever fluctuating, struggle between love and hate, between the affirmation of life and death, and between good and evil.

The recognition of humanity's endemic evildoing is one of the historic insights of Judaism. It is expressed in the universal, permanent, and most solemn observance of Atonement as well as the attribution of the sovereign prerogative of mercy to the Divine.

NOTES

1. See Bernard Wasserstein, *Britain and the Jews of Europe, 1939–1945* (Oxford: Clarendon Press, 1979), pp. 304–305.

2. D. Dombrowska, "Warsaw: Holocaust Period," in *Encyclopedia Judaica*, vol. 16 (Jerusalem: Keter Publishing, 1972), pp. 342, 348.

3. Tadeusz Bór-Komorowski, *Armia Podziemna* (Underground Army), 3d ed. (London: Vritas, 1951), p. 96. The Warsaw ghetto was actually connected to the outside world by a regular telephone network until late 1942. The ghetto was visible from many buildings in adjacent streets of the city. Many Polish workers daily

visited the ghetto to perform their jobs in Nazi-operated factories. Some Jewish workers were allowed to go outside the ghetto for analogous purposes. The ghetto was not really a "secret"—except perhaps to those who would rather not know about it.

4. As Jan Kmenta, *Elements of Econometrics*, 2d ed. (New York: Macmillan, 1986), p. 422, explains it: "The idea behind [beta coefficients] is to measure all variables in terms of their respective standard deviations. The . . . beta coefficients . . . measure the change in the dependent variable corresponding to a unit change in the respective explanatory variable, holding other explanatory variables constant and measuring all changes in standard . . . units." Jeffrey Wooldridge, *Introductory Econometrics: A Modern Approach* (Cincinnati: Southwestern College Publishing, 2000) p. 182, says: "In a standard OLS equation, it is not possible to simply look at the size of different coefficients and conclude that the explanatory variable with the largest coefficient is 'the most important.' . . . But when each x_j has been standardized, comparing the magnitudes of the resulting beta coefficients is more compelling."

5. Among others, see the works of Henry Feingold, Seymour Maxwell Finger, Hannah Klinger, and Walter P. Zenner, cited in earlier chapters.

p. 170

APPENDICES

APPENDIX A: Questionnaire

JUDGMENT OF THE SURVIVORS
Your opinions are welcome on any questions.
Please disregard any questions you do not wish to answer.
Your anonymity will be protected.
Circle the best answer or fill in the blank.

1. Where did you live when the Second World War broke out? _____

2. Age in 1939? _____

3. Gender: Male _____ Female _____

4. Current marital status: Single ___ Married ___ Widowed ___ Divorced ___

5. Was your place of residence before the Holocaust:
   a. A large city
   b. A small town
   c. A village
   d. The countryside

6. Occupation before the Second World War and/or at the beginning of the Holocaust:
   a. Your parent(s) _____
   b. Yourself, if applicable _____

   _____

7. Would you say that your family before the war was:
   a. Very well-off
   b. Moderately well-off
   c. Making ends meet
   d. Relatively poor

8. Would you describe your household before the Holocaust as:
   a. Very religious—observed shabatt, kashrut, all holidays
   b. Somewhat religious—observed major holidays, kashrut at home
   c. Not at all religious, but identifiably Jewish
   d. Other: _____

9. Before the Holocaust, were you:
   a. Working
   b. Attending school
   c. Too young to work or attend school
   d. A housewife
   e. Unemployed
   f. Other: _____

10. Was your family before the war assimilated into the non-Jewish society?
    a. Strongly assimilated
    b. Somewhat assimilated
    c. Not assimilated

11. What was the primary language spoken at home when you were at home?

    _____

12. What is the highest level of education you have completed?
    a. Primary school (first six grades)
    b. Middle school
    c. High school
    d. College
    e. Postgraduate education or degree
    f. None of the above

13. What was your main occupation in the years after the Holocaust?

    _____

14. How would you describe your own material welfare?
    a. Well-off or better
    b. Making ends meet
    c. Relatively difficult

15. Looking back on your life at this point, would you say you feel—all things considered:
    a. Highly satisfied
    b. Moderately satisfied
    c. Somewhat disappointed
    d. Seriously disappointed

16. With respect to your immediate family (grandparents, parents, siblings, spouse, children, aunts, uncles, nieces, and nephews) would you say that in the Holocaust, you lost:
    a. Virtually all such relatives
    b. Most of these relatives
    c. Some of these relatives
    d. None of these relatives

17. During the Holocaust, where or how did you survive?
    a. Under a Gentile identity
    b. In hiding
    c. In a partisan unit
    d. In a concentration camp
    e. Other—explain: _____

18. How did you estimate Nazi intentions toward Jews at the start of the war?
    a. I did not think that *in practice* the Nazis would be any worse in their treatment of Jews than anybody else.
    b. I did not know what to expect.
    c. They planned severe measures against Jews but not mass killings of innocent persons.
    d. They planned the total extermination of the Jews.
    e. Cannot recall.

19. In terms of the above expectations, do you think most *other* Jews in the country where you lived believed at the outset of the war that
    a. *In practice* the Nazis would be no worse in their treatment of the

Jews than anybody else.

b. The prospects for Jews were unclear.

c. Hitler planned severe measures against Jews but not mass killings of innocent persons.

d. Hitler planned the total extermination of the Jews.

e. Cannot recall.

20. Would you say that by the summer of 1942, you were aware of a Nazi attempt to exterminate all Jews?

a. Did not believe that the Nazis really could have such an intention

b. Did not really know what to expect

c. Believed the Nazis would want to kill some Jews, but not all or most

d. Suspected this, but was not yet sure

e. Definitely yes

f. Cannot recall

21. What was your impression of those Germans who assisted in the Final Solution?

a. Most did not relish their jobs, but feared opposing their superiors' orders.

b. Most were probably unaware of the results of their actions.

c. Most acted with indifference, rather than hatred.

d. Most acted willingly, as if enjoying the job.

e. Other or don't know.

22. Would you say that the responsibility for Nazi destruction of Jews is something that must be placed directly:

a. On top Nazi leaders only

b. Only upon the Nazis themselves

c. Upon many Germans, Nazi and non-Nazi, but not upon all Germans

d. Upon the whole German people

e. Other or don't know

23. What is your opinion of the claim sometimes made that most people in Germany did not know what was happening to the Jews of Europe, even as late as 1943 or 1944? You actually:

a. Believe it

b. Feel uncertain about it
c. Do not believe it
d. Have no opinion
e. Other—explain: _____

24. How do you believe that the German people of the 1940s, by and large, supported Hitler's program of extermination of the Jews?
   a. Generally knew nothing about it
   b. Did not support it, but were forced into it by the Nazis
   c. With reluctance
   d. With indifference
   e. With enthusiasm
   f. Other—specify: _____
   g. Don't know; cannot say

25. Looking back over the years, do you think that what the Nazis did to the Jews of Europe is strictly or especially *German*, or do you feel that other people might have possibly done it, too, given certain "appropriate circumstances"?
   a. Only Germans
   b. Possibly others as well
   c. Anyone
   d. Other or don't know

26. What is your opinion about a statute of limitations for prosecuting people who participated in the Nazi Final Solution?
   a. There should be a time limit on the prosecution of such persons.
   b. It should depend on the type of case involved.
   c. There should be no time limit on these crimes.
   d. Other or don't know.

27. If you were to travel to Germany, or stay there for an extended period of time (as perhaps you have done), would you say that personally you would feel:
   a. Quite comfortable about it
   b. Ambivalent about it
   c. Quite uncomfortable
   d. Unwilling to do it
   e. Other or don't know

28. How would you feel about travel or stay in Austria?
    a. Quite comfortable about it
    b. Ambivalent about it
    c. Quite uncomfortable
    d. Unwilling to do it
    e. Other or don't know

29. At any time during the Second World War, did you believe that Hitler and the Nazis would eventually win?
    a. Yes, throughout the whole war
    b. Yes, from time to time
    c. Yes, during the first few years of the war
    d. Never
    e. Cannot recall

30. How do you feel Jews should be disposed toward Germans after the war?
    a. They should deal with them as with anybody else, dealing with each situation separately.
    b. They should be on guard against them, but not shun all contacts with them.
    c. They should insist that they acknowledge their guilt and change their attitudes toward Jews as a condition of any individual contacts.
    d. They should refuse to have anything to do with any Germans—boycott them and their products.
    e. Don't know or other.

31. Have your feelings changed in more recent years?
    a. Yes, my feelings have softened.
    b. No, nothing has changed.
    c. Yes, my feelings have hardened.

32. How important, in your view, was anti-Semitism in the country where you lived in making it possible for the Nazis to carry out the extermination of the Jews as effectively as they did?
    a. Not particularly important/not relevant
    b. Somewhat important/relevant
    c. Very important/highly relevant
    d. Don't know; cannot say

33. How would you assess the strength of anti-Semitism in the country where you lived?
    a. Nonexistent
    b. Fairly weak
    c. Moderately strong
    d. Very strong
    e. Don't know; cannot say

34. Looking back over the Holocaust, how do you see the role of non-Jews in the country where you lived? In general, would you say that they:
    a. Effectively opposed the liquidation of Jews
    b. Opposed the liquidation, but were powerless to thwart it in any substantial way
    c. Were divided in their attitudes toward the liquidation
    d. Passively accepted the liquidation of Jews
    e. Cooperated with and supported the liquidation of Jews
    f. Don't know; cannot say

35. Do you think more Jews would have been willing to risk escape from ghettos and camps if they felt non-Jews were more sympathetic or less hostile to them?
    a. No
    b. Maybe
    c. Yes
    d. Don't know; cannot say

36. Do you think that Jews would have more effectively resisted Nazi extermination if they had had more support among non-Jews?
    a. No
    b. Maybe
    c. Yes
    d. Don't know; cannot say

37. Do you think the reason more assistance was *not* given to Jews was:
    a. Lack of information about the fate of the Jews
    b. Lack of resources
    c. Fear of Nazi terror and reprisals
    d. Ordinary human indifference
    e. Lack of sympathy for Jews stemming from anti-Semitism

f. A combination of the above: specify _____

g. Other: _____

38. As you look back on Gentile collaboration with Nazism aimed at the extermination of Jews, do you see its motives largely in terms of:

a. A desire to save oneself or prolong one's own life

b. A desire to *lessen* the impact of Nazi persecution

c. Mental disturbance

d. Desire for recognition from Nazis

e. Material profit or gain

f. Belief in Nazi ideals, including anti-Semitism

g. A combination of the above: specify _____

h. Other

i. Don't know; cannot say

39. How would you rank the intensity or prevalence of anti-Semitism among the following ethnic entities—start with the *most* anti-Semitic and list your top five:

1. _____

2. _____

3. _____

4. _____

5. _____

Austrians	Czechs	French	Latvians	Russians
Belgians	Danes	Germans	Lithuanians	Serbs
Bulgarians	Dutch	Greeks	Norwegians	Slovaks
Byelorussians	Estonians	Hungarians	Poles	Spaniards
Croatians	Finns	Italians	Rumanians	Swiss
Other: _____				Ukrainians

40. How would you rank the intensity or prevalence of sympathy toward Jews among the following ethnic entities—list the *most* sympathetic first:

1. _____

2. _____

3. _____

4. _____

5. _____

Austrians	Czechs	French	Latvians	Russians
Belgians	Danes	Germans	Lithuanians	Serbs
Bulgarians	Dutch	Greeks	Norwegians	Slovaks
Byelorussians	Estonians	Hungarians	Poles	Spaniards
Croatians	Finns	Italians	Rumanians	Swiss
Other: _____				Ukrainians

41. How effective were the efforts of non-Jews in rescuing Jews during the Holocaust?
    a. Very effective
    b. Effective
    c. Somewhat effective
    d. Not effective

42. Was your own survival, personally, assisted in any way by non-Jews?
    a. Yes
    b. No

43. In your estimation, did those persons who aided Jews, do so primarily because of:
    a. Humanitarian reasons
    b. Personal friendship
    c. Political reasons
    d. Financial or other personal gain
    e. Some combination of the above: specify _____
    f. Other
    g. Does not apply; cannot say

44. Among different *religious* groupings, which do you believe the *most* sympathetic toward Jews?
    a. Catholics
    b. Protestants
    c. Greek Orthodox
    d. Russian Orthodox
    e. Jehovah's Witnesses
    f. Nonbelievers
    g. Other
    h. Don't know; cannot say

45. Among different *religious* groupings, which do you believe the *least* sympathetic toward Jews?
    a. Catholics
    b. Protestants
    c. Greek Orthodox
    d. Russian Orthodox
    e. Jehovah's Witnesses
    f. Nonbelievers
    g. Other
    h. Don't know; cannot say

46. Which strata were most *hostile* to Jews? (Choose top three.)
    a. Workers
    b. Peasants
    c. Businesspeople/shopkeepers   1. _____
    d. Aristocracy   2. _____
    e. Clergy   3. _____
    f. Professionals/doctors/lawyers
    g. The rich
    h. The very poor
    i. Very religious people
    j. Trade unionists
    k. The intelligentsia
    l. Don't know; cannot say

47. Which strata were most *sympathetic* to Jews? (Choose top three.)
    a. Workers
    b. Peasants
    c. Businesspeople/shopkeepers   1. _____
    d. Aristocracy   2. _____
    e. Clergy   3. _____
    f. Professionals/doctors/lawyers
    g. The rich
    h. The very poor
    i. Very religious people
    j. Trade unionists
    k. The intelligentsia
    l. Don't know; cannot say

48. Among organizations of partisans politically affiliated with the following, which one was *most* sympathetic to Jews during the war, as far as you know?
    a. Peasant parties
    b. Nationalists
    c. Socialists
    d. Communists
    e. Liberal-democratic middle-class group
    f. Clerical elements
    g. Other
    h. Don't know; cannot say

49. Among organizations of partisans politically affiliated with the following, which one was *least* sympathetic to Jews during the war, as far as you know?
    a. Peasant parties
    b. Nationalists
    c. Socialists
    d. Communists
    e. Liberal-democratic middle-class group
    f. Clerical elements
    g. Other
    h. Don't know; cannot say

50. In retrospect, do you think that the attitude of the world at large would have been different if the victims of Nazism were *not* Jews?
    a. *Definitely* different—more concerned and willing to help non-Jewish victims
    b. *Probably* different—more helpful to non-Jews
    c. The same to all, no different
    d. Different—but even less concerned than about Jews
    e. Don't know; cannot say

51. Besides the Nazis, who would you say bears *major* responsibility for the Jewish tragedy in Europe?
    a. Western statesmen and public opinion
    b. Jews and Jewish organizations outside Europe
    c. Non-Jews in countries where the Final Solution was being carried out

d. All of these equally

e. None of these

f. A combination of the above: specify _____

g. Other

h. Don't know; cannot say

52. What are your feelings about the role of the pope in the Jewish tragedy? Do you believe that:

a. He did all he could to save Jewish lives.

b. He deplored it, but could not prevent it.

c. He was unaware of the true plight of the Jews.

d. He was a neutral observer throughout the war, trying to keep the church out of politics.

e. He held the power to save Jewish lives, but did not use it out of fear of Nazi reprisals.

f. He was indifferent toward Jews.

g. He was anti-Semitic and was not opposed to Nazi policies.

h. Other: _____

i. Don't know; cannot say.

53. What is your view about the claim that there was no reliable information about the fate of European Jewry in the free Western countries, even as late as 1943 and 1944? Do you believe that this claim is:

a. Genuine

b. Perhaps valid in some places, but not others

c. An excuse for passivity in the face of the Jewish catastrophe

d. No opinion

e. Other—explain: _____

54. Many people say that the "world at large," people outside the Nazi-occupied countries, could have done much more to help Jews than they did.

a. Agree

b. Unsure; cannot say

c. Disagree

55. What things in particular do you think they could or should have done?

a. Ransomed Jews from Nazi persecution

b. Threatened reprisals against Nazis/Germans

c. Allowed Jews entry into their country

    d.   Bombed concentration camps

    e.   Publicized Nazi atrocities more (or more effectively)

    f.   Raised money to aid Jews

    g.   All of the above

    h.   Other—explain: _____

56. If Roosevelt and Churchill did not do all they could have to help Jews, is this because:

    a.   They concentrated on fighting the war against the Nazis.

    b.   They did not know what was happening to Jews in Europe.

    c.   They were afraid of anti-Semites in their own countries.

    d.   They did not really care about Jews.

    e.   They were anti-Semites themselves.

    f.   A combination of the above: specify _____

    g.   Other—explain: _____

57. Given the failure of Allied governments, according to many observers, to help rescue the Jews from the Holocaust, what is your view of Franklin Roosevelt and Winston Churchill considering their role in the war against Hitler?

    a.   Largely positive

    b.   Mixed

    c.   Largely negative

    d.   Don't know

    e.   Other—explain:_____

58. Have your views regarding Roosevelt and Churchill changed since the end of the Second World War?

    a.   Yes, I feel more positive.

    b.   No, unchanged.

    c.   Yes, I feel more negative.

59. If you resided in a ghetto during the Second World War, how would you best describe the role of Jewish militia?

    a.   They often helped Jews to escape and mitigated Nazi orders.

    b.   They were in a difficult situation and did the best they could.

    c.   They did what they were forced to do by the Nazis.

    d.   Their behavior toward other Jews was inexcusable.

    e.   A combination of the above: specify _____

60. How would you best describe the role of Jewish community leaders in Nazi-occupied Europe?
    a. They did what they could under the circumstances.
    b. They acted differently in different places.
    c. They were generally weak, timid, and/or ineffectual.
    d. They tried to appease the Nazis at every turn.
    e. A combination of the above: specify _____
    f. Other or don't know.

61. Would you say that these Jewish leaders generally:
    a. Above all, tried to improve conditions for Jews while they could
    b. Did what they were forced to do by the Nazis
    c. Did not make much difference either way
    d. Looked out only for themselves
    e. Contributed their share to killing fellow Jews
    f. A combination of the above: specify _____
    g. Cannot say; do not recall
    h. Other

62. As you look back upon cases of Jewish collaboration with Nazism, do you attribute it mainly to:
    a. A desire to *lessen* the impact of Nazi persecution
    b. A desire to save oneself or to prolong one's own life
    c. Mental disturbance
    d. Desire for recognition from the Nazis
    e. Hope of material profit or gain
    f. A belief that he or she was not like other Jews
    g. Belief in Nazi ideals, including anti-Semitism
    h. A combination of the above: specify _____
    i. Other
    j. Don't know; cannot say

63. What do you think of the role of Jews in America and other areas of the free world? Do you think that they:
    a. Did all they could to help European Jews, given what they knew
    b. Were not in a position to make a big difference in the fate of European Jewry
    c. Could have done much more, given what they did know
    d. Other: specify _____
    e. Don't know; cannot say

64. How do you personally feel about Israel?
    a. Enthusiastically favorable and hopeful of its future
    b. In favor of its existence, but disagree with the politics
    c. Skeptical of its future but favorable to it
    d. Indifferent, Israel has no effect on me
    e. Opposed to the whole idea of a Jewish state
    f. Don't know; cannot say
    g. Other

65. Do you believe that the existence of the state of Israel will:
    a. Prevent a repetition of the Holocaust of 1939–45
    b. Not affect the future treatment of Jews in the world
    c. Help to encourage future destruction and persecution of Jews
    d. Don't know; cannot say

66. Since 1948, have you ever considered making aliyah to Israel?
    a. Yes, I thought about it.
    b. I tried it but came back.
    c. I did make aliyah.
    d. No, I never did.

67. Have you visited Israel since 1948?
    a. Yes
    b. No
    c. If yes, how many visits? _____

68. Looking back over the last fifty years or so, would you describe your-self as an active contributor to Jewish and/or Israeli causes either through personal service, or financially, or both?
    a. Regularly and frequently
    b. From time to time
    c. Rarely
    d. Never
    e. Other—comment: _____
        (e.g., UN activities, etc.)

69. Do you feel that the strength of anti-Semitism in the world has been:
    a. Weakening
    b. About the same since the end of the Second World War
    c. Increasing
    d. Don't know; cannot say

70. How do you think your Holocaust experience affected your feelings about being Jewish? Are you:
    a. More aware of your Jewish identity
    b. More religious
    c. More Zionist
    d. The same as before
    e. Less concerned about Jewish identity
    f. Other

71. Do you think that present-day Germany no longer poses the kind of danger to the world that Nazi Germany did?
    a. Agree, it does not pose a danger.
    b. Not sure.
    c. Disagree, it does pose a danger.

72. How likely in your opinion is the revival of a dominant new form of Nazism in present-day Germany?
    a. It is unlikely but possible.
    b. It is probable.
    c. It is already happening.
    d. Don't know; cannot say

73. If you had children, did you discuss the Holocaust with them?
    a. Frequently
    b. Occasionally
    c. Rarely
    d. Never
    e. Not applicable

74. If you had children who married, did:
    a. All marry Jewish
    b. Some marry Jewish
    c. None marry Jewish
    d. Not applicable

75. If any of your children who married did not marry Jewish, did any of their spouses convert to Judaism later?
    a. Yes
    b. No
    c. Not applicable

76. If any of your children married non-Jews who did not convert to Judaism, did they maintain anything that might be termed "a Jewish home"?
    a. Yes
    b. Some did, some did not
    c. No
    d. Not applicable

77. Given what happened in the Holocaust, what do you think about human nature?
    a. People are generally good.
    b. People are capable of being good one minute and evil the next, depending on the circumstances.
    c. People are generally bad.
    d. Too hard to categorize.
    e. Other—explain: _____

78. Do you think the world has really learned something from the experience of the Jewish Holocaust?
    a. Yes, a great deal has been learned about evil and suffering in this world.
    b. People have learned a little about man's inhumanity to man, at the very least.
    c. No, people hardly know what really happened to the Jews.
    d. In the case of most people, whatever they learned, very little has changed.
    e. Other.
    f. Don't know; cannot say.

79. How would you describe your current feelings with respect to the future of the world?
    a. Optimistic about chances for peace, prosperity, and progress for all people
    b. Unsure about peace, prosperity, and progress
    c. Pessimistic about peace, prosperity, and progress
    d. Don't know; cannot say

80. Some say that what happened to the Jews in the Second World War could never happen to them again. What is your opinion?

    a. It is probable that at some future time, it will happen again.
    b. It might happen again.
    c. It is not likely to happen again.
    d. It is certain that it will never happen again.
    e. Don't know; cannot say.

81. What is your view about teaching schoolchildren about the Holocaust? Do you think that this will:
    a. Help prevent a future Holocaust
    b. Not have much effect on what happens in the future
    c. Confuse young children, and I oppose it
    d. Don't know—hard to say
    e. Other—explain: _____

82. Some people say that if G-d existed, G-d would not have allowed the Holocaust to occur. Do you:
    a. Agree
    b. Disagree

83. Given your Holocaust experience, what are your feelings about G-d?
    a. I am a nonbeliever.
    b. I am a doubter.
    c. I am a believer.
    d. I don't know.
    e. Other—specify: _____

84. Some people compare tragic events in Bosnia, Rwanda, and Cambodia with the Holocaust. Do you see some or any equivalence to the Holocaust in these events?
    a. None
    b. Little
    c. Some
    d. Quite a lot
    e. Other—specify: _____

Optional:

An important question about the Holocaust that I feel has never been addressed is:

_____

_____

_____

Comments about the questionnaire or topic:

_____

_____

I would be interested in learning about the results of the survey: YES/NO
Please contact me as follows:

Name _____

Address _____

_____

I would like to have my name included in a list of those who participated in this survey and hereby give my permission:

Signature: _____ Date: _____

Please print your name: _____

APPENDIX B: Questions in Analysis

1. DEMOGRAPHIC AND BACKGROUND INDEPENDENT VARIABLES

Age in 1939
Assimilation of family into prewar non-Jewish society
Belief in God
Current/recent occupation
Current material welfare
Level of formal education attained
Family losses in the Holocaust
Prewar family wealth
View of world future
Gender
War residence, by country
Residence before Holocaust, by urban, small town, and rural
Satisfaction with one's own life
View of human nature
Assistance by Gentiles
Family religious background
Mode of survival: by camp, hiding, assumed identity, etc.

2. COMPOUND SCALES ("MODELS") USED AS INDEPENDENT VARIABLES

Culture: Assimilation of family into prewar non-Jewish society; family religious background; belief in God

Exposure to Suffering: Age in 1939; war residence, by country; assimilation of family into prewar non-Jewish society; mode of survival: by camp, hiding, assumed identity, etc.

Personality: Satisfaction with one's own life; view of world future

Socioeconomic Status (SES): Current/recent occupation; current material welfare; level of formal education attained

3. DEPENDENT VARIABLES (SCALES)

Cognition: Awareness/understanding of Holocaust and pre-Holocaust circumstances

Learning: Views of contemporary world

Identity: Sense of Jewish identification, attitudinal and behavioral
Blame: Degree of culpability for Holocaust events attributed to various actors
Comparison: Comparisons of Holocaust with later genocidal events

4. QUESTIONS RELEVANT TO PARTICULAR SCALES

Cognition:

   Estimate of Nazi intentions at beginning of war
   View of other Jews' estimate
   Awareness of Nazi intentions in summer 1942
   Importance of anti-Semitism
   Role of non-Jews in the Holocaust
   Attitude of non-Jews and possibilities of Jewish escape
   Jewish resistance and non-Jewish attitudes
   Strength of anti-Semitism in country of residence
   Impression of Germans who participated in the Final Solution

Learning:

   Strength of anti-Semitism today
   Danger of Germany today
   Likelihood of revival of Nazism in Germany
   What the world has learned from the Holocaust
   Could the Holocaust happen again?
   Feelings about Israel
   View of effect of Israel's existence on world Jewry
   Who might be capable of committing (another) Holocaust
   Feelings about visiting Germany
   Feelings about visiting Austria
   Postwar attitude toward Germany
   View of human nature
   Should there be a statute of limitations on Holocaust crimes?
   Value of teaching school children about the Holocaust
   Is it true that if God existed, the Holocaust would not have occurred?
   Opinion about God

Identity:

   Holocaust and sense of Jewishness
   Frequency of contributions to Jewish causes
   Frequency of discussions of Holocaust with own children

Marriage of children to Jews
Conversion of children's non-Jewish spouses
Maintenance of "Jewish homes" by children
Consideration of aliyah (immigration to Israel)
Number of visits to Israel
Feelings about Israel
View of effect of Israel's existence on world Jewry

Blame:

View of German people and Holocaust responsibility
View of German people's knowledge of Holocaust during war
View of German people's support of Holocaust
Attitude change toward Germans since war
View of claims that no reliable information concerning Holocaust was
    available in West during war
Could the world have done more?
Things that should have been done
View of Roosevelt and Churchill on issue of helping Jews
General view of Roosevelt and Churchill
Change in views about Roosevelt and Churchill
Role of Jewish militia in the ghettos
View of Jewish leaders in Nazi-occupied Europe
Religions least sympathetic to Jews during Holocaust
Religions most sympathetic to Jews during Holocaust
Social strata least sympathetic to Jews
Social strata most sympathetic to Jews
Political parties least sympathetic to Jews
Political parties most sympathetic to Jews
View of world opinion if Holocaust victims were not Jews
Who bears major responsibility for Holocaust other than the Nazis
Role of pope in Holocaust
Contributions of Jewish leaders in extermination of Jews
Motives of Jewish collaborator
Motives of non-Jewish collaborators
Role of American Jews

Comparison:

Survivor comparison of Holocaust with several post–Second World
    War genocidal events (single question).

APPENDIX C: Mean Scores of Seventeen Independent Variables for Men and Women and Percentage Difference between Them

Independent Variable	Men	Women	% Difference	Observations
Assimilation of family	2.67	2.42	9.4	Women are drawn from more assimilated backgrounds.
Culture scale	7.48	7.50	0.3	Women rank slightly higher on the composite Jewish culture scale.
Current material welfare	1.33	1.53	13.1	Women see themselves as currently poorer than men.
Education level attained	3.67	3.72	1.3	Women report slightly higher levels of education than men.
Family losses	3.43	3.47	1.2	Women report slightly higher family losses.
Prewar family wealth	2.20	1.94	12.0	Women report having richer prewar families than men.
View of world future	1.67	1.86	10.0	Women are currently more pessimistic.
Home residence before Holocaust	1.54	1.44	6.5	Women's prewar residences were more urban.
Satisfaction with own life	1.91	2.17	12.0	Women report more disappointment in life.
Assistance by Gentiles	0.31	0.33	6.0	Women report somewhat more assistance by non-Jews.
Family religious background	2.46	2.47	0.4	Women report slightly more religious family origins.
War residence	2.50	2.44	2.4	Women are slightly more "western" in their geographic roots.
Socioeconomic status (SES)	3.72	3.22	13.5	Women's socioeconomic status is lower.
Mode of survival	2.69	2.75	2.2	Women are slightly more likely to have been incarcerated in camps.
Age in 1939	16.20	15.33	5.4	Women are somewhat younger.
Suffering	9.96	9.64	3.2	Women's exposure to suffering was slightly lower than that of men.
Belief in God	2.35	2.61	10.0	Women are more often believers in God than men are.
Personality scale	3.57	4.03	11.4	Women's personalities are self-reportedly less positive.

APPENDIX D: Differences by Gender

Blame, Cognition, Learning, Identity, Comparison Scales: Variables Significant above or near 2.000 T Levels

BLAME SCALE

Men		Women	
War residence	2.822	War residence	1.913
Personality scale	2.250		

COGNITION SCALE

Men	Women
None	None

LEARNING SCALE

Men		Women	
Family religious background	−2.218	Belief in God	3.004
		War residence	2.780
Assistance by Gentiles	−2.066	Age in 1939	2.737
War residence	2.043	Suffering	−2.717
Belief in God	2.023	Mode of survival	2.551
		Assimilation	2.123

IDENTITY INDEX

Men	Women
None	None

COMPARISON INDEX

Men		Women	
Age in 1939	2.985	Future	3.026
Mode of survival	2.714	Belief in God	−2.461
Suffering	2.701		
War residence	−2.362		

APPENDIX E: Gender and Standardized Betas

For Each Dependent Variable, Four Largest Standardized Betas for Men and Women

BLAME

Men		Women	
Suffering	−0.520	Belief in God	0.549
War residence	0.492	Suffering	0.478
Res. before Holocaust	0.443	Assimilation	0.443
Personality scale	0.417	War residence	0.414

COGNITION

Men		Women	
Suffering	−0.923	War residence	0.467
Assimilation	0.669	Assimilation	0.370
War residence	0.589	Age in 1939	−0.332
Mode of survival	0.465	Belief in God	0.269

LEARNING SCALE

Men		Women	
Suffering	1.395	Suffering	−2.778
War residence	0.881	War residence	1.530
Age in 1939	0.541	Assimilation	1.132
Mode of survival	0.496	Mode of survival	0.959

IDENTITY

Men		Women	
Suffering	−0.468	Suffering	1.050
Assimilation	0.458	Assimilation	−0.597
SES	0.406	Curr. Material Welfare	0.447
War residence	0.328	Personality Scale	0.208

COMPARISON

Men		Women	
Suffering	2.331	Future	0.911
Mode of survival	−1.100	Suffering	0.760
War residence	1.007	Assimilation	−0.723
Age in 1939	−0.949	Belief in God	−0.617

APPENDIX F: Regression: "Bare-Bones" Model

Cognition Regression

Variables Entered/Removed[a]

Model	Variables Entered	Variables Removed	Method
1	recoded future, Recoded religion3, Suffering Scale, Socioeco Status[b]		Enter

a. Dependent variable: Cogindex
b. All requested variables entered.

Model Summary

Model	R	R Square	Adjusted R Square	Std. Error of the Estimate
1	.425[a]	.181	.149	3.10

a. Predictors: (Constant), recoded future, Recoded religion3, suffering scale, SES

ANOVA[a]

Model		Sum of Squares	df	Mean Square	F	Sig.
1	Regression	216.277	4	54.069	5.633	.000[b]
	Residual	1065.232	102	9.599		
	Total	1122.542	106			

a. Dependent variable: Cogindex
b. Predictors: (Constant), recoded future, Recoded religion3, suffering scale, SES

COEFFICIENTS[a]

Model		Unstandardized Coefficients		Standardized Coefficients		
		B	Std. Error	Beta	t	Sig.
1.	(Constant)	1.151	2.602		.443	.659
	Recoded religion3	.866	.483	.167	1.792	.076
	SES	.162	.283	.053	.574	.567
	Suffering scale	.824	.209	.364	3.952	.000
	recoded future	−1.577E-02	.416	−.003	−.038	.970

a. Dependent variable: Cogindex

Blame Regression

Variables Entered/Removed[a]

Model	Variables Entered	Variables Removed	Method
1	recoded future, Recoded religion3, Suffering Scale, Socioeco Status[b]		Enter

a. Dependent variable: Blame index
b. All requested variables entered.

Model Summary

Model	R	R Square	Adjusted R Square	Std. Error of the Estimate
1	.226[a]	.051	.014	3.23

a. Predictors: (Constant), recoded future, Recoded religion3, suffering scale, SES

ANOVA[a]

Model	Sum of Squares	df	Mean Square	F	Sig.
1 Regression	57.310	4	14.327	1.372	.249[b]
Residual	1065.232	102	10.443		
Total	1122.542	106			

a. Dependent variable: Blame index
b. Predictors: (Constant), recoded future, Recoded religion3, suffering scale, SES

COEFFICIENTS[a]

Model	Unstandardized Coefficients B	Std. Error	Standardized Coefficients Beta	t	Sig.
1. (Constant)	7.269	2.714		2.679	.009
Recoded religion3	.413	.504	.082	.820	.414
SES	.291	.295	.099	.988	.328
Suffering scale	.405	.217	.185	1.863	.065
recoded future	−.177	.434	−.040	−.407	.685

a. Dependent variable: Blame index

Learning Regression

Variables Entered/Removed[a]

Model	Variables Entered	Variables Removed	Method
1	recoded future, Recoded religion3, Suffering Scale, Socioeco Status[b]		Enter

a. Dependent variable: Learn index
b. All requested variables entered.

Model Summary

Model	R	R Square	Adjusted R Square	Std. Error of the Estimate
1	.183[a]	.033	−.005	2.19

a. Predictors: (Constant), recoded future, Recoded religion3, suffering scale, SES

ANOVA[a]

Model	Sum of Squares	df	Mean Square	F	Sig.
1 Regression	16.917	4	4.229	.880	.479[b]
Residual	490.148	102	4.805		
Total	507.065	106			

a. Dependent variable: Learn index
b. Predictors: (Constant), recoded future, Recoded religion3, suffering scale, SES

COEFFICIENTS[a]

Model	Unstandardized Coefficients		Standardized Coefficients		
	B	Std. Error	Beta	t	Sig.
1. (Constant)	5.907	1.841		3.209	.002
Recoded religion3	−.413	.342	−.122	−1.207	.230
SES	.190	.200	.096	.949	.345
Suffering scale	.163	.148	.110	1.104	.272
recoded future	−.129	.294	−.043	−.438	.662

a. Dependent variable: Learn index

Learning Regression

Variables Entered/Removed[a]

Model	Variables Entered	Variables Removed	Method
1	recoded future, Recoded religion3, Suffering Scale, Socioeco Status[b]		Enter

a. Dependent variable: Learn index
b. All requested variables entered.

Model Summary

Model	R	R Square	Adjusted R Square	Std. Error of the Estimate
1	.183[a]	.033	−.005	2.19

a. Predictors: (Constant), recoded future, Recoded religion3, suffering scale, SES

ANOVA[a]

Model	Sum of Squares	df	Mean Square	F	Sig.
1 Regression	16.917	4	4.229	.880	.479[b]
Residual	490.148	102	4.805		
Total	507.065	106			

a. Dependent variable: Learn index
b. Predictors: (Constant), recoded future, Recoded religion3, suffering scale, SES

COEFFICIENTS[a]

Model	Unstandardized Coefficients		Standardized Coefficients		
	B	Std. Error	Beta	t	Sig.
1. (Constant)	5.907	1.841		3.209	.002
Recoded religion3	−.413	.342	−.122	−1.207	.230
SES	.190	.200	.096	.949	.345
Suffering scale	.163	.148	.110	1.104	.272
recoded future	−.129	.294	−.043	−.438	.662

a. Dependent variable: Learn index

Comparison Regression

Variables Entered/Removed[a]

Model	Variables Entered	Variables Removed	Method
1	recoded future, Recoded religion3, Suffering Scale, Socioeco Status[b]		Enter

a. Dependent variable: Contemporary comparison with Holocaust
b. All requested variables entered.

Model Summary

Model	R	R Square	Adjusted R Square	Std. Error of the Estimate
1	.201[a]	.041	.003	1.09

a. Predictors: (Constant), recoded future, Recoded religion3, suffering scale, SES

ANOVA[a]

Model	Sum of Squares	df	Mean Square	F	Sig.
1 Regression	5.113	4	1.278	1.068	.376[b]
Residual	120.896	101	1.197		
Total	126.009	105			

a. Dependent variable: Contemporary comparison with Holocaust
b. Predictors: (Constant), recoded future, Recoded religion3, suffering scale, SES

COEFFICIENTS[a]

Model	Unstandardized Coefficients		Standardized Coefficients		
	B	Std. Error	Beta	t	Sig.
1. (Constant)	2.368	.933		2.537	.013
Recoded religion3	−.105	.171	−.062	−.614	.540
SES	9.402E-02	.101	.094	.931	.354
Suffering scale	−5.029E-02	.074	−.068	−.678	.499
recoded future	.164	.147	.111	1.117	.267

a. Dependent variable: Contemporary comparison with Holocaust

APPENDIX G: Table of Correlations

		Identity Index	Blame Index	Contempoary Comparison with Holocaust	Learn Index
Identity Index	Pearson Correlation	1.000	.104	.070	.235**
	Sig. (2-tailed)		.145	.329	.001
	N	.200	.199	.195	.200
Blame Index	Pearson Correlation	.104	1.000	.015	.197**
	Sig. (2-tailed)	.145		.835	.005
	N	.199	.200	.196	.200
Contemporary Comparison with Holocaust	Pearson Correlation	−.070	.015	1.000	−.150*
	Sig. (2-tailed)	.329	.835		.036
	N	.195	.196		.196
Learn Index	Pearson Correlation	.235**	.197**	−.150*	1.000
	Sig. (2-tailed)	.001	.005	.036	
	N	.200	.200	.196	.201
Cogindex	Pearson Correlation	.154*	.277**	−.166*	.117
	Sig. (2-tailed)	.030	.000	.020	.099
	N	.200	.200	.196	.201
recoded future	Pearson Correlation	.011	−.038	.099	.061
	Sig. (2-tailed)	.886	.611	.193	.417
	N	.179	.180	.176	.180
Recoded Religion3	Pearson Correlation	.189**	.051	−.103	−.064
	Sig. (2-tailed)	.008	.477	.151	.372
	N	.197	.198	.194	.196
Suffering Scale	Pearson Correlation	.156	.169*	−.197*	.107
	Sig. (2-tailed)	.054	.019	.014	.188
	N	.153	.154	.153	.154
SES	Pearson Correlation	.032	.027	.207*	.007
	Sig. (2-tailed)	.702	.749	.014	.932
	N	.143	.144	.142	.144

		Cogindex	recoded future	Recoded Religion3	Suffering Scale	SES
Identity Index	Pearson Correlation	.154*	.011	.189**	.156	.032
	Sig. (2-tailed)	.030	.886	.008	.054	.702
	N	.200	.179	.197	.153	.143
Blame Index	Pearson Correlation	.277**	−.038	.051	.189*	.027
	Sig. (2-tailed)	.000	.611	.477	−.019	.749
	N	.200	.180	.196	.154	.144
Contemporary Comparison with Holocaust	Pearson Correlation	−.166*	.099	−.103	−.197*	.207*
	Sig. (2-tailed)	.020	.193	.151	.014	.014
	N	.196	.176	.194	.153	.142
Learn Index	Pearson Correlation	.117	.061	−.064	.107	.007
	Sig. (2-tailed)	.099	.417	.372	.188	.932
	N	.201	.180	.196	.54	.144
Cogindex	Pearson Correlation	1.000	−.025	.243**	.391**	−.120
	Sig. (2-tailed)		.743	.001	.000	.153
	N	.201	.180	.196	.154	.144
recoded future	Pearson Correlation	−.025	1.000	−.066	−.029	.153
	Sig. (2-tailed)	.743		.251	.732	.078
	N	.180	.180	.178	.138	.134
Recoded Religion3	Pearson Correlation	.243**	−.066	1.000	.224**	−.165*
	Sig. (2-tailed)	.001	.251		.005	.048
	N	.196	.178	.196	.153	.144
Suffering Scale	Pearson Correlation	.391**	−.029	.224**	1.000	−.109
	Sig. (2-tailed)	.000	.732	.005		.245
	N	.154	.138	.153	.154	.116
SES	Pearson Correlation	−.120	.153	−.165*	−.109	1.000
	Sig. (2-tailed)	.153	.078	.046	.245	
	N	.144	.134	.144	.116	.144

*Correlation is significant at the at the 0.05 level (2-tailed)
**Correlation is significant at the at the 0.01 level (2-tailed)